Mastering Visual Studio 2017

Build windows apps using WPF and UWP, accelerate
cloud development with Azure, explore NuGet, and more

Kunal Chowdhury

BIRMINGHAM - MUMBAI

Mastering Visual Studio 2017

First published: July 2017

Production reference: 1250717

Published by Packt Publishing Ltd.
Livery Place
35 Livery Street
Birmingham
B3 2PB, UK.
ISBN 978-1-78728-190-5

www.packtpub.com

Credits

Author
Kunal Chowdhury

Reviewer
Dirk Strauss

Commissioning Editor
Merint Mathew

Acquisition Editor
Karan Sadawana

Content Development Editor
Siddhi Chavan

Technical Editor
Tiksha Sarang

Copy Editor
Safis Editing

Project Coordinator
Prajakta Naik

Proofreader
Safis Editing

Indexer
Mariammal Chettiyar

Graphics
Abhinash Sahu

Production Coordinator
Nilesh Mohite

About the Author

Kunal Chowdhury has been a Microsoft MVP (Most Valuable Professional) since 2010, starting with Silverlight to Windows app development. He is also a renowned public speaker, active blogger (by passion), and a software engineer (senior/technical lead) by profession. Over the years, he has acquired profound knowledge on various Microsoft products and helped developers throughout the world with his deep knowledge and experience.

As a technical buff, Kunal has in-depth knowledge of OOPs, C#, XAML, .NET, WPF, UWP, Visual Studio, Windows 10 and Microsoft Azure. He is also proficient in entire Software Development Life Cycle (SDLC) and Scrum methodology. He has written many articles, tips & tricks on his technical blog (*kunal-chowdhury*) for developers and consumers.

You can contact Kunal via email at books@kunal-chowdhury.com. You can also follow him on Twitter at @kunal2383 and become a part of his major fans on social media channels for the updates that he shares over there.

I would like to thank my wife, Manika Paul Chowdhury, and my parents for their continuous support throughout the period while writing this book. I would also like to thank the publisher and reviewers for their valuable feedback.

Lastly, thanks to all my friends and colleagues who helped me to learn all that I have gathered over the years.

About the Reviewer

Dirk Strauss is a software developer and Microsoft MVP from South Africa, with over 13 years of programming experience. He has extensive experience in SYSPRO Customization, an ERP system, with C# and web development being his main focus.

He works for Evolution Software, developing responsive web applications with incredibly inspirational and talented individuals.

He has authored the books *C# Programming Cookbook* and *C# 7 and .NET Core Cookbook – Second Edition*, published by Packt. He has written for Syncfusion, contributing to the Succinctly series of ebooks, and he also blogs at www.dirkstrauss.com whenever he gets a chance.

As always, to my wife and kids. Thank you for your love and support.

www.PacktPub.com

For support files and downloads related to your book, please visit www.PacktPub.com.

Did you know that Packt offers eBook versions of every book published, with PDF and ePub files available? You can upgrade to the eBook version at www.PacktPub.com and as a print book customer, you are entitled to a discount on the eBook copy. Get in touch with us at service@packtpub.com for more details.

At www.PacktPub.com, you can also read a collection of free technical articles, sign up for a range of free newsletters and receive exclusive discounts and offers on Packt books and eBooks.

https://www.packtpub.com/mapt

Get the most in-demand software skills with Mapt. Mapt gives you full access to all Packt books and video courses, as well as industry-leading tools to help you plan your personal development and advance your career.

Why subscribe?

- Fully searchable across every book published by Packt
- Copy and paste, print, and bookmark content
- On demand and accessible via a web browser

Customer Feedback

Thanks for purchasing this Packt book. At Packt, quality is at the heart of our editorial process. To help us improve, please leave us an honest review on this book's Amazon page at https://www.amazon.com/dp/1787281906.

If you'd like to join our team of regular reviewers, you can e-mail us at customerreviews@packtpub.com. We award our regular reviewers with free eBooks and videos in exchange for their valuable feedback. Help us be relentless in improving our products!

Table of Contents

Preface

Day by day, a revolution is happening in the computer world; existing technologies are becoming old and obsolete, opening up more space for newer ones. To learn and work on the modern technologies, you will need an updated IDE. Microsoft does the same with developers, most popular IDE named Visual Studio.

Microsoft released Visual Studio for developers in 1997. In 2002, it first received a flavor of .NET, and then it underwent a revolution with many new features in every major build. Along with Visual Studio 2015, Microsoft added support for .NET Core, which is a cross-platform, free, and open source managed software framework, such as .NET.

Visual Studio 2017, initially known as Visual Studio "15", was released on 7th March, 2017. It included a new installation experience, with which you will be able to install a specific workload or a component that you need to accomplish your work. As well as this, it also includes features such as .NET Core, and support for NGen, Editor Config, Docker, and Xamarin. Not only the Microsoft platforms, but Visual Studio 2017 also supports Linux app development, C/C++, Cordova, Python, Node.js, tooling for data science, and analytical applications.

As the industry is forwarding with latest technologies and IDE changes, it is not easy to cope with the latest changes. As a developer, it is very hard to learn everything that a new release brings.

In this book, we will cover most of the changes to move you one step ahead with the advancements. Ranging from the installation changes to new features introduced in the IDE, followed by features introduced in it, C# 7.0 will give you the base to start with Visual Studio 2017. Then, we will move on to learning how to build apps for Windows using XAML tools, UWP tools, and .NET Core; we will learn about NuGet, more on debugging and unit testing applications, cloud development with Azure, and source controls like Git/TFS.

The examples given in this book are simple, easy to understand, and provide you with a heads up to learn and master your skills with the new IDE, Visual Studio 2017. By the time you reach the end of this book, you will be proficient with deep knowledge about each of the chapters that it covers. You will enjoy reading this book with lots of graphical and textual steps to help you gain confidence in working with this IDE.

Choosing the right version of Visual Studio 2017 can be done as follows:

Visual Studio 2017 comes in three different editions and they are: Visual Studio Community 2017, Visual Studio Professional 2017, and Visual Studio Enterprise 2017.

The Visual Studio Community edition is a free, fully-featured IDE for students, open source developers, and individual developers. In all these cases, you can create your own free or paid apps using the Visual Studio 2017 Community edition. Organizations will also be able to use the Community edition, but only under the following conditions:

- In an enterprise organization, an unlimited number of users can use the Community edition, if they are using it in a classroom learning environment, academic research, or in an open source project. An organization is defined as an enterprise organization if they have more than 250 computers or $1 million annual revenue.
- In a non-enterprise organization, the Community edition is restricted to up to five users.

If you are a professional in a small team, you should go for Visual Studio Professional 2017. If you are a large organization building end-to-end solutions in a team of any size, and if the price does not matter to you, then Visual Studio Enterprise 2017 is the right choice as it includes all the features that it offers.

 A point to note is that you can install multiple editions of Visual Studio 2017 side by side. So, feel free to install any or all editions based on your need.

What this book covers

Chapter 1, *What is New in Visual Studio 2017 IDE?*, focuses on the new IDE-specific changes incorporated in Visual Studio 2017 and how these will help the developers to improve their productivity. Starting from installation, it will cover the various workloads and component parts of the installer, and then guide you through syncing your IDE settings, followed by the new features.

Chapter 2, *What is New in C# 7.0?*, provides in-depth knowledge to help you learn about the latest changes part of C# 7.0. This chapter will guide you through a number of simple code snippets to help you learn quickly and become proficient in delivering your code.

Chapter 3, *Building Applications for Windows Using XAML Tools*, focuses on XAML-based Windows Presentation Foundation (WPF) applications for Windows. This will help you learn the WPF architecture, XAML syntax, various layouts, data bindings, converters, and triggers, and guide you through building professional applications from scratch.

Chapter 4, *Building Applications for Windows 10 Using UWP Tools*, provides a deeper insight to build XAML-based applications targeting Universal Windows Platform (UWP). This is the latest technology platform from Microsoft and the base for Windows 10 specific devices, such as mobile, PC, Xbox, IoT, and so on. This chapter will guide you through learning the generic design principles of UWP apps, followed by designing and styling applications. Later in the chapter, it will guide you to prepare apps to publish to the Windows Store.

Chapter 5, *Building Applications with .NET Core*, gives you a quick lap around the new Framework and guides you to create, build, run, and publish .NET Core applications. This chapter will cover in-depth knowledge of Framework Dependent Deployments and Self-Contained Deployments. Later, it will guide you through publishing ASP.NET Core applications to Windows Azure.

Chapter 6, *Managing NuGet Packages*, focuses on the NuGet package manager for the Microsoft development platform including, .NET. The NuGet client tools provide the ability to produce and consume packages. The NuGet gallery is the central package repository used by all package authors and consumers. Here, you will learn how to create a NuGet package, publish it to a gallery, and test it.

Chapter 7, *Debugging Applications with Visual Studio 2017*, focuses on giving you an in-depth understanding on the different debugging tools present inside Visual Studio. It's the core part of every code development. The more comfortable you are with code debugging, the better the code that you can write/maintain. This chapter will help you learn the debugging process in Visual Studio 2017.

Chapter 8, *Live Unit Testing with Visual Studio 2017*, provides a deeper insight into Live Unit Testing, which is a new module in Visual Studio 2017. It automatically runs the impacted unit tests in the background as you edit code, and then visualizes the results with code coverage, live in the editor. This chapter will help you become proficient in building Live Unit Testing with Visual Studio 2017.

Chapter 9, *Accelerate Cloud Development with Microsoft Azure*, makes it easy for you to understand the cloud computing basics that includes Microsoft Azure, which is an open, flexible, enterprise-grade cloud computing platform. It basically delivers IaaS (Infrastructure as a Service), PaaS (Platform as a Service), and SaaS (Software as a Service). This chapter will guide you through creating Azure websites and mobile app services, and then integrating those with a Windows application.

Chapter 10, *Working with Source Controls*, demonstrates the steps to manage your code with versioning support in a source control repository. Source control is a component of software configuration management, source repositories, and version management systems. If you are building enterprise-level applications in a distributed environment, you must use it to keep your code in a safe vault. This chapter will guide you through how easy it is to use Git and TFS to manage your code directly from Visual Studio.

What you need for this book

The basic software requirements for this book are as follows:

- Microsoft Visual Studio 2017 (version 15.0 or above)
- Microsoft .NET Framework 4.5 and above (part of Visual Studio)
- Microsoft .NET Core 1.0 (part of Visual Studio)
- Windows 10 operating system
- An account on Windows DevCenter
- An account on Windows Azure
- An account on GitHub and/or Microsoft Team Services

Who this book is for

.NET developers who would like to master the new features of VS 2017, and would like to delve into newer areas such as cloud computing, would benefit from this book. Basic knowledge of previous versions of Visual Studio is assumed.

Conventions

In this book, you will find a number of text styles that distinguish between different kinds of information. Here are some examples of these styles and an explanation of their meaning. Code words in text, database table names, folder names, filenames, file extensions, pathnames, dummy URLs, user input, and Twitter handles are shown as follows: "The dotnet restore command restores the dependencies and tools of a project."

A block of code is set as follows:

```
public partial class MainWindow : Window
{
  public MainWindow()
  {
    InitializeComponent();
  }
}
```

Any command-line input or output is written as follows:

```
dotnet sln <SolutionName> add <ProjectName>
dotnet sln <SolutionName> add <ProjectOneName> <ProjectTwoName>
dotnet sln <SolutionName> add **/**
```

New terms and **important words** are shown in bold. Words that you see on the screen, for example, in menus or dialog boxes, appear in the text like this: "In the **New Project** dialog, navigate to **Installed** | **Templates** | **Visual C#** | **.NET Core**."

Warnings or important notes appear like this.

Tips and tricks appear like this.

Reader feedback

Feedback from our readers is always welcome. Let us know what you think about this book-what you liked or disliked. Reader feedback is important for us as it helps us develop titles that you will really get the most out of. To send us general feedback, simply e-mail feedback@packtpub.com, and mention the book's title in the subject of your message. If there is a topic that you have expertise in and you are interested in either writing or contributing to a book, see our author guide at www.packtpub.com/authors.

Customer support

Now that you are the proud owner of a Packt book, we have a number of things to help you to get the most from your purchase.

Downloading the example code

You can download the example code files for this book from your account at http://www.packtpub.com. If you purchased this book elsewhere, you can visit http://www.packtpub.com/support and register to have the files e-mailed directly to you. You can download the code files by following these steps:

1. Log in or register to our website using your e-mail address and password.
2. Hover the mouse pointer on the **SUPPORT** tab at the top.
3. Click on **Code Downloads & Errata**.
4. Enter the name of the book in the **Search** box.
5. Select the book for which you're looking to download the code files.
6. Choose from the drop-down menu where you purchased this book from.
7. Click on **Code Download**.

Once the file is downloaded, please make sure that you unzip or extract the folder using the latest version of:

- WinRAR / 7-Zip for Windows
- Zipeg / iZip / UnRarX for Mac
- 7-Zip / PeaZip for Linux

The code bundle for the book is also hosted on GitHub at https://github.com/PacktPublishing/Mastering-Visual-Studio-2017. We also have other code bundles from our rich catalog of books and videos available at https://github.com/PacktPublishing/. Check them out!

Downloading the color images of this book

We also provide you with a PDF file that has color images of the screenshots/diagrams used in this book. The color images will help you better understand the changes in the output. You can download this file from https://www.packtpub.com/sites/default/files/downloads/MasteringVisualStudio2017_ColorImages.pdf.

Errata

Although we have taken every care to ensure the accuracy of our content, mistakes do happen. If you find a mistake in one of our books-maybe a mistake in the text or the code-we would be grateful if you could report this to us. By doing so, you can save other readers from frustration and help us improve subsequent versions of this book. If you find any errata, please report them by visiting http://www.packtpub.com/submit-errata, selecting your book, clicking on the **Errata Submission Form** link, and entering the details of your errata. Once your errata are verified, your submission will be accepted and the errata will be uploaded to our website or added to any list of existing errata under the Errata section of that title. To view the previously submitted errata, go to https://www.packtpub.com/books/content/support and enter the name of the book in the search field. The required information will appear under the **Errata** section.

Piracy

Piracy of copyrighted material on the Internet is an ongoing problem across all media. At Packt, we take the protection of our copyright and licenses very seriously. If you come across any illegal copies of our works in any form on the Internet, please provide us with the location address or website name immediately so that we can pursue a remedy. Please contact us at copyright@packtpub.com with a link to the suspected pirated material. We appreciate your help in protecting our authors and our ability to bring you valuable content.

Questions

If you have a problem with any aspect of this book, you can contact us at questions@packtpub.com, and we will do our best to address the problem.

1

What is New in Visual Studio 2017 IDE?

Visual Studio 2017 is the new IDE for developers released by Microsoft. It not only focuses on building applications targeting the Microsoft platform, but it can also be used to build applications using C++, Python, and so on. In short, it will be an IDE for every developer who needs to build apps on any platform.

Visual Studio 2017 will help you save time and effort for all the tasks that you want to do with your code, be it code navigation, refactoring, code fixes, debugging, IntelliSense, or unit testing of your module. Not only from the code perspective, but it will also streamline your real-time architectural dependency validation and provide stronger support for the integration of source code repositories, such as **TFS** (**Team Foundation Server**) or Git.

It comes with a brand new lightweight installation experience that modularizes the need to improve your efficiency of the fundamental tasks with a faster IDE access to a new way of viewing, editing, debugging, and testing your code.

Not only the common code editing features, but Visual Studio 2017 also comes with Xamarin, which will help you build mobile applications for Android, iOS, and Windows, more quickly and easily than ever. You can also choose the path to build mobile apps with Visual C++ or Apache Cordova, the cloud's first applications powered by Microsoft Azure.

In this chapter, we will cover the new installation experience, as well as the new features and enhancements that Microsoft has added to Visual Studio 2017. The following are the topics that we will discuss in this chapter:

- The new installation experience:
  - Overview of the new installation experience
  - Installation using the online installer
  - Creating an offline installer of Visual Studio 2017
  - Installing Visual Studio 2017 from the command line
  - Modifying your existing Visual Studio 2017 installation
  - Uninstalling Visual Studio 2017 installation
  - Signing in to Visual Studio 2017
- The new features and enhancements to the Visual Studio IDE:
  - Overview of the redesigned start page
  - The improved code navigation tool
  - Changes to **Find All References** of an instance
  - Structural guidelines
  - Editor config
  - The **Roaming Extension Manager**
  - Open folders in a convenient way
  - The **Lightweight Solution Loading**
  - The **Connected Services**
  - Acquiring tools and features by using the **In-Product Acquisition**
  - The **Run to Click** feature
  - Improved **Attach to Process** with process filtering
  - The new **Exception Helper**
  - Adding conditions to **Exception Settings**
  - Updates to the **Diagnostic Tools**

The new installation experience

In this section, we will discuss the various workloads and components of Visual Studio 2017's new installation experience. The basic installer that comes in the web-only mode allows you to select the components that you want to install before it downloads them. This saves you a lot of bandwidth. We will cover them here.

Unlike the previous versions of Visual Studio, you will not find an Offline Installer for Visual Studio 2017. You need to manually create it, which you can use to install Visual Studio 2017 without internet connectivity. This can be done by creating a layout using the web installer. Although the download size of the offline installer is big, it saves you the time and bandwidth when you want to install it on multiple devices.

In this section, we will learn how to configure and install different workloads or components using the online and offline installers. We will then continue to learn the ways to modify or uninstall the Visual Studio installation, as well as signing in to the IDE for a synced workspace setting across devices.

Before going into depth, let's see the system requirements to install Visual Studio 2017:

- Visual Studio 2017 will install and run on the following operating systems:
    - Windows 10 version 1507 or higher to build apps for Universal Windows Platform (UWP)
    - Windows Server 2016
    - Windows 8.1 (with Update 2919355)
    - Windows Server 2012 R2 (with Update 2919355)
    - Windows 7 SP1 (with the latest Windows Updates)
- Here's the hardware requirements:
    - 1.8 GHz or faster processor. It's recommended to have dual core or higher.
    - At least 2 GB of RAM, minimum 2.5 GB if running in a Virtual Machine. It's recommended to have 4 GB of RAM.
    - It's recommended to have 1 GB to 40 GB HDD space, based on the features you are going to install.
    - Visual Studio will work best at a resolution of WXGA (1366 by 768) or higher.

Overview of the new installation experience

The new version of the installer that is used to install Visual Studio 2017 allows you to control the individual workload/module that you need. Unlike the previous versions of the installer, it does not take more installation space; rather, it allows you to do a basic installation, having a few hundred MBs only for the core editor to install. On a need basis, you can select the workload or the individual module.

The **Workloads** screen will allow you to select the module that you want to install. If you want to build applications targeting Windows 10 only, you should go with **Universal Windows Platform development**. Consider the following screenshot:

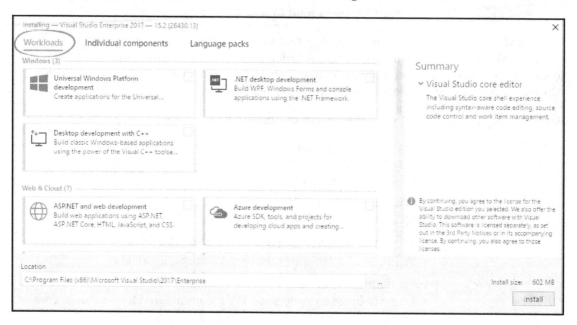

If you want to build applications for Python or Node.js, the respective workloads are there to help you install the required components. Consider the following screenshot:

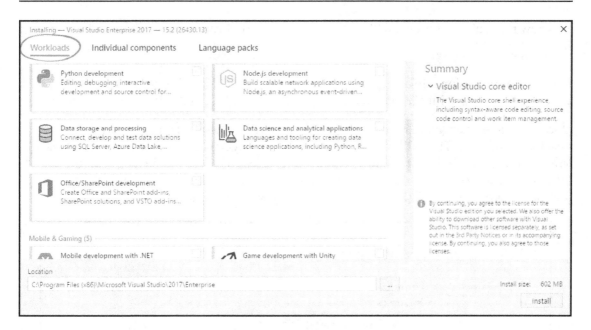

We will discuss more about the installation steps in the next point, where we will see how to install Visual Studio 2017 using the online installer.

Installation using the online installer

You can go to `https://www.visualstudio.com/downloads/` and select the Visual Studio 2017 edition that best suits your need and then download it. There are three different editions available--Visual Studio Community 2017, Visual Studio Professional 2017, and Visual Studio Enterprise 2017.

The Visual Studio Community edition is a free, fully-featured IDE for students, open source developers, and individual developers. In all these cases, you can create your own free or paid apps using the Visual Studio 2017 Community edition. Organizations will also be able to use the Community edition, but only under the following conditions:

- In an enterprise organization, an unlimited number of users can use the Community edition if they are using it in a classroom learning environment, academic research, or an open source project. An organization is defined as an enterprise organization if they have more than 250 computers or a 1 million dollar annual revenue.
- In a non-enterprise organization, the Community edition is restricted to up to five users.

To know more about the Visual Studio Community 2017 license terms, check out this page:

`https://www.visualstudio.com/license-terms/mlt553321/`

If you are a professional in a small team, you need to select Visual Studio Professional 2017, and for end-to-end solutions by a team of any size, select Visual Studio Enterprise 2017.

Once you have downloaded the online/web installer, double-click on it to start the installation process. This will first show a screen where you can read the **License Terms** and **Microsoft Privacy Statement**, which you need to agree to before continuing with the installation process. Once you click on the **Continue** button, the installer will take a few minutes to prepare itself. This is shown in the following screenshot:

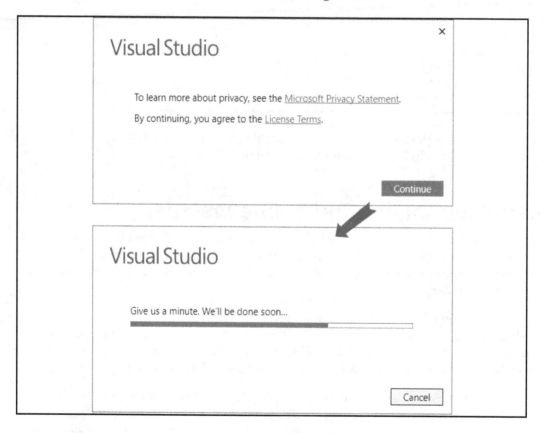

The main screen of the installer has three different tab contents--**Workloads, Individual components**, and **Language packs**.

The **Workloads** tab allows you to select the group of components that comes under a single module. In other words, each workload contains the features you need for the programming language or platform you prefer.

For example, if you like to build **Windows Presentation Foundation (WPF)** applications, you need to select **.NET desktop development**, and to build ASP.NET web applications, you need to select the **ASP.NET and web development** module under the workloads.

To install and build applications for both WPF and Windows 10, select **.NET desktop development** and **Universal Windows Platform development**, as shown in the following screenshot. For each individual workload, the selected components will be listed in the panel on the right-hand side of the screen:

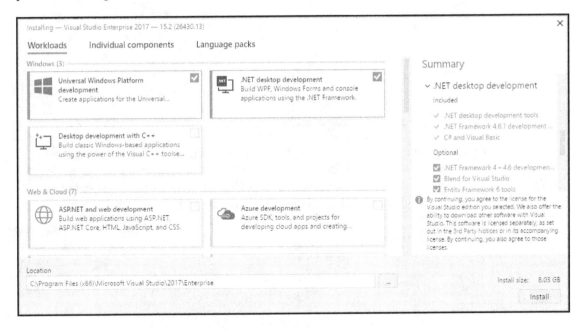

The **Individual components** tab lists all the component parts of individual workloads, category wise, for you. The components part of the selected workloads will be auto-checked by default.

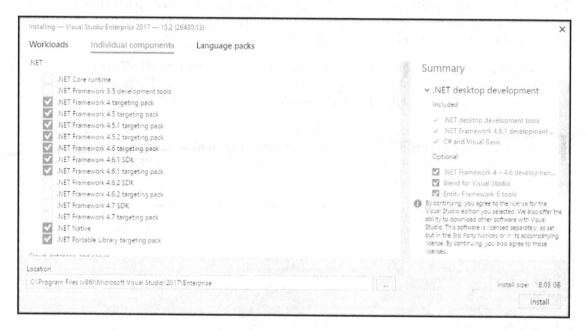

 Only use this section if you are an advanced user. Some components may have dependencies with one or more workloads. Deselecting one of them can cause the other workloads to unload from the installation process. So, be cautious while selecting/deselecting any one of them.

The third tab is the **Language packs** tab, which allows you to choose the language that you want to use with Visual Studio 2017. By default, it's the system's default language selected on the screen; however, you can opt for **Czech**, **French**, **German**, or any other languages from the available list shown in the following screenshot:

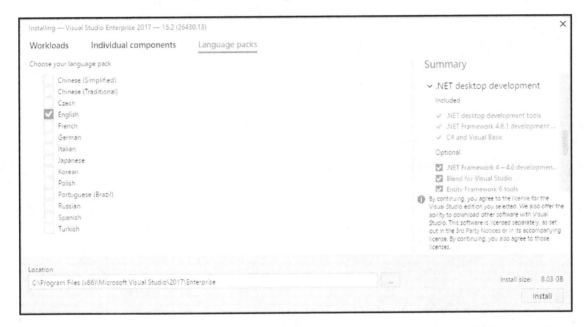

By default, a location is prepopulated for the installer to install Visual Studio 2017, but you can change it to a different folder. Once you are done, click on the **Install** button.

This will start the actual installation process. If you are using the web installer, it will download an individual module from the Microsoft server and install them gradually. This may take some time, based on your selected workloads/components and internet bandwidth. Consider the following screenshot:

This will be fast and take less time than the previous IDE installers. Once it completes the installation, it may ask you to restart your system to take into effect the changes that it made to start the Visual Studio instance. If you see such a message on the screen, as shown in the following screenshot, make sure to restart your computer by clicking on the **Restart** button:

From the same page, you will be allowed to modify the existing installation, launch the Visual Studio 2017 IDE, or uninstall the complete installation.

Creating an offline installer of Visual Studio 2017

Sometimes, we may need to have an offline copy of the installer so that we can install it to multiple devices without an active or fast internet connection. This will save your bandwidth from downloading the same copy multiple times over the network. The offline installer is big. So, before going further to create the offline copy, make sure that you have an active internet connection available with no limitation of download bandwidth.

1. First, download the Visual Studio setup executable file (web installer) to a drive on your local machine.
2. Now, run the downloaded setup executable with the following arguments (switches) from a command prompt:
   - Add `--layout <path>`, where `<path>` is the location where you want the layout to be downloaded. By default, all languages will be downloaded along with all the packages.
   - In case you want to restrict the download to a single language only, you can do so by providing the `--lang <language>` argument, where `<language>` is one of the ISO country codes given in the following list. If not specified, support for all localized languages will be downloaded.

ISO CODE	LANGUAGE
cs-CZ	Czech
de-DE	German
en-US	English
es-ES	Spanish
fr-FR	French
it-IT	Italian
ja-JP	Japanese
ko-KR	Korean
pl-PL	Polish

pt-BR	Portuguese - Brazil
ru-RU	Russian
tr-TR	Turkish
zh-CN	Chinese - Simplified
zh-TW	Chinese - Traditional

For example, to download the Visual Studio 2017 Enterprise edition under the local path C:\VS2017\, you need to provide the following command:

```
vs_enterprise.exe --layout "C:\VS2017\"
```

To download the English localized edition to local path C:\VS2017\, provide the following command:

```
vs_enterprise.exe --layout "C:\VS2017\" --lang "en-US"
```

To download only the .NET desktop development workload, run:

```
vs_enterprise.exe --layout "C:\VS2017\" --add
Microsoft.VisualStudio.Workload.ManagedDesktop
```

To download the .NET desktop development and Azure development workloads, provide the following command:

```
vs_enterprise.exe --layout "C:\VS2017\" --add
Microsoft.VisualStudio.Workload.ManagedDesktop
Microsoft.VisualStudio.Workload.Azure
```

As shown in the following screenshot, it will start downloading all the packages part of Visual Studio 2017. As the offline installer is big, it will take plenty of time, depending on the speed of your internet network:

Once the download completes, go to the folder where you downloaded the packages (in our case, it's `C:\VS2017\`) and run the installer file, that is, `vs_enterprise.exe`, for example. Then, follow the same steps as mentioned earlier to select the required **Workloads** and/or **Individual components** to start the installation process.

Installing Visual Studio 2017 from the command line

You can use command-line parameters/switches to install Visual Studio 2017. Be sure to use the actual installer, for example, `vs_enterprise.exe` for the Visual Studio 2017 Enterprise edition, and not the bootstrapper file, which is named `vs_setup.exe`. The bootstrapper file loads the **MSI** for actual installation. You can also run `C:\Program Files (x86)\Microsoft Visual Studio\Installer\vs_installershell.exe` to install the Visual Studio components from the command line.

Here is a list of the command-line parameters/switches:

Parameters/Switch	Description
`[--catalog] <uri> [<uri> ...]`	Required -- One or more file paths or URIs to catalogs.
`--installDir <dir>` `--installationDirectory <dir>`	Required -- The target installation directory.
`-l <path>, --log <path>`	Specify the log file; otherwise, one is automatically generated.
`-v, --verbose`	Display verbose messages.
`-?, -h, --help`	Display parameter usage.
`--instanceId <id>`	Optional -- The instance ID to install or repair.
`--productId <id>`	Optional -- The product ID to install. Otherwise, the first product found is installed.
`--all`	Optional -- Whether to install all workloads and components for a product.

`--add <workload or component ID> ...`	Optional -- One or more workload or component IDs to add.
`--remove <workload or component ID> ...`	Optional -- One or more workload or component IDs to remove.
`--optional, --includeOptional`	Optional -- Whether to install all optional workloads and components for selected workload.
`--lang, --language <language-locale> ...`	Optional -- Install/uninstall resource packages with the specified languages.
`--sharedInstallDir <dir>`	Optional -- The target installation directory for shared payloads.
`--compatInstallDir <dir>`	Optional -- The target installation directory for legacy compatibility payloads.
`--layoutDir <dir>` `--layoutDirectory <dir>`	Optional -- The layout directory in which to find packages.
`--locale <language-locale>`	Optional -- Change the display language of the user interface for the installer. Setting will be persisted.
`--quiet`	Optional -- Do not display any user interface while performing the installation.
`--passive`	Optional -- Display the user interface, but do not request any interaction from the user.

Here is a list of workload IDs that you need to provide while installing Visual Studio 2017 from the command line:

- **Microsoft.VisualStudio.Workload.CoreEditor**: This is the core part of Visual Studio 2017 containing the core shell experience, syntax-aware code editing, source code control, and work item management.
- **Microsoft.VisualStudio.Workload.Azure**: This contains the Azure SDK tools and projects to develop cloud apps and create resources.
- **Microsoft.VisualStudio.Workload.Data**: Using this workload, you can connect, develop, and test data solutions using SQL Server, Azure Data Lake, Hadoop, or Azure Machine Learning.

- **Microsoft.VisualStudio.Workload.ManagedDesktop**: This workload will help you build WPF, Windows Forms, and console applications using the .NET Framework.

- **Microsoft.VisualStudio.Workload.ManagedGame**: If you are a game developer, you can create 2D and 3D games with Unity, a powerful cross-platform development environment.

- **Microsoft.VisualStudio.Workload.NativeCrossPlat**: Want to create and debug applications running in a Linux environment? This workload will allow you to build native cross platform apps.

- **Microsoft.VisualStudio.Workload.NativeDesktop**: Classic Windows-based applications using the power of the Visual C++ toolset, ATL, and optional features such as MFC and C++/CLI can be built using this workload.

- **Microsoft.VisualStudio.Workload.NativeGame**: If you are a game developer, you can use the full power of C++ to build professional games powered by DirectX, Unreal, or Cocos2d.

- **Microsoft.VisualStudio.Workload.NativeMobile**: Using this, you can build cross-platform applications for iOS, Android, or Windows using the C++ APIs.

- **Microsoft.VisualStudio.Workload.NetCoreTools**: .NET Core is a new addition to Visual Studio. You can build cross-platform applications using .NET Core, ASP.NET Core, HTML, JavaScript, and CSS.

- **Microsoft.VisualStudio.Workload.NetCrossPlat**: To build cross-platform applications for iOS, Android, or Windows using Xamarin, you will need to have this workload installed on your development environment.

- **Microsoft.VisualStudio.Workload.NetWeb**: You can build web applications using ASP.NET, ASP.NET Core, HTML, JavaScript, and CSS using the NetWeb workload.

- **Microsoft.VisualStudio.Workload.Node**: To build scalable network applications using Node.js and asynchronous event-driven JavaScript runtime, you will need this workload.

- **Microsoft.VisualStudio.Workload.Office**: To create Office and SharePoint add-ins, SharePoint solutions, and VSTO add-ins using C#, VB, and JavaScript, you will need this Office workload.

- **Microsoft.VisualStudio.Workload.Universal**: To create applications targeting the Universal Windows Platform with C#, VB, JavaScript, or, optionally, C++, you need to install this workload.

- **Microsoft.VisualStudio.Workload.VisualStudioExtension**: If you want to create add-ons and extensions for Visual Studio, you will need to install this workload. This also includes new commands, code analyzers, and tool windows.

- **Microsoft.VisualStudio.Workload.WebCrossPlat**: To build Android, iOS, and UWP apps using Tools for Apache Cordova, you will need this.

Each of the preceding workloads has its own set of components, which you can refer to from the official Microsoft page (https://aka.ms/vs2017componentids).

Modifying your existing Visual Studio 2017 installation

After the installation ends, if you later decide to modify the existing installation to add or remove any components or uninstall the installation, you can do so from the control panel - **Add/Remove Programs**. Alternatively, you can launch the **Microsoft Visual Studio Installer** and click on **Modify**, as shown in the following screenshot:

To add new modules, check the new workloads, or to remove modules, uncheck the existing workloads, and proceed toward modifying the existing installation.

Uninstalling Visual Studio 2017 installation

If you have set your mind to uninstall all the packages that Visual Studio 2017 installed, the new installer that comes with it can help you uninstall the entire packages completely, without keeping any trace of the components.

You can also launch the Microsoft Visual Studio Installer, click the ☰ icon, then **Uninstall**, as shown in the following screenshot, and then click on **OK** when asked:

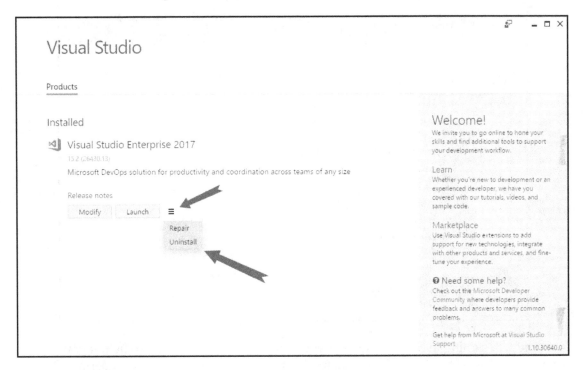

Signing in to Visual Studio 2017

Once you are done with the installation, open your Visual Studio 2017 IDE. When you open it for the first time, it will ask you to sign in. Be sure to sign in with your **MSA (Microsoft Account)** ID or a work/school account that best represents you. If you don't have an existing account, you can create a personal account for free.

Although it is optional to sign in, it is good to keep all your Visual Studio settings and personalization settings synced in the cloud. Doing so will help you use the same settings from any other devices. If you are working on multiple devices, syncing your settings will help you in many ways (includes Theme).

Here is the screenshot of the sign-in screen of Visual Studio, where you need to provide your account credentials:

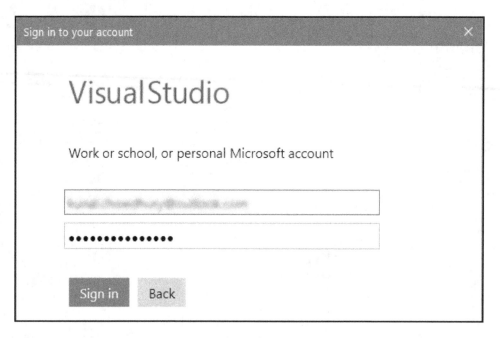

Not only will signing in help you extend your trial license, but it will also help if you installed the Visual Studio trial version. By default, it will have a 30 day trial period. Once you sign in to Visual Studio 2017, you will get an additional 90 days to try it.

If you have an account that's associated with the MSDN or **VSO** (**Visual Studio Online**) subscription, signing in to Visual Studio will automatically unlock your installation. It will also connect to services such as Microsoft Azure and Visual Studio Team Services in the IDE without prompting again for credentials for the same account.

If you missed logging in to Visual Studio at the first start of the IDE, you can do so later from the Visual Studio by using this path: **Help | Register Product | Sign in**, or by clicking on the **Sign in** link available at the top-right corner of the screen, as shown in the following screenshot:

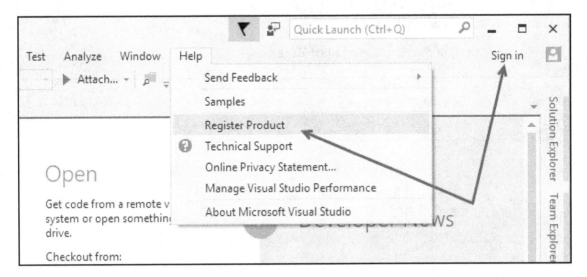

Unless you sign out, you will be automatically signed in to Visual Studio whenever you start it. This will synchronize all your changes to the settings in the cloud.

The new features and enhancements to the Visual Studio IDE

Every new product comes with new features and enhancements to the existing one, to give you more control over what you need. It's the same with Visual Studio 2017 having product version 15. Microsoft has changed many things in this new redesigned IDE and added many things to improve your productivity.

Ranging from the installation point of view to the IDE level, many things have been incorporated. We have already discussed the new installation experience. Now we will discuss the new features/enhancements at this point. Starting from the redesigned start page, we will cover the improved navigation tool, the changes that have been made in the **Find All References** window, structural guidelines, editor config, the roaming extension manager, lightweight solution loading, connected services, run to click feature, and many more.

Overview to the redesigned start page

In Visual Studio 2017, Microsoft has brought you a faster installation experience, better performance, and new/enhanced productivity features. One of these productivity features is a **Start Page** redesigned by the Microsoft team. This will help you start working on your code faster, with easy access to whatever you need.

Here is a quick peek of the redesigned **Start Page**:

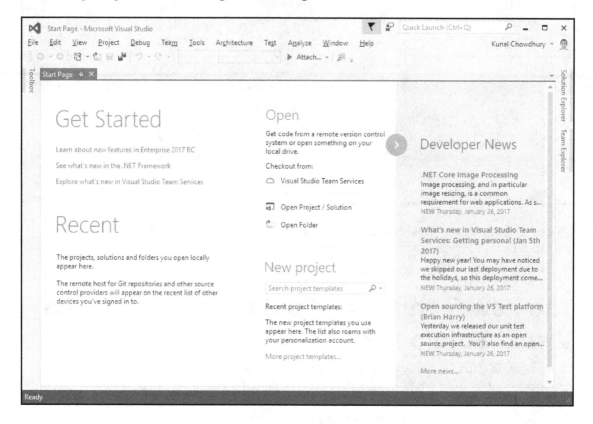

The first item here is the **Get Started** section having a few links to get you started, but this is not always helpful and covers part of your **Start Page**. To get out of it, hover on the **Get Started** section to see a close (**x**) button. Clicking on it will collapse the said section and, thus, will give more space to the **Recent / Most Recently Used** (**MRU**) list.

The MRU list in the **Start Page** will allow you to quickly find what you're looking for. Each MRU item will display an icon denoting it as a project, a solution, a folder, a file path for local resources, or a remote URL for remote items not yet on the local system.

To help you stay more productive in your daily work, the MRU on the **Start Page** has some additional features:

- Along with **Projects** and **Solutions**, it also lists recently opened folders.
- It groups the list by date and can accommodate a longer history of files, folders, projects, and solutions.
- You can pin an MRU item to the top of the list so that you can easily access your most important items.
- If you are using multiple devices and are already signed into your Visual Studio installation on all the devices, the MRU list will also show you a roaming item.
- If you cloned a remote repository, Visual Studio will roam the item in any of your devices that have the same associated account, and clicking on any of them will automatically clone it down for you to continue your work. Consider the following screenshot:

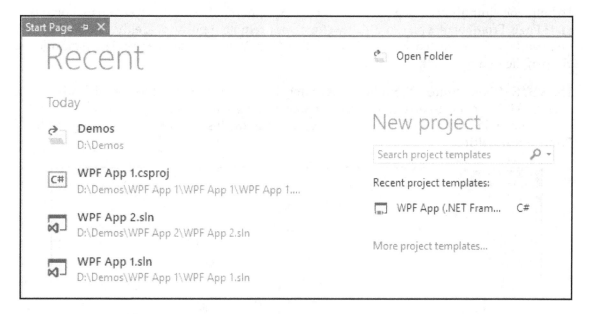

The **New Project** section in the Visual Studio 2017 start screen will allow you to get easy access to the project templates. If you have recently created any projects out of any templates, it will list all those recently used project templates.

You can also search for any project templates and use the one from the list. This is to help you speed up the process of creating new projects using the new IDE by bypassing the steps to find and select the desired template in the **New Project** dialog. If you sign into Visual Studio, this list will also roam with you across your devices:

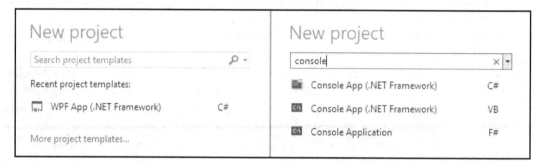

To help you simplify the open project/solution experience, Microsoft placed a panel on the **Start Page**. From there, you can directly clone your remote repositories, either from on-premise TFS, cloud-hosted TFS, or shared on GitHub. You can also open projects/solution or open the folder from this screen.

The **VSTS** (**Visual Studio Team Services**) extension is already in built to Visual Studio 2017; GitHub is a third-party extension, but comes along with it as an optional download. If you are not able to find GitHub on the **Start Page**, run the installer or install it using the **In-Product acquisition**:

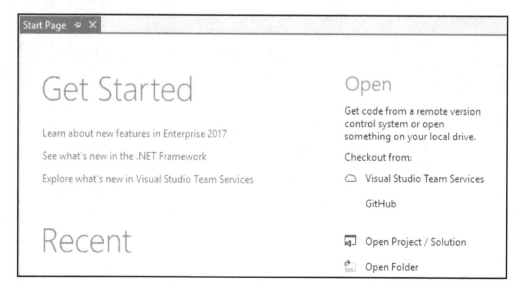

The **Developer News** section is the place where you can stay updated with the latest news. Although some developers like to read it every day, not everyone does. Hence, Microsoft now allows you to collapse this section and stay focused on your code-related stuff on the start page. A small badge will be there on the arrow circle to notify you of new posts in the news feed. Consider the following screenshot:

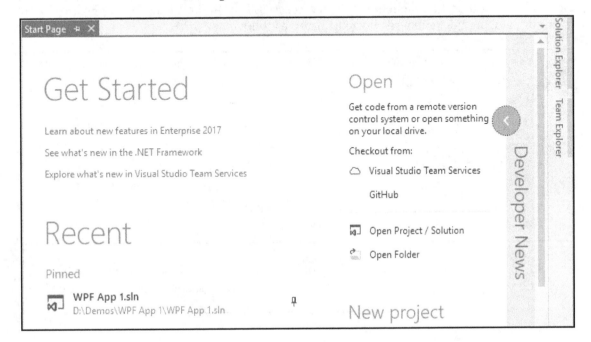

 Did you know? Hovering your mouse over the **Get Started** section provides you with an **x** button to close the same and gain more space for the **Recent**/MRU list.

The improved code navigation tool

With Visual Studio 2017, Microsoft has improved the code navigation feature to let you quickly find and go to line, files, types, methods, and other elements in your code. It gives you a one-stop way to go to any kind of item that you are looking for, even in a large code base, helping you find the item easily. You can access it from the Visual Studio **Edit** | **Go To** menu or by using the keyboard shortcuts listed as follows:

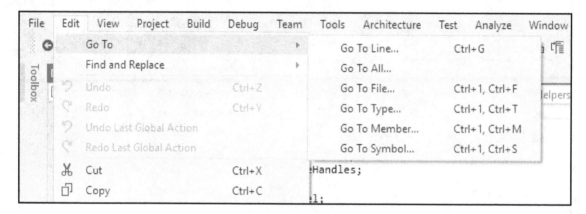

The **Go To** toolbox that pops up has a few toolbox buttons to easily switch between the navigational types, such as line, files, types, symbols, members, and so on, and a search box:

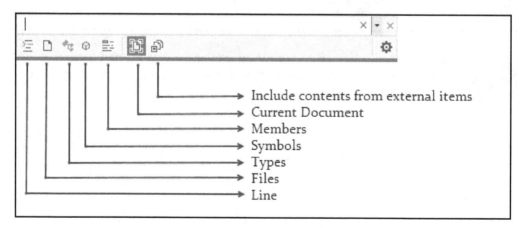

It also offers you easy access to the toolbox buttons with shortcuts. The shortcuts are actually a character that you start the search with. For example, starting a search with t will directly navigate you to **Types** search. To find out the search key shortcut, enter ? in the search box. It will show help, as shown in the following screenshot:

If you want to navigate to a specific line, enter : <LineNo> (for example, : 25) to see a quick view of the line, and confirming it will directly navigate you to that specific line number. You can also access it using the keyboard shortcut, *Ctrl + G*.

The **Go to line** was already there in earlier versions of Visual Studio, but the quick preview of the same before navigating has been added with Visual Studio 2017.

Take a look at the following screenshot to grasp an idea of previewing the line before confirming it:

If you start the search with f, followed by the key term, it will search the term in the file name and show you a quick preview of the selected file along with the file path. For example, to list all the C# files having **Helper** at the end of their names, enter f helper.cs in the search box, as shown in the following screenshot; interestingly, you will see the result along with the file path, which is blurred in this screenshot. Use the up/down arrow keys to select the result for a quick view of the selected file:

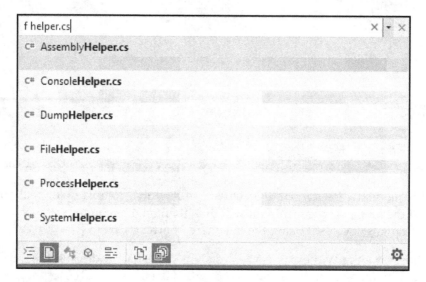

If you want to search for types such as class, interface, enum, and so on, you can start the search with the character t, as shown here:

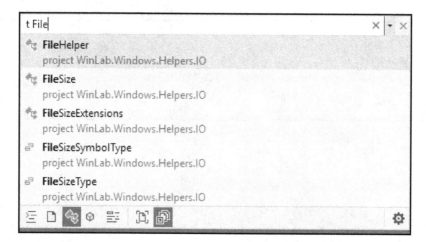

To start a symbol search, begin the search term with the # character and you will find the result having entered term like this:

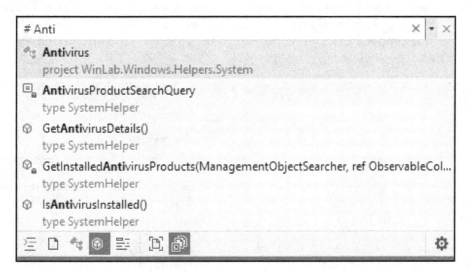

Similarly, to search for a member, begin the search with m and your search key; you will get the result matching the key for any members in the solution, as shown in the following screenshot:

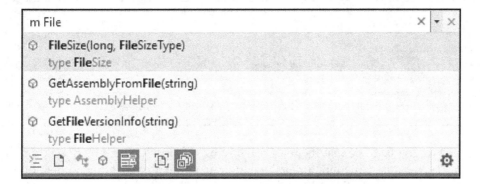

You can also search by clicking on the respective buttons, which will automatically add the contextual search character at the beginning of the search key. However, if you remember the character, it will be very quick for you to access the required resource without using your mouse cursor.

The last two toolbox buttons will help you switch between Current Document and external items. You can quickly switch between them using the keyboard shortcut *Ctrl + Alt + C*.

Changes to Find All References of an instance

The **Find All References** command in Visual Studio is not a new thing. It's used to find out all the references of a member or symbol. In earlier versions of Visual Studio, the UI of the result dialog was simple, having only the results in a grouped list. You can find the previous result dialog here:

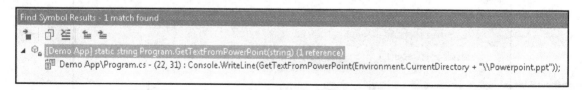

However, there was always a demand to improve it, as most developers use it regularly to check for references of a member, type, or symbols. Microsoft worked on it in Visual Studio 2017 and have provided a rich UI for developers to improve their daily productivity.

It now has an advanced grouping, filtering, sorting, and searching within the reference result. It now also has a colorization of the term in the result, giving you a clear understanding of the references and directly moving you into the line of code that you are looking for. Here, you can see the new result dialog:

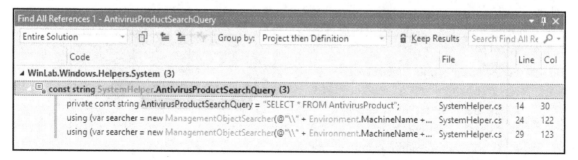

The resultant dialog lists the results in a grid, having column headers to give you clear visibility of the records, which includes the code, file name, line number, and so on for your easy reference. You can use the column headers to sort the result based on your need.

When you hover your mouse over a resultant item in the grid, a tooltip is displayed with the context of the reference in source code. This gives you a quick peek of what you are looking for.

The toolbar of the dialog has many new toolbox items. Let's understand each one of them, as follows:

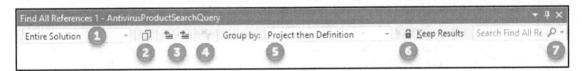

1. This list has a few entries with which you can filter the records to solution level, project level, and so on. The list consists of the following entries:
   - **Entire Solution**
   - **Open Documents**
   - **Current Project**
   - **Current Document**
   - **Changed Documents**

2. This is the Copy button that copies the content of the selected record.
3. These are the two buttons for navigation purposes. This will navigate you to the previous and next location in the list.
4. This button is used to clear all the filters.
5. This combination list allows you to change the **Group by** definition. You can choose any one of the following:
   - **Project then Definition**
   - **Definition only**
   - **Definition then Project**
   - **Definition then Path**
   - **Definition, Project then Path**

6. This is another new toggle button to help you keep the current result on the screen when you trigger another **Find All Reference** command. When the **Keep Results** button is turned ON, the next invocation of **Find All References** will populate the reference results in a new window.
7. The search box will allow you to search within the result set to give you the perfect result that you are looking for.

Structural guide lines

Visual Studio 2017 also focuses on a new feature called **Structural guide lines**. The Structural Guide Lines are drawn in the editor so that you can easily visualize the structure of the code that you are currently working on. When you mouse hover on the guideline, a tooltip containing the context of the current code block relative to its ancestor blocks is displayed. Here, in the following screenshot, you can see how the lines are drawn and how the tooltip is displayed with its ancestor blocks when you hover over the guide lines of the using block:

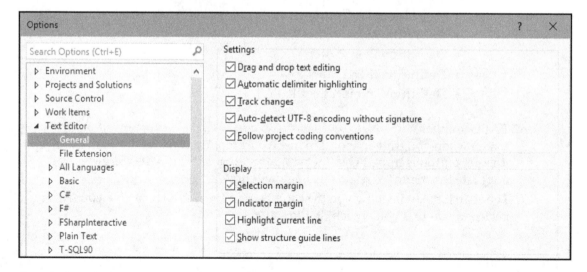

This feature is enabled by default. If you want to disable it, you can navigate to the Visual Studio options dialog at the path: **Tools | Options | Text Editor | General**, and uncheck the checkbox labelled **Show structure guide lines**.

To enable it again, follow the same path and check the same box, as shown in the preceding screenshot.

Editor config

Editor config helps developers define and maintain consistent coding styles between different editors and/or IDEs. Microsoft has added support of **Editor config** in Visual Studio 2017.

The default text editor settings in Visual Studio applies to all projects of a given type. For example, if you change a C# or VB.NET text editor's settings, those settings will apply to all C# projects and VB.NET projects respectively. However, in general, the coding conventions that you use in your personal projects may differ from those used in your team's projects.

Here comes the Editor Config that enables you to do this on a per project basis and/or per folder level. In this case, the settings are contained in a .editorconfig file added to your code base. As the settings are contained in a file in the code base, they travel along with the code base:

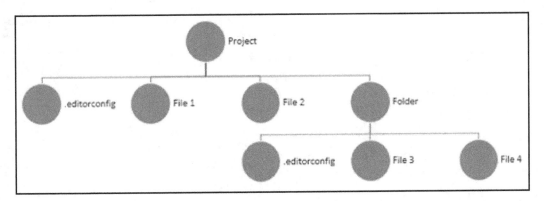

The Editor Config doesn't support a full set of C# formatting rules and, hence, it's not a replacement for format settings in Visual Studio. Currently, it supports the following settings only in Visual Studio 2017:

- **indent_style**
- **indent_size**
- **tab_width**
- **end_of_line**
- **charset**
- **root**
- **trim_trailing_whitespace**
- **insert_final_newline**
- **Code style conventions**

You can create an editor configuration file at the project level or at any folder level. When you add it to the project's root level, its settings are applied across all the files in the project. If you add it to any specific folder level inside the project, the root settings will be overridden and will apply to all applicable files at that level and below.

Did you know? Adding an `.editorconfig` file to your project or code base will not convert the existing styles to new ones. It will apply the settings to only newly added lines in that code base. To make an entire document adhere to the code formatting rules defined in your editor configuration, you can use the **Format Document** (*Ctrl + K, D*) command.

To create an Editor Config (`.editorconfig`) file, right-click on a project or folder where you want to apply the settings, and then, from the context menu, click on **Add | New Item...**, as shown in the following screenshot:

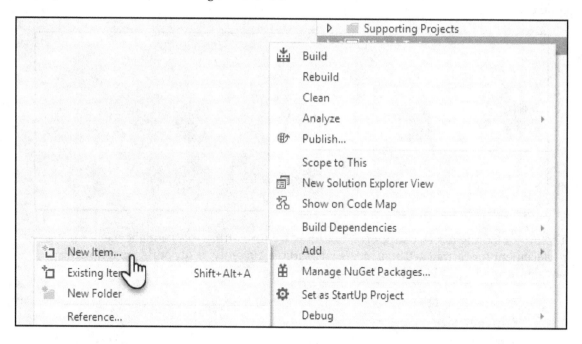

Now, from the **Add New Item** dialog box, select the **Text File** template and give it a name, for example, **.editorconfig**, as shown in the following screenshot, to add the file. Note that the file name only consists of the extension of the file:

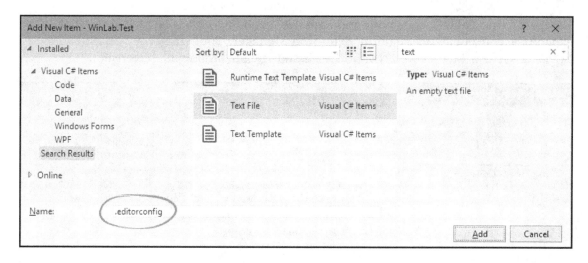

The .NET code style settings allow you to enforce the style that you want to use in your code base. Depending on the severity set in the Editor Config, it can show you a suggestion, a compiler warning, or compiler error. This can be written in the following fashion:

```
options_name = false|true : none|suggestion|warning|error
```

The option must specify `true` (preferable) or `false`; a colon, `:`, and a severity of `none`, `suggestion`, `warning`, or `error`. The default is `none`.

If you set the severity as `none`, it will not show anything to the user when this style is not being followed. If you set it as a `suggestion`, it will show a suggestion (underlying dots on the first two characters) when the style is not being followed. In case of `warning` or `error`, it will either show compiler warning or compiler error if the code does not match the style being applied to it.

The Roaming Extension Manager feature

The **Roaming Extension Manager** is a new feature in Visual Studio 2017 and can be seen under the **Extensions and Updates** dialog box. This allows you to keep a track of all your favorite extensions. It allows you to sync the installed extensions by creating a synchronized list in the cloud if you have already signed in on all your Visual Studio IDEs across all your development environments.

Navigate to the **Tools | Extensions and Updates** menu in your Visual Studio instance and expand the entry that says **Roaming Extension Manager**. Under this, you will find all the extensions roamed with your account. This is shown in the following screenshot:

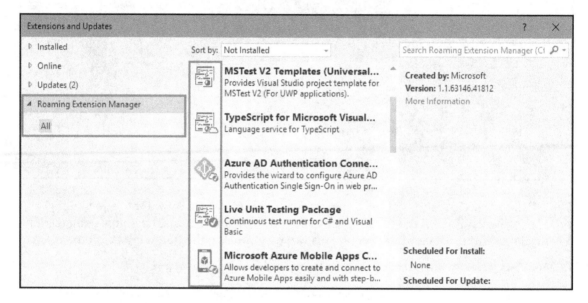

Here, you will find three kinds of icons:

- **Roamed icon** (⌓): If the extension is a part of your roaming list, but not installed on this machine, you will get this roamed icon overlayed on it. Click on the **Download** button to install the extension.
- **Roamed and installed icon** (⌓): This icon will be set as an overlay, when an extension is part of your roaming list and is installed on this system too.
- **Installed icon** (✓): When an extension is not a part of your roaming list, but present on this machine, it will get this installed icon overlay.

If you want to add any extensions to the roaming list to roam along with your account, select the specific extension and click on the **Start Roaming** button. When the extension is roaming, it will auto-install on the other system, where you sign in to Visual Studio with the same personalized account:

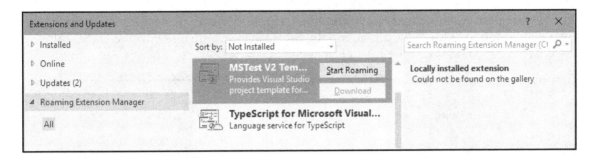

If you do not want to roam an extension for any reason, you can remove it from the roaming list by clicking on the **Stop Roaming** button of that extension, which is shown in the following screenshot:

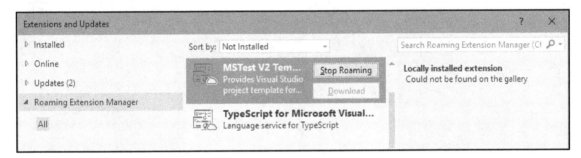

If you have any favorite extensions that you use regularly on all your devices, you will love to sync them with your account. This way, you don't have to manually search and install them on the new system where you will write your code.

 Did you know? If you download an extension when you are already signed in to Visual Studio 2017, it will be added to your roaming list, giving you easy access to it from any of your development environments.

Open folders in a convenient way

In Visual Studio 2017, Microsoft has provided a convenient way to work with the code base. You can now directly open a folder instead of opening the solution/project explicitly. When you open a folder, you can easily navigate to all files by structural folders using the **Solution Explorer**. Not only this, but you can also build your projects from the **Solution Explorer**; right-click on context menu.

In order to open a folder, you can click on **File | Open | Folder...** from the Visual Studio menu or the **Open Folder** link present on the **Start Page**. Alternatively, you can press the keyboard shortcut: *Ctrl + Shift + Alt + O*:

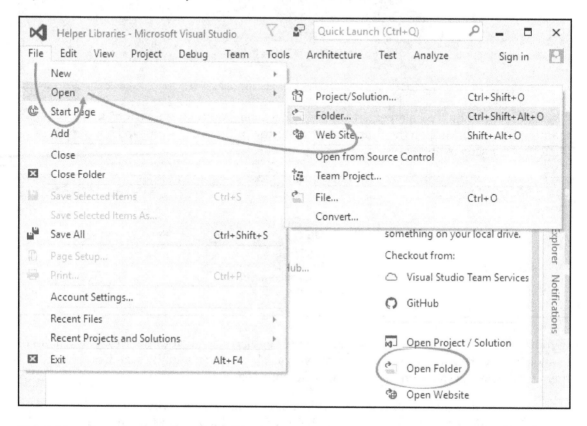

The folder view also supports the following:

- Searching across the code in your folder with the **Go To** (*Ctrl + ,*) command.
- Scoping the **Solution Explorer** folder view to subfolders. To scope your current context to a specific project/folder, right click on it and then click on **Scope To This** from the context menu.
- Opening folders in Explorer or the Command Prompt from the **Solution Explorer** itself.
- Easily toggle between solutions with the **Solution** selection dropdown.
- Configuring the debug and launch settings with `launch.json`. Right-click on a debuggable file and select **Debug and Launch Settings**.

- Configuring tasks and customizing the build with **tasks.json**. Right-click on any file and select **Configure Task Settings**.
- `Launch.vs.json` and `tasks.vs.json` have IntelliSense in the JSON editor.
- Integration with supported source control repositories. This will provide you the current status of the file. As shown in the following screenshot, a + or a tick mark provides you the status of the local file in comparison with the version available in source control repository:

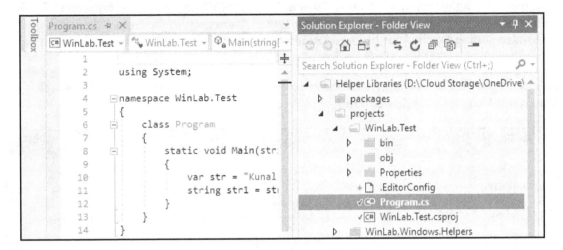

You can also open a folder from the Windows Explorer window by right-clicking on any folder and then clicking the **Open in Visual Studio** context menu item, as shown in the following screenshot:

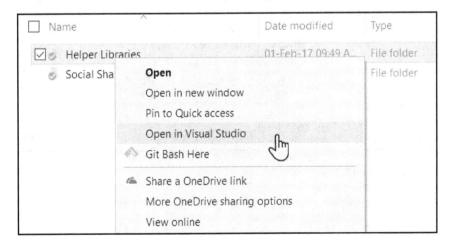

Lightweight solution loading

Lightweight solution loading is yet another feature of Visual Studio 2017 that enables you to load large solutions faster, reducing the load time and memory usages, as it loads only the files that are needed (per need basis). It is best suited to large solutions that contain C# or a mix of C# and C++ projects. If Visual Studio decides that you are working with large solutions, it will prompt you to enable this feature.

This feature is not enabled by default. To enable it, open Visual Studio Options from **Tools | Options** and navigate to **Projects and Solutions | General**. On the right-side panel, you will find a setting labelled **Lightweight solution load for all solutions**. Check it to enable the feature. Uncheck it if you decide to go back to the previous settings.

Alternatively, you can search for `Lightweight Solution load` in the **Quick Launch** search box to directly navigate to it:

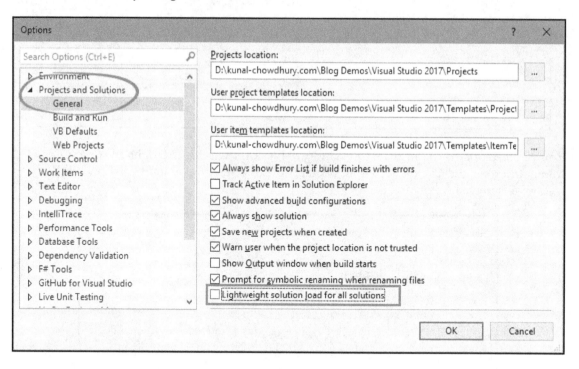

Once you enable the feature, it will apply the lightweight solution loading to all solutions that you open using Visual Studio 2017. If you don't want this but would like to open a solution only, you can enable it for that specific solution by right-clicking on the solution file in the **Solution Explorer**. There, you will find a context menu entry that says **Enable Lightweight Solution Load**. This is shown in the following screenshot:

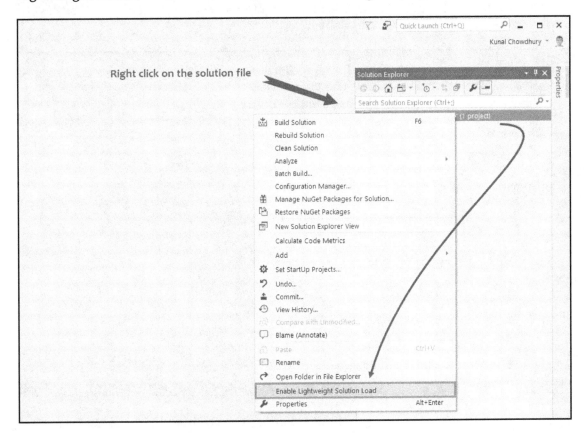

Connected Services

Microsoft added a new **Getting Started** experience for freshly created projects in Visual Studio 2017. It replaced existing **Getting Started** pages with an **Overview** tab in the new App Configuration Designer and focused the page on the actions that will get you started quickly to build your app, add an application insight/other connected services, publish your app to Azure, and set up continuous delivery:

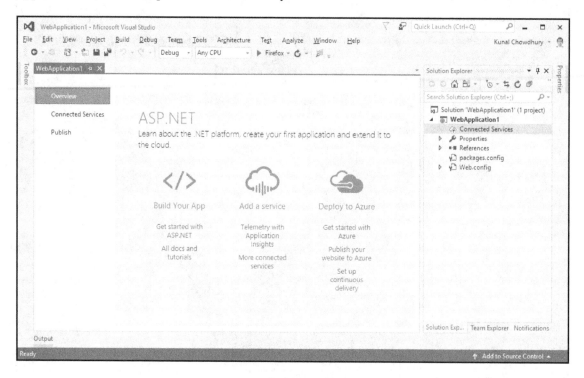

In Visual Studio 2015, we saw a section called **Service Capabilities**. In Visual Studio 2017, they have changed it to **Connected Service** to modernize the **Add Connected Service** and **Add Service Reference** features.

This will allow you to connect your app to services. A new node called **Connected Services** is available in the **Solution Explorer** for web and mobile applications. Double-clicking on this node will open a new full-page tab in Visual Studio where you can configure popular Microsoft services available for you to connect to.

Using **Monitoring with Application Insights**, you can gain insights through telemetry, analytics, and smart detection in the following ways:

- Detect and diagnose exceptions and application performance issues
- Monitor the website insights hosted on Azure, containers, on-premises, and on other cloud providers
- Integrate with your DevOps pipeline using Visual Studio, VSTS, GitHub, and Webhooks

Here is the screenshot of the **Connected Services** screen present inside Visual Studio 2017:

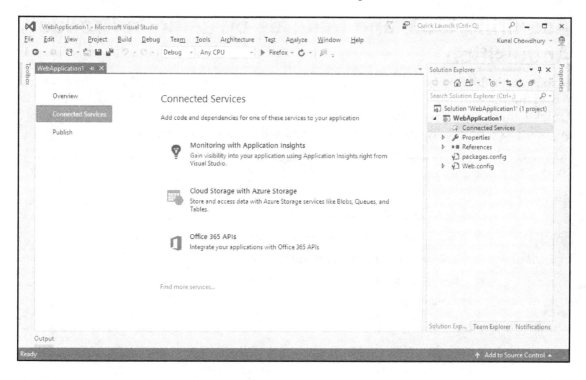

The **Cloud Storage with Azure Storage** feature will allow you to store and access data with Azure Storage services, such as Blobs, Queues, and Tables. If you have an Azure subscription, you can connect to it and start using it on your web or mobile apps. You can also connect to the Azure App Service to add authentication and deliver push notifications for mobile apps.

The other popular service, **Office 365 APIs**, will allow you to integrate your applications with Office 365 Services. A wizard is there to help you easily configure your project to connect with services such as mail, calendar, contacts, files, and more. You can also create an application in the Azure Active Directory associated with your Office 365 domain. To get started, you should have a valid Office 365 subscription available.

There is a **Find more services** link at the bottom of the page, which will open the Visual Studio Marketplace under the **Extensions and Updates** option, where you will be able to connect to more services.

Acquiring tools and features by using In-Product Acquisition

Visual Studio 2017 makes it easier to acquire any missing components using **In-Product Acquisition**. Using this, you don't have to leave the IDE to start the installer. Using the **Quick Launch** search bar, you can kick off the installer to start an in-product acquisition of any workload or individual component. Consider the following screenshot:

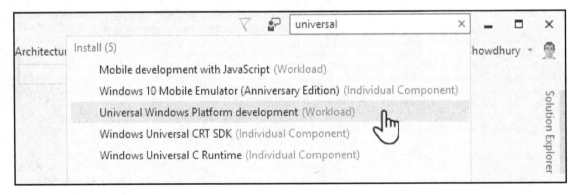

The preceding image shows us how to use Visual Studio to acquire a **Universal Windows Platform development** workflow and other related components. This will directly launch the installer and proceed towards the installation of said workflow.

If you cannot find the templates that you are looking for, the Visual Studio 2017 installer can also be opened from the **New Project** dialog box, as shown in the following screenshot:

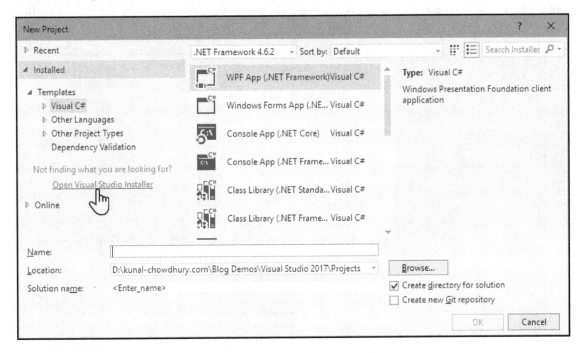

The Run to Click feature

Debugging now becomes easier with Visual Studio 2017. You can simply click on an icon next to a line of code to run to that line while debugging. When you have stopped at a breakpoint, just click on the green **Run to Click** icon that subtly appears next to the line of code that your mouse is hovered over. This will reduce the burden of adding temporary breakpoints and several steps that need to be performed to break the debugger to a specific line on the fly:

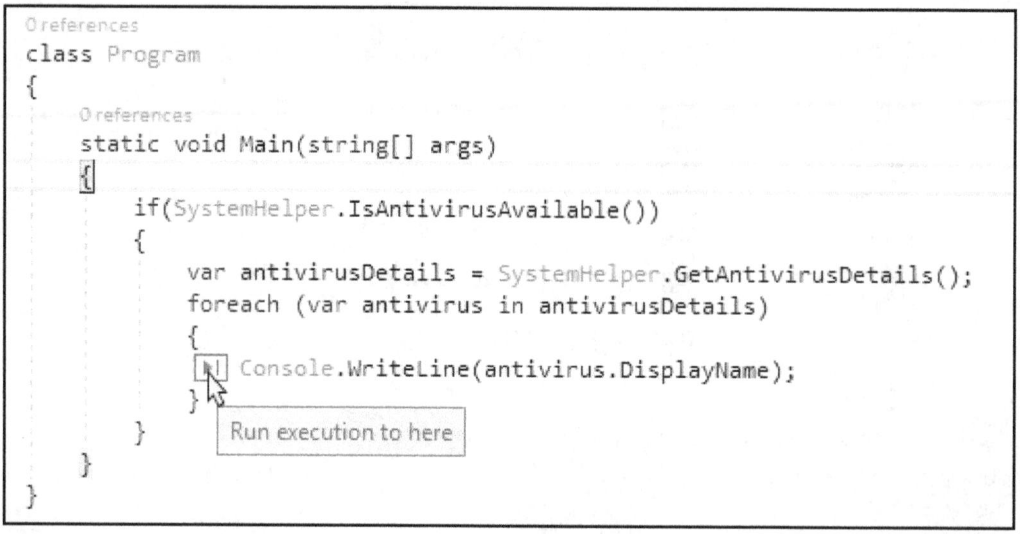

```
0 references
class Program
{
    0 references
    static void Main(string[] args)
    {
        if(SystemHelper.IsAntivirusAvailable())
        {
            var antivirusDetails = SystemHelper.GetAntivirusDetails();
            foreach (var antivirus in antivirusDetails)
            {
                    Console.WriteLine(antivirus.DisplayName);
            }
        }              Run execution to here
    }
}
```

This feature is enabled by default. To disable it, click on the menu item **Tools | Options** and then navigate to **Debugging | General**. Alternatively, you can directly navigate there by clicking on the menu item **Debug | Options**. Scroll to the end of the right-side panel and find an option labelled **Show run to click button in editor while debugging**. Uncheck it to disable the feature.

If you want to re-enable it later, follow the same steps and check the aforementioned option. Consider the following screenshot:

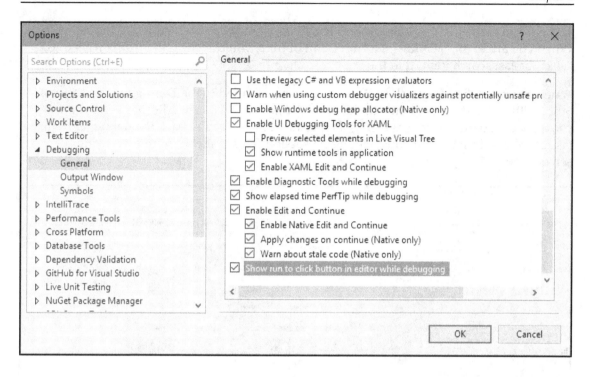

Improved Attach to Process with process filtering

In the earlier versions of Visual Studio, it was quite difficult to search for a particular process in the **Available Processes** list of the **Attach to Process** dialog box. To overcome this, Microsoft has added a search box in the top-right corner of the list. It will help you filter the list and find out the exact process that you are looking for:

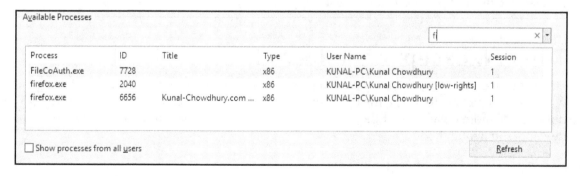

To help you further in this long process list, history entry has been added to the search box. When you are in this window at a later point of time, you can click on the arrowhead to select the last search item from the list.

A new entry labelled **Reattach to Process...** has been added to the **Debug** menu of Visual Studio 2017 to help you reattach to the process that you used last. Alternatively, you can press the keyboard shortcut, which is *Shift + Alt + P*, to directly attach the debugger to the last processes from the previous debugging session. This is shown in the following screenshot:

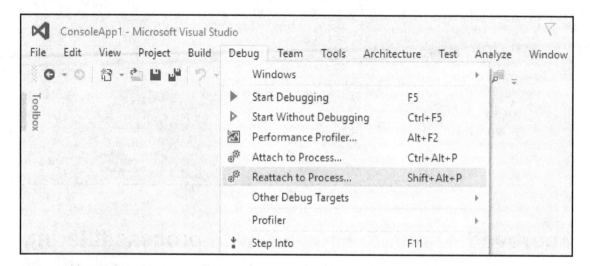

The debugger will first try to reattach to the process by matching the previous process ID, and then by matching to the previous process name. If no matches are found, or if there are multiple processes with the same name, the **Attach to Process** dialog will open to allow you to select the desired process from the list.

The new exception helper

Handling an exception is the most crucial part for a developer and it becomes frustrating when you are unable to define the cause of the same. Previous versions of Visual Studio do not provide more details about the exception other than a generic contextual UI to the developer in debug mode.

Microsoft worked on a redesigned UI for the exception helper to give you more details of the exception in a compact non-modal dialog with quick access to the inner exception. When there is a `NullReferenceException`, the new UI shows you what was null. Take a look at the following screenshot that shows **antivirusList** was null, which caused the issue:

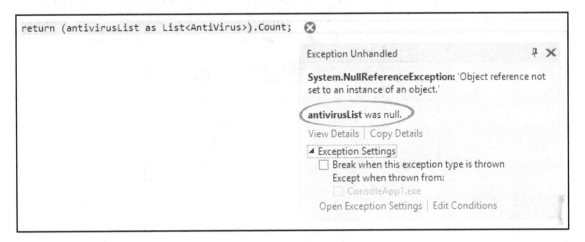

Add conditions to Exception Settings

Visual Studio 2017 allows you to add conditions when you configure the debugger to break on thrown exceptions from a specific module. Thus, the breakpoint will hit only when the specified condition is met. You can use the asterisk/wildcards to broaden the conditions, as shown in the following screenshot:

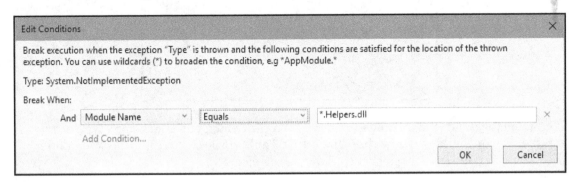

Updates to Diagnostic Tools

When you start your debugging session inside Visual Studio, the **Diagnostic Tools** window becomes visible, having many details on the screen. With Visual Studio 2017, you can now view the number of Application Insights and UI Analysis events (UWP apps only) that occurred in your application, along with the number of Exceptions and IntelliTrace events. You can also take a memory snapshot of your heap and enable or disable the CPU profiling:

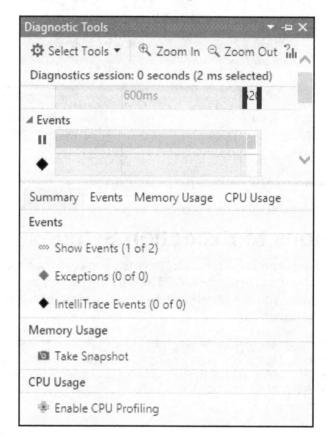

If you don't want to load **Diagnostic Tools** when the debugger session starts, you can disable it by unchecking the **Enable Diagnostic Tools while debugging** checkbox under the debugging options. Consider the following screenshot:

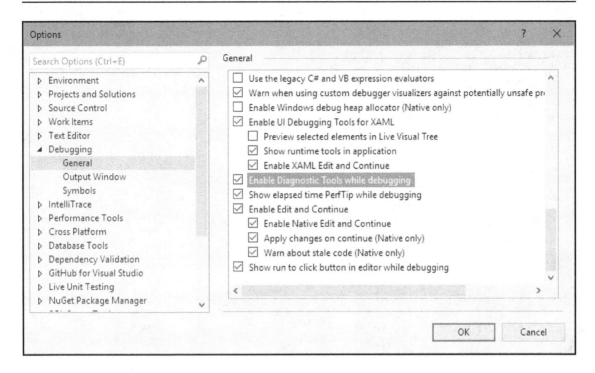

Summary

By the end of this chapter, you will have learned many things that have been newly added/modified in Visual Studio 2017. You learned about the workloads and the individual components part of the new installation experience. You also learned how to create an offline layout of the installer and the step-by-step instructions to install Visual Studio 2017 on your system.

Apart from those, we also covered the new and improved changes in Visual Studio 2017 IDE that will improve the productivity of developers. Whether you want to create a new project, open an existing one, or work with code, find the references of any symbol, or debug, you will find it useful and easy to use everywhere. Also, the convenient way to open a folder, load the solution in a lightweight manner, or acquire additional components using the In-Product Acquisition is second to none.

In the next chapter, we will discuss the new features introduced in C# 7.0 that have been introduced with Visual Studio 2017 for developers to build rapid and robust applications without spending too much time on code.

2
What is New in C# 7.0?

C# is a simple, modern, object-oriented programming language with support for component-oriented programming. It constructs robust applications using automatic garbage collection of unused objects, proper exception handling, and type-safe design.

Along with Visual Studio 2017, Microsoft introduces the next version of C#, that is, C# 7.0, which provides several changes and new features for developers to build rapid and robust applications without spending more time on code.

In this chapter, we will learn about the following new features introduced in C# 7.0, guided through the code:

- Local functions or nested functions
- Literal improvements in C# 7.0
- The new digit separators
- Getting to know about pattern matching
- The `ref` returns and locals
- New changes to tuples
- Changes to the throw expression
- Changes to Expression-bodied members
- New changes to the out variables
- Getting to know about the Deconstruction syntax
- Uses of the generalized `async` return types

Local functions or nested functions

C# 7.0, which comes with Visual Studio 2017, allows you to write local functions or nested functions. The local function provides you with the ability to declare methods/functions inside an already defined methods body. It has the same capability as normal methods, but it will be scoped to the method block where they are declared.

In earlier versions of C#, we needed to write the method bodies separately and then we needed to call one method from the other. Here is the old way to write a method called by another method:

```
public static Person GetBloggerDetails()
{
  return new Person
  {
    FirstName = "Kunal",
    LastName = "Chowdhury",
    Blogs = GetBlogs()
  };
}

private static List<string> GetBlogs()
{
  return new List<string> { "http://www.kunal-chowdhury.com" };
}
```

In the preceding example, although the GetBlogs method is private, it is accessible to the other members of the same class and is being detected by IntelliSense. To overcome this, C# 7.0 introduced **local functions** (**nested functions**), by which you will be able to add a number of local/nested functions within a function/method body, constructor, or property's getter and setter. Here's how to do it:

```
public static void CalculateOne()
{
  double a = 5, b = 3;

  double Sum(double x, double y) { return x + y; }
  double Subtract(double x, double y) { return x - y; }
  double Multiply(double x, double y) { return x * y; }

  void Print(string msg, double value)
  {
    Console.WriteLine(msg + value);
  }

  Print(string.Format("Sum of {0}, {1} is: ", a, b), Sum(a, b));
```

```
        Print(string.Format("Difference of {0}, {1} is: ", a, b),
          Subtract(a, b));
        Print(string.Format("Multiplication of {0}, {1} is: ", a, b),
          Multiply(a, b));
    }
```

Here you can see that the Sum, Subtract, Multiply, and Print methods are local to the CalculateOne method. So, no one other than the callee will have access to it. That means, only the CalculateOne method from the preceding example will have access to those local methods, thus, making your code more secure:

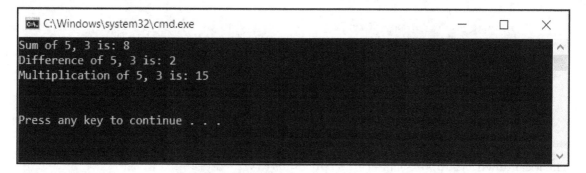

It's not mandatory to pass a parameter to the inline method. You can use the variables already in scope of the main method (callee). Here's an example for your quick reference:

```
        public static void CalculateTwo(int a, int b)
        {
          Print();
          void Print()
          {
            Console.WriteLine("Sum of {0}, {1}: {2}", a, b, (a + b));
          }
        }
```

Once you run the preceding code snippet, you will see the following output in console window:

You can also utilize the same capabilities as a normal function here. For example, you can easily use generics, ref and out parameters, dynamic, async and await within a local function and achieve all the things that a normal function does. The following code block returns an out parameter from a local function:

```
public static void CalculateThree()
{
    void Sum(int x, int y, out int result) => result = x + y;

    int retValue = 0;
    Sum(5, 3, out retValue);

    Console.WriteLine("Result: " + retValue);
}
```

Remember that a local function cannot be static and it does not maintain any of the call stack information that a normal function does. That's why, if you are using recursive calls and the call stack becomes too high, you may sometime get StackOverflowException. As the local function does not have any call stack, it is better to use it in such scenarios.

The local function supports Caller Info Attributes (CallerMemberName, CallerLineNumber, CallerFilePath). Here's an example:

```
public static void PrintMethodDetails()
{
    void Print([CallerMemberName] string name = null,
               [CallerLineNumber] int line = 0,
               [CallerFilePath] string filePath = null)
    {
        Console.WriteLine("The method name is: " + name);
        Console.WriteLine("The method line no. is: " + line);
        Console.WriteLine("The file path is: " + filePath);
    }
    Print();
}
```

The preceding code snippet will result in the following output:

You can declare a local function with the same name as the member method and the local function will hide it:

```csharp
public static void DisplayText()
{
  void Print()
  {
    Console.WriteLine("Print from local function");
  }
  Print();
}

public static void Print()
{
  Console.WriteLine("Print from member method");
}
```

Here you can see that, although a member method named Print is there, it called the local function instead of the member method:

Literal improvements in C# 7.0

There were two types of literals supported in C# prior to C# 7.0. They are **decimal literals** and **hexadecimal literals**. For example, 490 is a decimal literal, whereas 0x50A or 0X50A is a hexadecimal literal, equivalent to the decimal value 490. Please note that the prefixes 0x and 0X define the same thing.

Here's an example for you to easily understand how a hexadecimal literal is used in C#:

```
class Program
{
  static void Main(string[] args)
  {
    double height = 490;
    double width = 1290;

    double heightInHex = 0x1EA; // equivalent to decimal 490
    double widthInHex = 0x50A; // equivalent to decimal 1290

    Console.WriteLine("Height: " + heightInHex + " Width: " +
widthInHex);
    }
  }
```

Along with C# 7.0, Microsoft added more support to literals, and they have now introduced binary literals in C# to handle the binary value. The binary literals prefixed with 0b or 0B have the same meaning.

In the following example, the decimal value of the binary literal 0b1110110110 is 950:

```
class Program
{
  static void Main(string[] args)
  {
    double height = 950;
    double width = 5046;

    double heightInBinary = 0b1110110110; // decimal 950
    double widthInBinary = 0b1001110110110; // decimal 5046

    Console.WriteLine("Height: " + heightInBinary + " Width: " +
widthInBinary);
    }
  }
```

Remember that, whether your representation is decimal, hexadecimal, or binary in code, the output is always in decimal form only.

Once you run the preceding code snippet, you will see the following output in console window:

The new digit separators

Digit separator is a new feature in C# 7.0. You can use _ (underscore) inside numeric literals as a digit separator. The purpose of it is none other than improving the readability of the value in code.

You can put a digit separator (_) wherever you want between digits. You can have multiple underscores (____) too. They will have no effect on the value. This is shown in the following code snippet:

```
var decimalValue1 = 1_50_000; // better than 150000
var decimalValue2 = 25_91_50_000; // better than 259150000

// you can use multiple underscores too
var decimalValue3 = 25_91__50___000; // better than 259150000
```

You can also add digit separators to a binary literal and/or hexadecimal literals:

```
var binaryValue = 0b1010_1011_1100_1101_1110_1111;
var hexadecimalValue = 0xAB_C_0_D_EF_578;
```

Please note that the following conventions are invalid:

- _1_50_000, as it starts with _
- 1_50_000_ or 1_50_000.25_, as it ends with _
- 5000_._25, as the decimal point can't be associated with _

- _0b1100, 0b_1100, or 0_b_1100, as 0b should be prefixed with a valid binary number
- _0xFEB1, 0x_FEB1, or 0_x_FEB1, as 0x should be prefixed with a valid hexadecimal value

Here is the complete code for you to try:

```
class Program
{
  static void Main(string[] args)
  {
    var decimalValue1 = 1_50_000; // better than 150000
    var decimalValue2 = 25_91_50_000; // better than 259150000

    // you can use multiple underscores too
    var decimalValue3 = 25_91__50___000;

    Console.WriteLine("Decimal Value 1: " + decimalValue1);
    Console.WriteLine("Decimal Value 2: " + decimalValue2);
    Console.WriteLine("Decimal Value 3: " + decimalValue3);

    var binaryValue = 0b1010_1011_1100_1101_1110_1111;
    var hexadecimalValue = 0xAB_C_0_D_EF_578;

    Console.WriteLine("Binary Value: " + binaryValue);
    Console.WriteLine("Hexadecimal Value: " + hexadecimalValue);
  }
}
```

Here's the output of the preceding code:

```
C:\Windows\system32\cmd.exe                       —    □    ×
Decimal Value 1: 150000
Decimal Value 2: 259150000
Decimal Value 3: 259150000

Binary Value: 11259375
Hexadecimal Value: 737675244920


Press any key to continue . . .
```

Getting to know about pattern matching

Pattern matching is a new notion introduced in C# 7.0, which adds some power to the existing operators and statements. You can perform pattern matching on any data type and from that statement you can extract the value of that data type. There are two different types of pattern matching in C# 7.0:

- The Is expression with pattern matching
- Switch statements with pattern matching

The Is expression with pattern matching

In this type of pattern matching, it introduces a new pattern variable out of the expression, allowing you to extract the value of the type. It is similar to the out variable, but with a limited scope to the surroundings.

Let's look at an example. In the old method, we need to check for the data type, and then we must convert the variable to the specified data type to get the value out of it. Here, if the person is of type Employee, we can type cast it to Employee to get the values of the employee object:

```
if (person is Employee)
{
  Employee employee = (Employee)person;
  Console.WriteLine("Person '{0}' is an Employee",
                    employee.Firstname);
}
else if (person is Customer)
{
  Customer customer = (Customer)person;
  Console.WriteLine("Person '{0}' is a Customer",
                    customer.Firstname);
}
```

In C# 7.0, you can do that in the same line while validating the expression. It allows you to extract the is expression by adding a pattern to the right side of the expression and extracting the value from it. The preceding example can be rewritten in C# 7.0 as follows:

```
if (person is Employee employee)
{
  Console.WriteLine("Person '{0}' is an Employee",
                    employee.Firstname);
}
else if (person is Customer customer)
```

```
    {
        Console.WriteLine("Person '{0}' is a Customer",
                          customer.Firstname);
    }
```

Here you can see that `employee` is a value extracted from the same line as the expression, which you can use in subsequent lines of the block.

You can also use the extracted variable just like an `out` variable with a limited scope to the surrounded blocks. The following code snippet shows you how to do this:

```
    if (!(obj is int i))
    {
        return;
    }
    Console.WriteLine("Value of i: " + i);
```

Here you can see that the value i, which is derived after the conversion in the expression, acts like an `out` parameter and has access to it within the next code lines outside the expression block. If you run the preceding example, it will print the value of i (where `obj` is 50, in our case) in the console window:

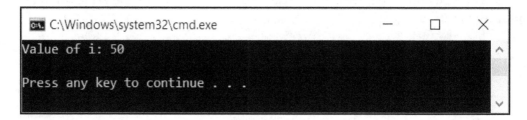

Switch statements with pattern matching

The new switch case statement pattern enhances the case blocks by comparing the value, not just by constants, but also by an expression. In C# 7.0, you can generalize the switch statement in the following manner:

- You can put `switch` on any type, in addition to primitive data types
- You can use patterns on case clauses
- You can have additional conditions on case clauses using the keyword `when`

Let's look at the following example, where we have the base `Person` reference passed to the `switch` statement:

```
public static void Validate(Person person)
{
  switch (person)
  {
    case Employee e:
      Console.WriteLine($"{e.Firstname} is an Employee");
      break;

    case Customer c when (c.IsPremium):
      Console.WriteLine($"{c.Firstname} is a Premium Customer");
      break;

    case Customer c:
      Console.WriteLine($"{c.Firstname} is a Customer");
      break;

    default:
      Console.WriteLine($"{person.Firstname} is a Person");
      break;

    case null:
      Console.WriteLine("Null value specified\n");
      break;
  }
}

// satisfies the first case of type Employee
Validate(new Employee { Firstname = "Kunal" });

// satisfies the second case where the person is a Premium Customer
Validate(new Customer { Firstname = "Kunal", IsPremium = true });

// satisfies the third case where the person is a Normal Customer
Validate(new Customer { Firstname = "Kunal" });

// satisfies the fourth case where the person does not fit any of the
above cases
Validate(new Person { Firstname = "Kunal" });

// satisfies the fifth case when the person is set as 'null'
Validate(null);
```

In this example, if the person is an `Employee`, the first case clause will execute. When the person is a `Customer`, the second or third case clause will execute based on the condition satisfied by the `when` expression. If no other case satisfies, it will execute the default case.

When the object passed to the switch statement is `null`, it will get higher preference on top of the default case, jump directly to the `case null`, and display **Null value specified** in the console window. This will reduce your additional code to checking whether the object is null and giving you the option to handle the null check within the switch case:

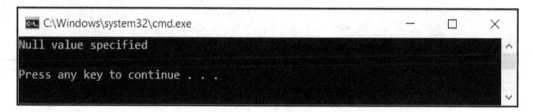

Some important points on switch statements in C# 7.0:

- Just like the `catch` clauses, the order of the `case` clauses now matters. The first clause that matches, gets picked. For example, the first clause of the following code snippet gets picked up when a customer is a premium user. This is a valid case for the compiler:

```
case Customer c when (c.IsPremium):
    Console.WriteLine($"{c.Firstname} is a Premium Customer");
    break;

case Customer c:
    Console.WriteLine($"{c.Firstname} is a Customer");
    break;
```

- The following case becomes invalid as the more generic one gets picked up before checking the condition within the `case` statement. The compiler will give an error in such cases, as it has already been handled by the previous case:

```
case Customer c:
    Console.WriteLine($"{c.Firstname} is a Customer");
    break;

case Customer c when (c.IsPremium):
    Con                                              omer");
    bre
            class Packtpub.KunalChowdhury.Demos.Customer
default
            The switch case has already been handled by a previous case.
    Console.WriteLine($"{person.Firstname} is a Person");
    break;
```

- Also, the compiler will give you an error for such obvious cases having unreachable codes. The following code snippet is invalid as well:

```
case Customer c:
    Console.WriteLine($"{c.Firstname} is a Customer");
    break;

case Customer c when (c.IsPremium):
    index++;
    Cons                      name} is a Premium Customer");
    brea    [#] (local variable) int index

default:      Unreachable code detected
    Console.WriteLine($"{person.Firstname} is a Person");
    break;
```

- Even though you write the `null` case at the end, the `default` case always gets evaluated at the end, giving higher preference to the null check.
- The pattern variables introduced by a case are always in the scope of the corresponding switch section only.

Visual Studio 2015 and C# 6.0 included a similar kind of when-clause pattern as part of a structured error handling system:

```
try
{
    // perform your error prone code
}
catch (Exception ex) when (logExceptionDetails)
{
    // handle the exception only if you want to log
    Console.WriteLine("Catch block when logExceptionDetails=true");
}
catch
{
    // all other cases
    Console.WriteLine("Catch block when logExceptionDetails=false");
}
```

The ref returns and locals

Since C# 1.0, the language has supported passing parameters to a method by reference using the `ref`, but there exists no mechanism to return a safe reference to stack or heap memory locations.

In C# 7.0, Microsoft has provided the option for developers to return values by reference and store them in local variables as a reference pointer.

Before going into an example of return by reference, let us first look at an example of how the return by value works with a pass by reference parameter. In the following example, the `GetAsValue` method accepts a third parameter of type integer as a reference, and returns a value to the callee, which gets stored in the local variable `name`:

```
public static void DemoReturnAsValue()
{
    var count = 0;
    var index = 0;
    string[] names = { "Kunal", "Manika", "Dwijen" };
    string name = GetAsValue(names, index, ref count);
```

```
        Console.WriteLine("No. of strings in the array: " + count);
        Console.WriteLine("Name at {0}th index is: {1}\n", index, name);
        name = "Rajat";
        Console.WriteLine("The value of 'name' variable changed to:" + name);
        Console.WriteLine("The new name at {0}th index is still: {1}\n",
            index, GetAsValue(names, index, ref count));
    }
    public static string GetAsValue(string[] names, int index,
        ref int count)
    {
        count = names.Length;
        return names[index];
    }
}
```

Now, when we change the value of the variable name, it does not change the original string of the array, as it returned by value and there's no reference between them. If you run the preceding example, you will see the following output, where the zeroth position of the array still has the previous/original value. The count variable that we passed as reference parameter will have the length of the array as it is marked as ref:

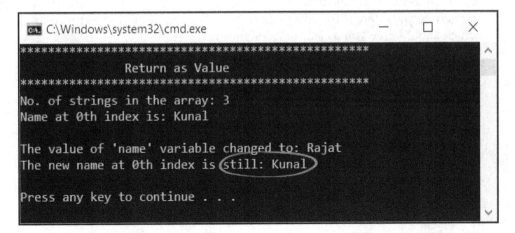

In C# 7.0, if you want to return something from a method by reference, you should mark the return type with the `ref` keyword and put it as a reference in a local variable. This is how the preceding implementation of the `GetAsValue` will change, along with the implementation of storing it:

```
public static ref string GetAsReference(string[] names, int index, ref int count)
{
    count = names.Length;
    return ref names[index];
}

ref string name = ref GetAsReference(names, index, ref count);
```
Store by reference in local variable

Now, when you change the value of the variable `name`, it will change the original value of the array as we are referencing its memory address. Printing the value of the array will give you the changed output. Here is the complete code implementation for the preceding changes, which should give you a clear understanding:

```
public static void DemoReturnAsReference()
{
    var count = 0;
    var index = 0;
    string[] names = { "Kunal", "Manika", "Dwijen" };
    ref string name = ref GetAsReference(names, index, ref count);

    Console.WriteLine("No. of strings in the array: " + count);
    Console.WriteLine("Name at {0}th index is: {1}\n", index, name);

    name = "Rajat";
    Console.WriteLine("The value of 'name' variable changed to: " +
name);
    Console.WriteLine("The new name at {0}th index is now: {1}\n", index,
                    GetAsReference(names, index, ref count));
}

public static ref string GetAsReference(string[] names,
    int index, ref int count)
{
    count = names.Length;
    return ref names[index];
}
```

When you run the code, you will get the preceding output, where the zeroth index of the array now has the new name, which we have changed by reference.

New changes to tuples

A **tuple** is a finite ordered list of elements. In C#, it's not a new thing, having been available since .NET Framework 4.0. It is useful when you want to return multiple values from a method without creating a separate class or collection to hold the data. Tuples are declared in the manner, Tuple<T1, T2, T3, ...> and are available under the System namespace.

By default, a tuple can hold up to eight value types, but you can extend it by adding the reference of System.Runtime.

Although this is useful when returning multiple values, you need to create an allocation for the System.Tuple<...> object. The following example demonstrates how to return multiple values using a tuple:

```
public static Tuple<string, string> GetAuthor()
{
    return new Tuple<string, string>("Kunal Chowdhury",
                              "www.kunal-chowdhury.com");
}
```

Based on the number of elements, the returned value generates properties dynamically to get the individual values. For example, if you return two values using a tuple, the returned object will have **Item1** and **Item2** properties to access the individual values. If the tuple object has three values, the properties will be Item1, Item2, Item3, and Item4.

Here you can see an example of how to access the returned values:

```
var authorDetails = GetAuthor();
Console.WriteLine(authorDetails.Item1 + authorDetails.Item2);
```

Equals	
GetHashCode	
GetType	
Item1	
Item2	
ToString	
ToValueTuple<>	

In C# 7.0, you don't need to specify it by explicitly creating the tuple object. Rather, you can specify the return types within brackets, as shown in the following code snippet:

```
public static (string, string) GetAuthor()
{
    return ("Kunal Chowdhury", "www.kunal-chowdhury.com");
}
```

If you receive an error using the new way of using tuples in C# 7.0, you must explicitly reference System.ValueTuple from the NuGet package library. To install the package, either open the NuGet package manager or the NuGet package manager console; or you can simply click the **Install package 'System.ValueTuple'** menu item from the tooltip, as shown in the following screenshot. This is the simplest way to download and install the package:

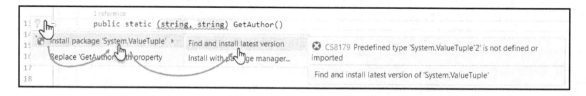

Alternatively, you can find the package here:
http://www.nuget.org/packages/System.ValueTuple/.

Once you have installed the package, you can see that the DLL reference to the **System.ValueTuple** has already been added to your project:

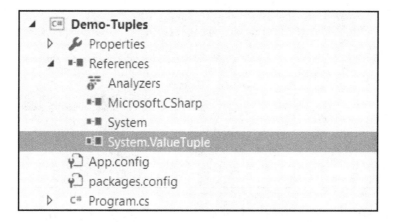

Apart from the preceding simplest way, C# 7.0 also allows you to define the name to the tuple elements to describe them easily:

```
public static (string AuthorName, string Blog) GetAuthor()
{
    return ("Kunal Chowdhury", "www.kunal-chowdhury.com");
}
```

You can also specify the element names directly to the tuple literals, making it simpler and error free while assigning:

```
public static (string AuthorName, string Blog) GetAuthor()
{
    return (AuthorName: "Kunal Chowdhury",
            Blog: "www.kunal-chowdhury.com");
}
```

Setting a descriptive name to the tuple element makes it easily identifiable while accessing from the returned object. In the preceding example, AuthorName and Blog are better than **Item1** and **Item2**.

When you make the changes to your existing tuple definition, you can easily rename it in the accessible method by following the step given here:

```
9              var authorDetails = GetAuthor();
10             Console.WriteLine(authorDetails.Item1 + authorDetails.Item2);
11
12   Use explicitly provided tuple name  ►    IDE0032 Prefer explicitly provided tuple element name

     Suppress IDE0032              ►    ...
13       public static (s       var authorDetails = GetAuthor();
14       {                       Console.WriteLine(authorDetails.Item1 + authorDetails.Item2);
15           return ("Kuna }     Console.WriteLine(authorDetails.AuthorName + authorDetails.Item2);
16       }                       ...
17
18                          Preview changes
19
                           Fix all occurrences in: Document | Project | Solution
```

When you are directly using tuples in Visual Studio editor window, you can see them appear in IntelliSense to use in your code.

Points to remember:

- Tuples are value types
- Elements of tuples are public and mutable
- Two tuples are equal, if their elements are pairwise equal

Changes to the throw expression

The earlier versions of C# had some limitations on throwing exceptions from certain places, which caused developers to write more code to validate and raise exceptions. In C# 7.0, those limitations have been removed to reduce the overload.

The **Null Coalescing** operator now allows you to throw an exception in the middle of the expression without explicitly checking for `null`:

```
m_designation = designation ??
        throw new ArgumentNullException(designation);
```

It is now possible to throw an exception from the **Conditional operator** too:

```
m_department = department == null ?
        throw new ArgumentNullException(department) :
        department;
```

C# 7.0 also allows you to throw an exception from **expression-bodied member**, as shown in the following code snippet:

```
public void SetSalary(double salary) =>
        throw new NotImplementedException();
```

Changes to the expression-bodied members

In C# 6.0, Microsoft introduced the expression-bodied methods and properties, but these had a few limitations, which didn't allow us to use them in the constructors, destructors, and getters/setters of properties.

With C# 7.0, these limitations are no more, and you can now write them for single-liner constructors and destructors, as well as the getter and setter of a property. Here's how you can use them:

```
public class Person
{
  private string m_name;

  // constructor
  public Person() => Console.WriteLine("Constructor called");

  // destructor
  ~Person() => Console.WriteLine("Destructor called");

  // getter/setter properties
  public string Name
  {
    get => m_name;
    set => m_name = value;
  }
}
```

When you run the preceding code, the following output can be seen in the console window:

New changes with the out variables

Currently in C#, we need to first declare a variable before we pass it as an out parameter to a method. You can use a var while declaration if you initialize them in the same line, but when you don't want to initialize explicitly, you must declare them, specifying the full type:

```
// predeclaration of 'out' variable was mandatory
int result; // or, var result = 0;
string value = "125";

int.TryParse(value, out result);

Console.WriteLine("The result is: " + result);
```

In C# 7.0, the out variables can be declared right at the point where they are passed as an out parameter to a method. You can now directly write int.TryParse(value, out int result); and get the value of the out parameter, to use it in the scope of the enclosing block:

```
static void Main(string[] args)
{
  string value = "125";
  int.TryParse(value, out int result);
  Console.WriteLine("Result:  " + result);
}
```

You can also use var instead of a strong type declaration, like int.TryParse(value, out var result);, and the compiler will define it properly:

```
static void Main(string[] args)
{
  string value = "125";
  int.TryParse(value, out var result);
  Console.WriteLine("Result:  " + result);
}
```

To use an out parameter, both the method definition and the calling method must explicitly use the out keyword.

If you have already written code in the existing way of declaration before passing the out parameter to a method, Visual Studio 2017 will allow you to leverage this new feature of C# 7.0 from the light bulb icon:

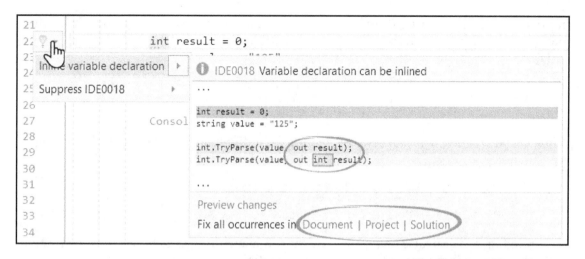

From the popup, you can fix all the similar occurrences, in the current document, the entire project, or at the solution level, by clicking the links highlighted as shown in the preceding screenshot.

Getting to know about deconstruction syntax

Deconstruction is a syntax to split a value into multiple parts and store those parts individually into new variables. For example, tuples that return multiple values. Let us take the following method as an example, which returns a tuple of two string variables, Title and Author (see the *New changes to tuples* section):

```
public (string Title, string Author) GetBookDetails()
{
    return (Title: "Mastering Visual Studio 2017",
            Author: "Kunal Chowdhury");
}
```

Now, when you call the method GetBookDetails(), it will return a tuple. You can access its elements by calling the element name, as follows:

```
var bookDetails = GetBookDetails(); // returns Tuple
Console.WriteLine("Title  : " + bookDetails.Title);
Console.WriteLine("Author : " + bookDetails.Author);
```

In a deconstructing declaration, you can split the tuple into parts and assign them directly into new variables. You can then access those variables individually, just like a local variable:

```
(string title, string author) = GetBookDetails();
Console.WriteLine("Title  : " + title);
Console.WriteLine("Author : " + author);
```

While deconstructing, you can also use `var` for the individual variables, instead of strong type names:

```
(var title, var author) = GetBookDetails();
Console.WriteLine("Title  : " + title);
Console.WriteLine("Author : " + author);
```

The preceding code can also be replaced by the following deconstruction syntax, by putting a single `var` outside the parentheses as an abbreviation:

```
var (title, author) = GetBookDetails();
Console.WriteLine("Title  : " + title);
Console.WriteLine("Author : " + author);
```

If you have existing variables with a deconstructing assignment, you can use the same variables to store the return values of a new call:

```
var (title, author) = GetBookDetails();
// deconstruct to existing variables
(title, author) = GetAnotherBookDetails();
Console.WriteLine("Title  : " + title);
Console.WriteLine("Author : " + author);
```

Until now, we have learned how to write the syntax to deconstruct a tuple. In C# 7.0, it's not limited to tuples only. You can use deconstructing assignments for any type, as long as it has a `Deconstruct` method in the following form: `public void Deconstruct (out T1 x1, ..., out Tn xn) { ... }`.

 A `Deconstruct` method should use `out` parameters to return the values instead of using tuples. This is to enable you to have multiple overloads for different numbers of values.

For example, let us create a class named `Book` exposing the `Deconstruct` method with two `out` variables:

```
public class Book
{
```

```
public void Deconstruct (out string Title, out string Author)
{
  Title = "Mastering Visual Studio 2017";
  Author = "Kunal Chowdhury";
}
}
```

As we didn't expose any properties to access the values of `Title` and `Author` from the `Book` class, we will not find them generally in the IntelliSense popup when trying to access an instance of the class. Refer to the following screenshot:

```
var book = new Book();
Console.WriteLine("Title  : " + book.);
```

  ⚲ Deconstruct
  ⚲ Equals
  ⚲ GetHashCode
  ⚲ GetType
  ⚲ ToString

As we have declared the `Deconstruct` method in the class, you can directly deconstruct the instance into multiple variables to get the desired output of the return values:

```
var book = new Book();
var (title, author) = book; //var (title, author) = new Book();
Console.WriteLine("Title  : " + title);
Console.WriteLine("Author : " + author);
```

When you run the preceding code, you will get the following output in the console window:

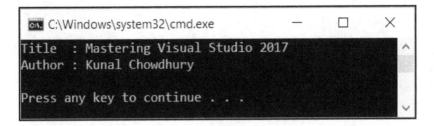

Uses of the generalized async return types

Prior to C# 7.0, `async` methods had to return either `void`, `Task`, or `Task<T>`. As `Task` is a reference type, returning such an object from `async` methods can impact performance because it allocates an object into memory even though it returns a cached object or runs asynchronously.

To overcome this, C# 7.0 introduces the `ValueTask` type, which is set to prevent the allocation of a `Task<T>` object when the result of the `async` operation is already available. Using it, the `async` methods can return types other than `Task`, `Task<T>`, and `void`:

```
public async ValueTask<long> GetValue()
{
   return await Task.Run<long>(() => 5000);
}
```

If you receive an error accessing `ValueTask` in C# 7.0, you must explicitly reference `System.Threading.Tasks.Extensions` from the `NuGet` package library. To install the package, either open the `NuGet` package manager or the `NuGet` package manager console; or you can simply click the **Install package 'System.Threading.Tasks.Extensions'** menu item from the tooltip, as shown in the following screenshot. This is the simplest way to download and install the package:

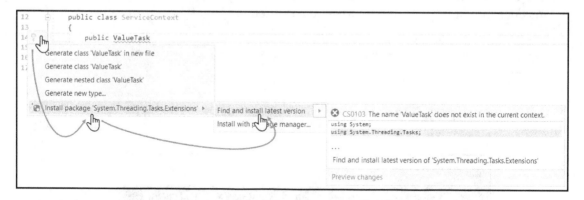

Alternatively, you can find the package here:
`http://www.nuget.org/packages/System.Threading.Tasks.Extensions/`.

Once you have installed the package, you can see that the DLL reference to
System.Threading.Tasks.Extensions has already been added to your project:

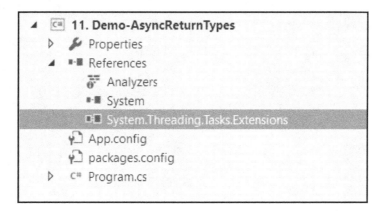

Summary

In this chapter, we have learned about the new features introduced in C# 7.0, along with the
release of Visual Studio 2017. We have also demonstrated each of them with examples/code.

At a glance, we have learned about local or nested functions, literal improvements, the new
digit separators, pattern matching, `ref` returns and locals, changes in tuples, changes to the
`throw` expression, and expression-bodied members. We also learned about the new changes
to the `out` variables, deconstruction syntax, and the uses of generalized `async` return types.

As we have become familiar with the features of C# 7.0, let's move on to the next chapter,
where we will learn about building applications for Windows using Windows Presentation
Foundation. We will also learn how to design a XAML UI, do data bindings, and much
more.

3

Building Applications for Windows Using XAML Tools

The **Windows Presentation Foundation** (**WPF**) provides developers a unified programming model to build dynamic, data-driven desktop applications for Windows. It supports a broad set of features that includes application models, controls, layouts, graphics, resources, security, and more. It is a graphical subsystem for rendering rich **UI** (**User Interfaces**) and is part of the .NET Framework, which was first released along with .NET 3.0.

The WPF is a resolution-independent framework that uses vector-based rendering engine using the **eXtendable Application Markup Language** (**XAML**) to create stunning user interfaces.

The runtime libraries for it to execute are included with Windows since Windows Vista and Windows Server 2008. If you are using Windows XP with SP2/SP3 and Windows Server 2003, you can optionally install the necessary libraries.

In this chapter, we will discuss on the following points and start building Windows applications using the WPF framework:

- The WPF architecture
- The XAML overview
  - Object element syntax
  - Property attribute syntax
  - Property element syntax
  - Content syntax
  - Collection syntax
  - Event attribute syntax

- Understanding the XAML namespaces
- Working with inline code in XAML pages
- The code behind file of an XAML page
- Build your first WPF application
  - Get started with WPF project
  - Understanding the WPF project structure
  - Get familiar with XAML Designer
  - Adding controls in XAML
  - Command-line parameters in WPF application
- Layouts in WPF
  - Using Grid as a WPF panel
  - Using Stack Panel to define stacked layout
  - Using Canvas as a panel
  - Using WPF Dock Panel to dock child elements
  - Using the WrapPanel to automatically reposition
  - Using UniformGrid to place elements in uniform cells
- WPF property system
- Data binding in WPF
- Using Converters while data binding
- Using triggers in WPF
  - Property trigger
  - Multi trigger
  - Data trigger
  - Multidata trigger
  - Event trigger

The WPF architecture

The architecture of WPF is a layered architecture, which includes managed, unmanaged, and the core APIs as shown in the following diagram, where the programming model is exposed through the managed code:

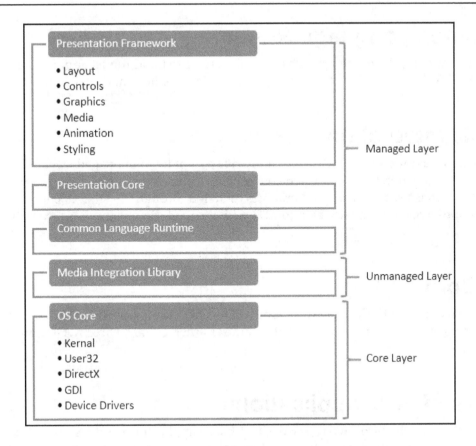

Presentation Framework

The **Presentation Framework** (`presentationframework.dll`) provides the required components (such as layouts, controls, graphics, media, data bindings, documents, animations, and styling) to build WPF applications.

Presentation Core

The **Presentation Core** layer (`presentationcore.dll`) provides you the wrapper around the Media Integration Library to provide you public interface to access the MIL Core. It also provides you the Visual System to develop the visual tree, which contains visual elements and rendering instructions.

Common Language Runtime

Common Language Runtime provides several features to build robust applications. This includes **CTS** (**Common Type System**), error handling, memory management, and more.

Media Integration Library

The **Media Integration Library** (`milcore.dll`) is part of the unmanaged layer and provides you access to the unmanaged components to enable tight integrations with DirectX, which is used to display all graphics rendered through the DirectX engine. MILCore provides performance gain to CLR with the rendering instructions from the Visual System.

OS Core

The next layer is the **OS Core** that provides you access to low-level APIs to handle the core components of the operating system that includes Kernel, User32, DirectX, GDI, and Device Drivers.

Types of WPF applications

WPF applications can be of two types: desktop-based applications and web-based applications. The desktop applications are normal `.EXE` executables, whereas the web-based browser applications are the `.XBAP` files which can be deployed in web servers and run inside any supported browser. The .NET framework is mandatory to run any of these application outputs.

Each WPF application starts with two threads. The UI thread uses `System.Threading.DispatcherObject` to create the messaging system to maintain the queue of UI operations. Just like Win32 message pumping, it performs the UI operation sorted by the priority set to it. The other thread is the background thread to handle the rendering engine, which is being managed by WPF. It picks up a copy of the visual tree and performs action to show the visual components in the Direct 3D surface. After that, it calls all UI elements to determine the size and arranges the child elements by their parents.

The XAML overview

XAML (eXtensible Application Markup Language), is an XML-based markup language to declaratively create the UI of the WPF applications. You can create visible UI elements in the declarative XAML syntax and then write the code behind to perform the run-time logic.

Though it is not mandatory to use XAML to create the UI, it is well accepted to make the things easier as creation of the entire application UI is much more difficult using C# or VB.NET. It is as simple as writing an XML node with few attributes (optional) to create a simple button in the UI. The following examples show you how you can create a button using XAML:

```
<Button />
<Button Content="Click Here" />
<Button Height="36" Width="120" />
```

You can either compile an XAML page or render directly on the UI. When you compile an XAML file, it produces a binary file known as **BAML (Binary Application Markup Language)**, stored as resource inside the assembly file. When it loads into the memory, the BAML is parsed at runtime:

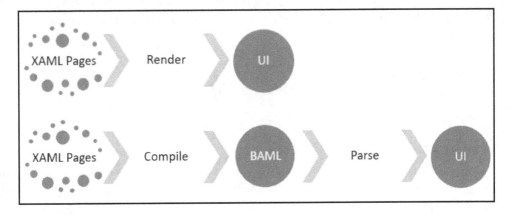

There are few syntax terminologies available to define an element in the XAML to create the instance of it. We'll take a look at few of them next to get started with it.

Object element syntax

The XAML object element declares an instance of a type. Each object element starts with an opening angular bracket (<) followed by the name of it. Optionally, it can have a prefix to define its namespace outside of the default scope. The object element can be closed by a closing angular bracket (>) or with a self-closing angular bracket (/>). When the object element has a child element, we use the first one followed by the end tag (`<Button>Click Here</Button>`), and for the other case, a self-closing element (`<Button Content="Click Here" />`) is used.

When you specify the object element in an XAML page, the instruction to create an instant of the element is being generated and when you load the XAML, it creates the instance by calling the default constructor of the same.

Property attribute syntax

Each element can have one or more properties. You can set the properties in XAML as an attribute. The syntax of it starts with the property name, an assignment operator and a value within quotes. For example, in the following code snippet, the first example defines a button element without specifying a property attribute whereas the other two elements have the attribute defined:

```
<Button />
<Button Content="Click Here" />
<Button Content="Click Here" Background="Red" />
```

Property element syntax

The properties can also be defined as an element when you cannot assign the value within the quotes. This generally starts with `<element.PropertyName>` and ends with `</element.PropertyName>`. The following example shows you how to write the `Background` property as an element to the Button:

```
<Button>
  <Button.Background>
    <SolidColorBrush Color="Red" />
  </Button.Background>
</Button>
```

Content syntax

An XAML element can have content within it. It can be set as the value of child elements of root. Refer to the following code blocks. The first example shows how to set the text content property of a button instead of specifying it in an attribute syntax (`<Button Content="Click Here" />`):

```
<Button>
    <Button.Content>
        Click Here
    </Button.Content>
</Button>
```

In the following example, when the `Button` element is wrapped by a `Border` panel, it is defined as element content of the said panel and omits the explicit definition of the content property:

```
<Border>
    <Button Content="Click Here" />
</Border>
```

The preceding code can be rewritten with a `Content` property (`Border.Child`) having a single element in it:

```
<Border>
    <Border.Child>
        <Button Content="Click Here" />
    </Border.Child>
</Border>
```

The value of an XAML content property must be contiguous and hence the following definition is incorrect:

```
<Button>
    Click
    <Button.Content>this</Button.Content>          ✕
    content
</Button>
```

Also, you cannot define an XAML content property like this, where you are trying to put the content twice:

```
<Button>
    <Button.Content>Click Here</Button.Content>
    <Button.Content>Click Here too</Button.Content>    ✗
</Button>
```

Collection syntax

Sometimes it's required to define a collection of elements in the XAML. This is done using the Collection syntax to make it more readable. For example, a **StackPanel** can have multiple elements defined inside the `Children` property :

```
<StackPanel>
    <StackPanel.Children>
        <Button Content="1" />
        <Button Content="2" />
    </StackPanel.Children>
</StackPanel>
```

The preceding example can also be written as follows, where the parser knows how to create and assign it:

```
<StackPanel>
    <Button Content="1" />
    <Button Content="2" />
</StackPanel>
```

Event attribute syntax

In XAML, you can also define events for a specific object element. Though it looks like property attribute, but is used to assign the event. If the attribute value of an element is the name of an event, it is treated as an event. In the following code snippet, the `Click` attribute defines the click event of the buttons:

```
<Button Click="Button_Click">Click Here</Button>
<Button Click="Button_Click" Content="Click Here" />
```

The implementation of the event handler is generally defined in the code behind of the XAML page. The event implementation for the preceding button click event looks like this:

```
void Button_Click(object sender, RoutedEventArgs e)
{
    // event implementation
}
```

Understanding the XAML namespaces

An XAML namespace is an extension to the XML namespace syntax, providing you the concept to use markup entities from referenced assemblies or different modules. When you create a new Windows UserControl or any other XAML pages, you will see that there are two XAML namespace declarations within the root tag of the XAML.

The first namespace
xmlns="http://schemas.microsoft.com/winfx/2006/xaml/presentation" maps the client/framework-specific XAML namespaces as default.

The second namespace declaration
xmlns:x="http://schemas.microsoft.com/winfx/2006/xaml" maps a different XAML namespace with the prefix x:, to provide you intrinsic supports to the XAML language definition. It defines many commonly used features, which are required for basic WPF applications. For example, the x:Class attribute in the root element of the XAML file defines the code behind the class name that you want to use as a partial class:

```
1  <Window x:Class="Demo_Basic.MainWindow"
2          xmlns="http://schemas.microsoft.com/winfx/2006/xaml/presentation"
3          xmlns:x="http://schemas.microsoft.com/winfx/2006/xaml"
4          Title="MainWindow" Height="350" Width="525">
5      <Grid>
6
7      </Grid>
8  </Window>
```

You can also map XAML namespaces to an assembly using a series of tokens in an xmlns declaration. The syntax has two token names: `clr-namespace` and `assembly`. For example, `xmlns:controls="clr-namespace:Packt.KunalChowdhury.Demo.Controls;assembly=MyAssembly"`.

The first token, that is, the `clr-namespace` defines the CLR namespace of the public element that you want to access from the second token, that is, `assembly`. The second token should pass the name of the assembly (without the file extension) and not the path of it. Once you have defined it, you can access the public type/element within that XAML.

Let's discuss this with a simple example:

```
<Window x:Class="MyWpfApplication.MainWindow"
  xmlns="http://schemas.microsoft.com/winfx/2006/xaml/presentation"
  xmlns:x="http://schemas.microsoft.com/winfx/2006/xaml"
  xmlns:controls="clr-namespace:Packt.KunalChowdhury.Demo.Controls;
  assembly=MyAssembly" Title="Main Window" Height="350" Width="525">
  <Grid>
    <controls:MyUserControl />
  </Grid>
</Window>
```

Here we have defined the XMLNS namespace to `clr-namespace:Packt.KunalChowdhury.Demo.Controls;assembly=MyAssembly` and assigned a prefix controls, so that we can access the public type `MyUserControl`, which is already available in it under the `Packt.KunalChowdhury.Demo.Controls` namespace with the `<controls:MyUserControl />` XAML tag.

 You can omit the `assembly` if the `clr-namespace` referenced is being defined within the same assembly as the application. Alternatively, you can specify `assembly=` without defining any string token.

Working with inline code in XAML pages

You can write inline programming code (C# or VB.NET) within the XAML page, using the `x:Code` directive and must be surrounded by `<![CDATA[...]]>` to escape the contents for XML. This can interact within the same XAML page:

```
<Window x:Class="MyWpfApplication.MainWindow"
xmlns="http://schemas.microsoft.com/winfx/2006/xaml/presentation"
xmlns:x="http://schemas.microsoft.com/winfx/2006/xaml"
  Title="Main Window" Height="350" Width="525">
```

```
<Grid>
  <Button Click="Button_Click" Content="Click Here" />
  <x:Code>
    <![CDATA[
      void Button_Click(object sender, RoutedEventArgs e)
      {
        // event implementation
      }
    ]]>
  </x:Code>
</Grid>
</Window>
```

Try to avoid using the inline code in the XAML page, as it violates the separation between the designer and the code behind. Also, other language-specific programming features are not supported in inline coding.

The code behind file of an XAML page

When an XAML is markup compiled, it has an associated code behind class file. The code behind is a partial class and derives from the same class, which is the root of the XAML page element:

```
public partial class MainWindow : Window
{
  public MainWindow()
  {
    InitializeComponent();
  }
}
```

The constructor of the class gives a call to the `InitializeComponent` method available in another partial class implementation, which resides in a `.g.i.cs` file. For example, if your XAML page name is `MainWindow.xaml`, its associated code behind is `MainWindow.xaml.cs` and the core partial implementation is in an autogenerated file named `MainWindow.g.i.cs`. The `.g.i.cs` file can be located in the obj folder under the project. It loads your XAML page and defines the UI elements placed in the designer.

Here's how the `InitializeComponent()` method looks like:

```
[System.Diagnostics.DebuggerNonUserCodeAttribute()]
[System.CodeDom.Compiler.GeneratedCodeAttribute("PresentationBuildTasks", "4.0.0.0")]
public void InitializeComponent()
{
    if (_contentLoaded)
    {
        return;
    }
    _contentLoaded = true;
    System.Uri resourceLocater = new System.Uri("/Demo-Basic;component/mainwindow.xaml",
                                    System.UriKind.Relative);

#line 1 "..\..\MainWindow.xaml"
        System.Windows.Application.LoadComponent(this, resourceLocater);

#line default
#line hidden
    }
```

Building your first WPF application

Before starting with the WPF application development, make sure that you have installed the **.NET desktop development** workload on your system. Run your Visual Studio 2017 installer and confirm that the **.NET desktop development** workload is already checked. If not, check it and proceed towards installation of the required components.

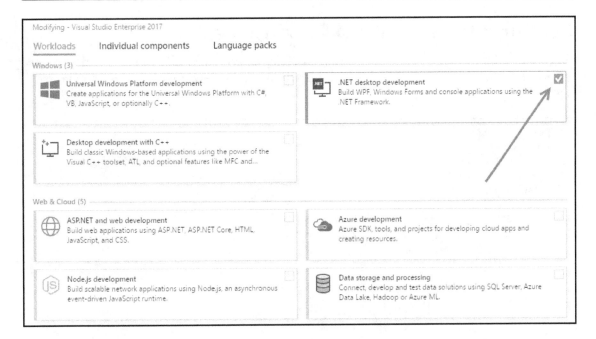

Hope you have already configured your Visual Studio installation to build desktop applications using Windows Presentation Foundation. Let's start building our first WPF app using XAML and C#.

Getting started with WPF project

To get started, open your Visual Studio 2017 IDE and navigate to **File** | **New** | **Project...** (or press keyboard shortcut *Ctrl + Shift + N*). This will open the new project window on your screen:

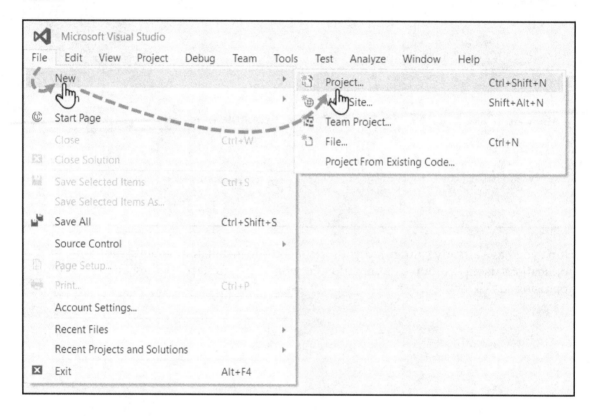

In the **New Project** dialog window, navigate to **Installed** | **Templates** | **Visual C#** | **Windows Classic Desktop**, and select the **WPF App** template from the list. Select the appropriate .NET Framework that you are targeting your app for (must be 3.5 or higher). Here we have selected the **.NET Framework 4.6.1**.

Enter the name of the solution, the location of the project code base, and the project name. Once you have filled up all the necessary details on the screen, click on the **OK** button. This will start creating the project from the selected project template:

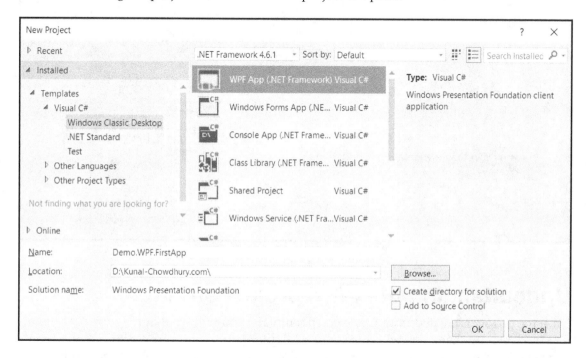

Alternatively, you can search for `wpf app` in the search box under the **New Project** section of the Visual Studio 2017 **Start Page** to bring the preceding dialog, selecting the correct project automatically:

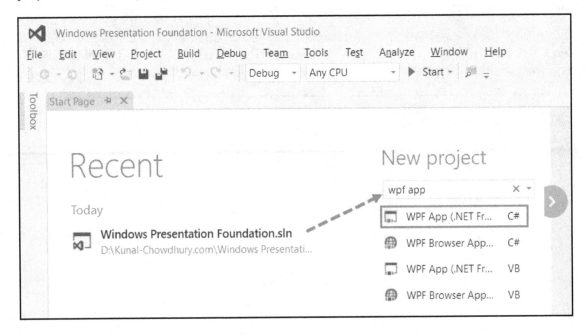

Understanding the WPF project structure

Once the project is created from the selected template, you will see that the project has few files in it. Among them, you will find two XAML files (`App.xaml` and `MainWindow.xaml`) and two associated C# files (`App.xaml.cs` and `MainWindow.xaml.cs`) automatically created by Visual Studio:

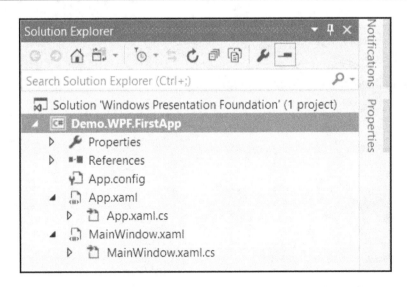

The `App.xaml` file is the declarative start point of your application, which extends the `Application` class and subscribes to application-specific events, unhandled exception, and more. From this class, it gets the starting instruction to navigate to the initial window or page.

Here's the structure of the `App.xaml` file:

```
<Application x:Class="Demo.WPF.FirstApp.App"
xmlns="http://schemas.microsoft.com/winfx/2006/xaml/presentation"
xmlns:x="http://schemas.microsoft.com/winfx/2006/xaml"
xmlns:local="clr-namespace:Demo.WPF.FirstApp"
StartupUri="MainWindow.xaml">
  <Application.Resources>
  </Application.Resources>
</Application>
```

Here you can see that `StartupUri` is set to `MainWindow.xaml`, which means that the `MainWindow.xaml` file will launch on startup. If you want to launch a different window/page at startup, replace the same with the desired filename.

Instead of defining `StartupUri` in the `App.xaml` file, you can also dynamically set it by subscribing to the application `Startup` event.

```
<Application x:Class="Demo.WPF.FirstApp.App"
xmlns="http://schemas.microsoft.com/winfx/2006/xaml/presentation"
xmlns:x="http://schemas.microsoft.com/winfx/2006/xaml"
xmlns:local="clr-namespace:Demo.WPF.FirstApp"
Startup="Application_Startup">
```

```
      <Application.Resources>
      </Application.Resources>
  </Application>
```

Here is the associated code behind, implementing the `Startup` event to launch a window named `MainWindow` on the user screen:

```
using System.Windows;
namespace Demo.WPF.FirstApp
{
  /// <summary>
  /// Interaction logic for App.xaml
  /// </summary>
  public partial class App : Application
  {
    private void Application_Startup(object sender,
      StartupEventArgs e)
    {
      var mainWindow = new MainWindow();
      mainWindow.Show();
    }
  }
}
```

The other file, `MainWindow.xaml`, by default consists of a blank `Grid` (one of the WPF panels), where you can specify your layouts and put your desired controls to design the UI:

```
<Window x:Class="Demo.WPF.FirstApp.MainWindow"
    xmlns="http://schemas.microsoft.com/winfx/2006/xaml/presentation"
    xmlns:x="http://schemas.microsoft.com/winfx/2006/xaml"
    xmlns:d="http://schemas.microsoft.com/expression/blend/2008"
    xmlns:mc="http://schemas.openxmlformats.org/markup-compatibility/2006"
    xmlns:local="clr-namespace:Demo.WPF.FirstApp"
    mc:Ignorable="d"
    Title="MainWindow" Height="350" Width="525">
    <Grid>
    </Grid>
</Window>
```

The related logics, properties, events, and so on, you can define in the associated code behind class file `MainWindow.xaml.cs`. It's a partial class and all the autogenerated UI-related initialization is written in the `InitializeComponent()` method defined in the other partial class `MainWindow.g.i.cs` file that we have already discussed earlier:

```
using System.Windows;
namespace Demo.WPF.FirstApp
{
```

```
/// <summary>
/// Interaction logic for MainWindow.xaml
/// </summary>
public partial class MainWindow : Window
{
  public MainWindow()
  {
    InitializeComponent();
  }
}
}
```

When you build any WPF desktop application project, it generates an `.exe` file along with `.dll` (if you have any in-house class libraries and/or third-party libraries) files.

Getting familiar with XAML Designer

When you open an XAML page, the Visual Studio 2017 editor opens it in two different views side-by-side within the same screen. These two views are named as **Designer View** and **XAML View**. In the designer view, you will be able to design your UI by drag, drop, resize, and so on and on the other side, the XAML view will allow you to write XAML codes directly to create the UI:

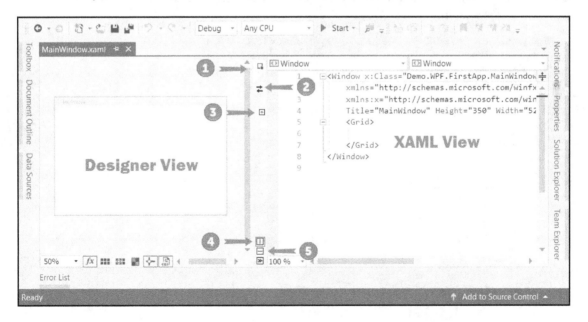

Check out the preceding screenshot to have a glimpse on how the Visual Studio loads the XAML page and provides you the option to change the view as follows:

1. **Switch to design view**: Double-clicking on this icon will change the view to full screen designer view, hiding the XAML editor
2. **Swap panes**: This will allow you to swap the views, left to right (vertical split) or up to down (horizontal split)
3. **Switch to XAML view**: If you double-click on this icon, it will change the view to full screen XAML view, hiding the designer
4. **Vertical Split**: When you do a vertical split, the designer view and the XAML editor view will set side by side (as shown in the preceding screenshot) left and right
5. **Horizontal Split**: When you do a horizontal split, the designer view and the XAML editor view will align top and bottom positions in a stack fashion

Adding controls in XAML

Let's add a button control on the UI of our WPF application. To do this, open the `MainPage.xaml` file and inside the `Grid` panel, add the `Button` tag with its content and dimension as shown in the following highlighted code snippet and it will show you a preview in the designer view:

```
<Window x:Class="Demo.WPF.FirstApp.MainWindow"
xmlns="http://schemas.microsoft.com/winfx/2006/xaml/presentation"
xmlns:x="http://schemas.microsoft.com/winfx/2006/xaml"
Title="MainWindow" Height="350" Width="525">
  <Grid>
    <Button Content="Click Here" Width="100" Height="26" />
  </Grid>
</Window>
```

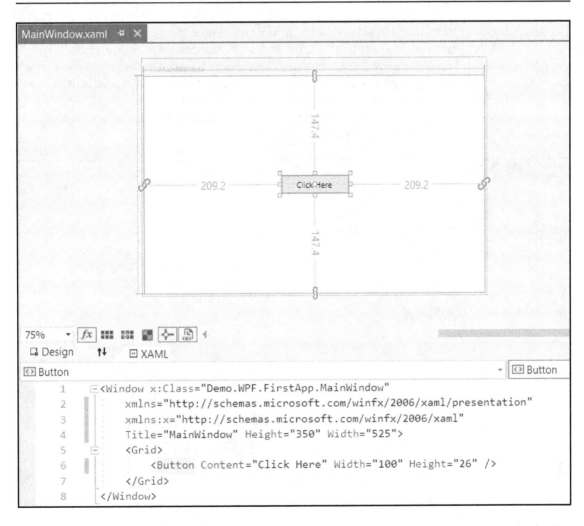

```
1   <Window x:Class="Demo.WPF.FirstApp.MainWindow"
2       xmlns="http://schemas.microsoft.com/winfx/2006/xaml/presentation"
3       xmlns:x="http://schemas.microsoft.com/winfx/2006/xaml"
4       Title="MainWindow" Height="350" Width="525">
5       <Grid>
6           <Button Content="Click Here" Width="100" Height="26" />
7       </Grid>
8   </Window>
```

Now, let's add some color to the button. You can either do it by writing XAML attributes for the button in the XAML view or you can utilize the Visual Studio property window from the designer view.

Let's add the color from the property window and will see how the Visual Studio editor adds the XAML attributes. To do this, select the button in the designer view and open the properties window. There you will see a category labeled as **Brush**. Under this, you will be able to change the color of the selected UI element. First, select the **Background** and move the color slider to select Red. Then, select **Foreground** and choose an appropriate foreground/text color to white. You will notice that the preview in the designer view automatically gets updated with the selected colors:

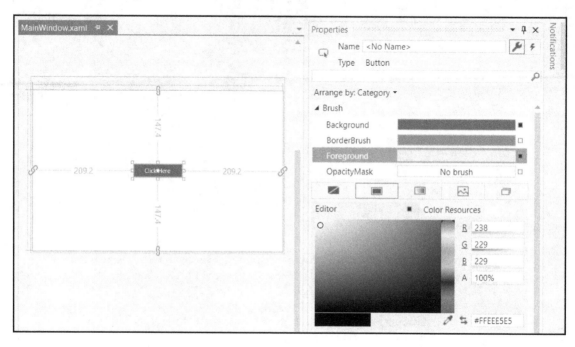

Here's the XAML code for your reference:

```
<Grid>
  <Button Content="Click Here" Width="100" Height="26"
    Background="Red" Foreground="#FFEEE5E5" />
</Grid>
```

Now, when you build and run the app, you will see a button having red background and white text color on the screen. If you click on that button, there will be no action as we have not added any event handler to it. To do this, go to the design view, select the button control, navigate to the **Properties** window, and click on the Navigate Event Handler icon present at the right corner, as shown in the following screenshot:

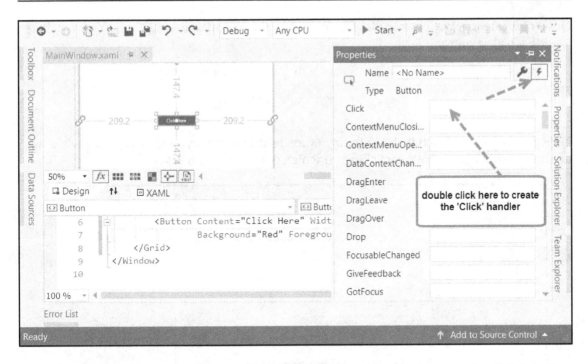

Here, you will find an input box labeled **Click**. Double-click on it to create the click handler of the button in the associated code file and register it in the XAML page.

Alternatively, you can write `Click="Button_Click"` in the XAML, against the button tag to register the event first and press the *F12* keyboard shortcut on the event name to generate the associated event handler in the code behind:

```
<0> Button                                    ⌄  🔧 Click                                    ⌄
    1   ⊟<Window x:Class="Demo.WPF.FirstApp.MainWindow"                                      ╪
    2        xmlns="http://schemas.microsoft.com/winfx/2006/xaml/presentation"
    3        xmlns:x="http://schemas.microsoft.com/winfx/2006/xaml"
    4        Title="MainWindow" Height="350" Width="525">
    5   ⊟    <Grid>
    6   ⊟        <Button Content="Click Here" Width="100" Height="26"
    7                    Background="Red" Foreground="#FFEEE5E5"
    8                    Click="Button_Click"
    9        </Grid>                          Select and press  [ F12 ]  to create the handler
   10   </Window>
100 %   ⌄ ◂
```

Now, navigate to the event handler implementation and add a message box to show when you click on the button:

```
private void Button_Click(object sender, RoutedEventArgs e)
{
    MessageBox.Show("Hello WPF Message Box");
}
```

Let's build and run the code. If the build succeeds, it will show you the following window on the screen with the button, clicking on which will display a message:

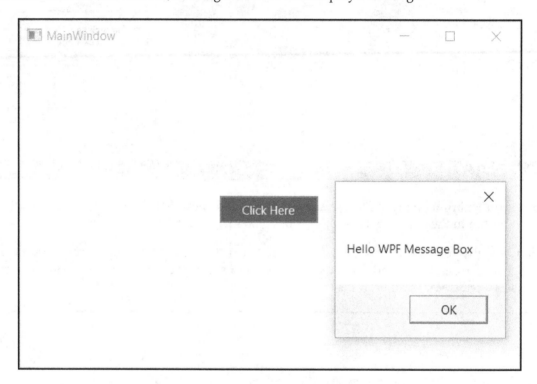

Command-line parameters in WPF application

You can also pass command-line parameters to a WPF application. These will be captured in the Startup event of the App.xaml file. The StartupEventArgs e has a property named Args that returns the command-line parameters as an array of strings.

The following example demonstrates how to retrieve the command-line arguments in WPF application:

```
private void Application_Startup(object sender,
 StartupEventArgs e)
{
  var args = e.Args;
  if (args != null && args.Count() > 0)
  {
    foreach (var arg in args)
    {
     // write code to use the command line arg value
    }
  }
}
```

You can go to the project properties by navigating to **Debug | Command line arguments** (as shown in the following screenshot) to set the arguments for debugging purpose:

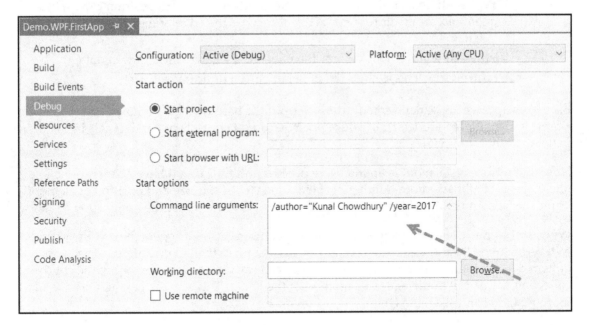

Layouts in WPF

Layout is an important part of any GUI-based application, for usability purpose. You must arrange your controls in a proper position, so that, the user can find it easy to work. You should also keep arranging your controls properly to scale them in different screen resolutions and/or different font sizes. WPF provides a built-in support of various panels to help you on this:

- **Grid**: This defines a flexible area to position UI elements in rows and columns.
- **StackPanel**: This defines an area where the child elements can arrange in stack fashion horizontally or vertically.
- **Canvas**: This defines an area to set the UI elements by coordinates relative to the area specified.
- **DockPanel**: This defines an area which you can arrange horizontally or vertically, relative to each other.
- **WrapPanel**: This defines an area where child elements can position themselves sequentially from left to right. When it reaches the edge of the panel box, it breaks to the next line.
- **VirtualizingPanel**: This defines the panel to virtualize the children data.
- **UniformGrid**: This defines the panel to have a uniform cell size.

Each of the preceding panel elements derives from the base Panel and allows you to create a simple and better layout design of your app. You can set controls or child panels inside a panel to design your view.

Note that designing a layout is an intensive process and thus if you have a large collection of children, it will have more number of calculations to set the size and position of elements. Thus, the UI complexity will increase impacting the performance of the application.

Whenever a child element changes its position, it automatically triggers the layout system to revalidate the UI and arranges the children according to the layout defined. The layout system does this in two phases. The Measure pass recalculates each member of the children collection with a call to the `Measure` method of the panel. This sets the height, width, and margin of the controls in the UI.

The Arrange pass, which generally begins with the call to the `Arrange` method, generates the bounds of the child and passes to the `ArrangeCore` method for processing. It then evaluates the desired size of the child and calls the `ArrangeOverride` method to determine the final size. Finally, it allocates the desired space and completes the process of layouting.

The following are some quick tips to remember:

- Canvas is a simple panel and has better performance than a complex panel such as Grid.
- Avoid fixed positioning of UI elements. Rather align them in combination to margin and padding.
- Whenever possible, set the `Height` and `Width` property to `Auto` instead of a fixed size.
- Avoid unnecessary calls to `UpdateLayout` as it forces a recursive layout update.
- Use a **StackPanel** to layout a list of elements horizontally or vertically.
- When working with a large Children collection, consider using a **VirtualizingStackPanel**.
- Use a **GridPanel** to layout static data in the UI.
- **ItemControl** can be used with a grid panel in a **DataTemplate** to layout dynamic data.
- Use `Margin` to add extra space around the control.
- Use `Padding` to add extra space inside the control.

As we have already seen that, there exists many panels in WPF to create the UI layout; let's discuss each of them in detail. This will help you to decide which one to choose when and how to use them.

Using Grid as a WPF panel

Let's start with the Grid layout panel. It is the most useful panel you will ever use in your application, and is the default panel inserted inside every XAML page when you create a Window, Page, or User Control. You could see that there was a Grid panel inserted when we created our first WPF application. A button control was placed inside it.

The Grid layout control allows you to define the Grid structure to place individual elements in rows and columns structure in a matrix format:

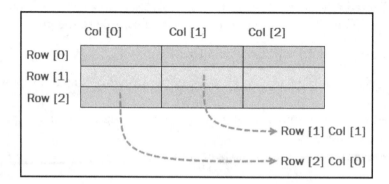

In XAML, you need to design your Grid cells using **RowDefinitions** and **ColumnDefinitions**. Each definition group can have multiple definitions. The **RowDefinition** can have height set to it and the **ColumnDefinition** can have width set to it. Each can have three different sets of values:

- **Auto**: When set to `Auto` the row height or the column width will set based on the content.
- **A numeric value**: When you set a positive numeric value, it will have a fixed size.
- *** (asterisk)**: When you provide asterisk (*), it will take the maximum available space in the ratio specified. Consider the following cases for example:
    - If you have two rows and you specify both of their heights to *, they will have the row height equally distributed on the available space.
    - If you have two rows and you specify one as * and the other as 2*, then the row height will be divided in the 1:2 ratio of the available space.

 In case you don't specify any height or width, the row or column will by default have equal distribution of the available space.

Let's discuss on the following code snippet, where it has four row definitions and three column definitions. The first two rows will automatically set their heights based on the dimension of their contents, the fourth row will have 30 px height and the third row will have the remaining space as its height. Similarly, the first column will have auto width based on its contents, the second column will have 20 px space, and the third column will occupy the remaining space available to it:

```
<Grid>
    <Grid.RowDefinitions>
        <RowDefinition Height="Auto"/>   <!-- auto layout based on content -->
        <RowDefinition Height="Auto"/>   <!-- auto layout based on content -->
        <RowDefinition Height="*"/>      <!-- take entire available space -->
        <RowDefinition Height="30"/>     <!-- take only 30px height -->
    </Grid.RowDefinitions>
    <Grid.ColumnDefinitions>
        <ColumnDefinition Width="Auto"/> <!-- auto layout based on content -->
        <ColumnDefinition Width="20"/>   <!-- take only 20px width -->
        <ColumnDefinition Width="*"/>    <!-- take entire available space -->
    </Grid.ColumnDefinitions>

    <!-- First Row -->
    <TextBlock Text="First Name" Grid.Row="0" Grid.Column="0"/>
    <TextBlock Text=":" Grid.Row="0" Grid.Column="1"/>
    <TextBox Grid.Row="0" Grid.Column="2"/>

    <!-- Second Row -->
    <TextBlock Text="Last Name" Grid.Row="1" Grid.Column="0"/>
    <TextBlock Text=":" Grid.Row="1" Grid.Column="1"/>
    <TextBox Grid.Row="1" Grid.Column="2"/>

</Grid>
```

Once you divide your Grid panel in rows and columns, you can place your elements in the appropriate cell by using the `Grid.Row` or `Grid.Column` property. The `Grid.RowSpan` and `Grid.ColumnSpan` properties are used to span an element across multiple rows and columns.

Using StackPanel to define stacked layout

When you want to add elements in a stack fashion, either horizontally or vertically, you need to use the **StackPanel**. You need to specify the `Orientation` property to set whether it will be a horizontal stack panel or a vertical stack panel. The following figure demonstrates a horizontal and a vertical StackPanel:

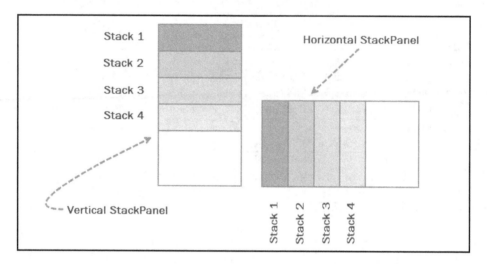

If you don't specify any orientation, it will by default be set as a vertical stack panel. You can add multiple UI elements (controls or panels) as children to it:

```xml
<!-- Horizontal StackPanel -->

<StackPanel Orientation="Horizontal">
  <TextBlock Text="Stack 1"/>
  <TextBlock Text="Stack 2"/>
  <TextBlock Text="Stack 3"/>
  <TextBlock Text="Stack 4"/>
</StackPanel>
<!-- Vertical StackPanel -->
<StackPanel Orientation="Vertical">
  <TextBlock Text="Stack 1"/>
  <TextBlock Text="Stack 2"/>
  <TextBlock Text="Stack 3"/>
  <TextBlock Text="Stack 4"/>
</StackPanel>
```

Using Canvas as a panel

Canvas is the lightweight panel and can be used to position the children at a specific coordinate position within the view. You can imagine it as a HTML div element and position the elements at (x, y) coordinate. The attached properties `Canvas.Left`, `Canvas.Top` can be used to position the elements relative to left and top corners, whereas the `Canvas.Right` and `Canvas.Bottom` can be used to position the child elements relative to right and bottom corners:

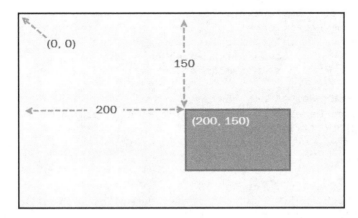

Here's a simple example that demonstrates the TextBlocks positioned at (75, 30) and (220, 75) respectively:

```
<Canvas>
  <TextBlock Text="(75, 30)" Canvas.Left="75" Canvas.Top="30"/>
  <TextBlock Text="(220, 75)" Canvas.Left="220" Canvas.Top="75"/>
</Canvas>
```

This is not very flexible as you have to manually move the child controls around and make them align the way you want them to. Use it only when you want complete control over the position of the child controls.

Using WPF DockPanel to dock child elements

The `DockPanel` allows you to dock the child elements to any one of the four sides (top, right, bottom, or left). By default, the last element (if not given any specific dock position) fills the remaining space. You can use it when you need to divide your window to regions and/or use when you want to place one or more elements to any of the sides.

As shown in the following code snippet, you need to set the `DockPanel.Dock` attribute of the child elements to one of the four values:

```xml
<DockPanel Background="LightCyan">
  <Border Width="150" Height="50"
          DockPanel.Dock="Bottom" Background="YellowGreen">
    <TextBlock Text="Bottom Docking"
               HorizontalAlignment="Center"
               VerticalAlignment="Center"/>
  </Border>
  <Border Width="150" Height="50"
          DockPanel.Dock="Top" Background="YellowGreen">
    <TextBlock Text="Top Docking"
               HorizontalAlignment="Center"
               VerticalAlignment="Center"/>
  </Border>
  <Border Width="150" Height="50"
          DockPanel.Dock="Right" Background="YellowGreen">
    <TextBlock Text="Right Docking"
               HorizontalAlignment="Center"
               VerticalAlignment="Center"/>
  </Border>
  <Border Width="150" Height="50"
          DockPanel.Dock="Left" Background="YellowGreen">
    <TextBlock Text="Left Docking"
               HorizontalAlignment="Center"
               VerticalAlignment="Center"/>
  </Border>
  <Border Width="150" Height="50"
          Background="White">
    <TextBlock Text="No Docking"
               HorizontalAlignment="Center"
               VerticalAlignment="Center"/>
  </Border>
</DockPanel>
```

When you run the preceding example, the result will look like the following diagram, positioning all the child elements based on the value specified as the `DockPanel.Dock` attribute:

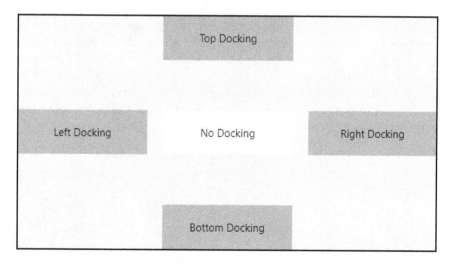

Note that the last element, which does not have any docking position set, has taken the remaining space and is placed at the center position of the Window.

Using the WrapPanel to automatically reposition

Inside a panel, when you want to position each of its child elements next to the other, either horizontally (default) or vertically, until there is no more room and then wrap to the next line to continue, you need to use **WrapPanel**. It just looks like a combination of **GridPanel** and **StackPanel**, having variable cell size. Use it when you want a vertical or horizontal list automatically wrapped to next line if there's no more room for the controls to accommodate in the same line.

Let's see the following diagram as an example of WrapPanel:

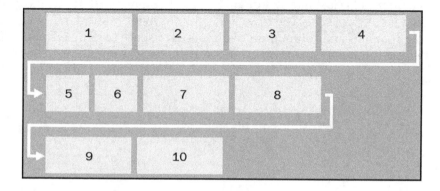

Here you can see that the child elements positioned themselves in a row and when it does not have room to accommodate in the same line, it wraps itself into a new line. For example, in the preceding diagram, the fifth element wrapped itself into second line due to lack of space in the first line. Similarly, the ninth element positioned itself on the third line as the second line does not have sufficient space for that element. You can also see that the items can have variable size and that does not affect the behavior of the positioning and as a result, there are no big gaps in between that we can see in a Grid.

Here's an XAML code snippet to demonstrate the preceding example:

```xml
<WrapPanel Background="DarkOrange">
  <Border Width="120" Height="50"
          Background="Yellow" Margin="4"/>
  <Border Width="120" Height="50"
          Background="Yellow" Margin="4"/>
  <Border Width="120" Height="50"
          Background="Yellow" Margin="4"/>
  <Border Width="60" Height="50"
          Background="Yellow" Margin="4"/>
  <Border Width="60" Height="50"
          Background="Yellow" Margin="4"/>
  <Border Width="120" Height="50"
          Background="Yellow" Margin="4"/>
  <Border Width="120" Height="50"
          Background="Yellow" Margin="4"/>
</WrapPanel>
```

Using UniformGrid to place elements in uniform cells

The **UniformGrid** panel is just like WrapPanel, but with a catch that, it will have child elements placed in uniform cells. The rows and columns in a UniformGrid have the same size. By default, the rows and columns autoresize to give space to more elements. The elements also resize automatically to accommodate themselves within that space:

```xml
<UniformGrid>
  <Border Width="150" Height="40"
          Background="DarkOrange" Margin="4"/>
  <Border Width="150" Height="40"
          Background="DarkOrange" Margin="4"/>
    .
    .
    .
  <Border Width="150" Height="40"
```

```
          Background="DarkOrange" Margin="4"/>
   <Border Width="150" Height="40"
          Background="DarkOrange" Margin="4"/>
</UniformGrid>
```

The following diagram is a UniformGrid panel, having all the columns autoresized to a same size x:

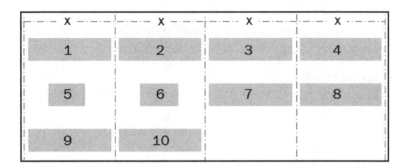

In the preceding example, notice elements **5** and **6**. Unlike WrapPanel, they don't set side by side in a condensed manner to reduce the gap between them; rather they still position themselves in their original defined column cells.

You can define how many rows or columns you want to show in the Grid by specifying the Rows and Columns properties of the UniformGrid.

When you mention the rows count to 1, all the elements inside a UniformGrid will accommodate themselves in a single row by reducing their size. When you define more rows, based on the number of row counts, it will reduce the column count:

```
<UniformGrid Rows="1">
   <Border Width="150" Height="40"
          Background="DarkOrange" Margin="4"/>
          .
          .
   <Border Width="150" Height="40"
          Background="DarkOrange" Margin="4"/>
</UniformGrid>
```

Similarly, you can specify the column count; when specified, based on the column count, it will generate the number of rows.

WPF property system

WPF provides a new property system, which extends the functionality of the default **CLR** (**Common Language Runtime**) property and is known as a **dependency property**. A normal CLR property is a wrapper to its getter and setter implementation of its private variable; whereas a dependency property extends it to provide you a way to compute the value based on the value of other inputs.

In addition to this, it also provides you with a way to do self-contained validation, set default values, monitor changes to its value, and do a callback.

To work with a dependency property, you must derive the class from `DependencyObject`, which will work as the observer. It holds the new property system defined within the `DependencyObject` class:

A CLR property looks like this:

```
private string m_AuthorName;

public string AuthorName
{
    get { return m_AuthorName; }
    set { m_AuthorName = value; }
}


public string BookName { get; set; } // auto properties
```

A dependency property extends it further and provides you with more options to set the default value, pass a callback method, and so on:

```
public static readonly DependencyProperty AuthorNameProperty =
DependencyProperty.Register("AuthorName", typeof(string),
typeof(MainWindow),
new PropertyMetadata("Kunal Chowdhury"));

public string AuthorName
{
    get { return (string)GetValue(AuthorNameProperty); }
    set { SetValue(AuthorNameProperty, value); }
}
```

The first line is used to register the dependency property into the WPF property system. This is done to ensure that the object contains the property in it and we can easily call the getter or setter to access the value of the property.

We can even use a normal CLR property to wrap a dependency property and use the `GetValue` and `SetValue` methods to get and set the values passed to the dependency property.

The `Register` method takes four parameters to it. The first one is the CLR property name that you defined for the getter and setter. The second parameter is the return type of the property. The third is the class handler (derived from `DependencyObject`), where you are declaring it. The fourth one is the extended property metadata, where you can set the default value.

You can further extend the property metadata to associate a callback method to it, just like the following code snippet extended from the preceding example:

```
public static readonly DependencyProperty AuthorNameProperty =
  DependencyProperty.Register("AuthorName", typeof(string),
typeof(MainWindow),
  new PropertyMetadata("Kunal Chowdhury", OnAuthorNamePropertyChanged));

private static void OnAuthorNamePropertyChanged(DependencyObject d,
  DependencyPropertyChangedEventArgs e)
{
   // your code here to handle the data
}

public string AuthorName
{
   get { return (string)GetValue(AuthorNameProperty); }
   set { SetValue(AuthorNameProperty, value); }
}
```

Each of the dependency property internally invokes the `INotifyPropertyChanged` event whenever the value of the property is modified, and thus, we can use it to provide notification to the UI that the data associated with it has been changed. When you need to use a data binding to a property target, you must define it as a dependency property.

Data binding in WPF

Data binding is a technique to establish a connection between the UI of the application and the business logic to have data synchronization between them. Though you can directly access UI controls from code behind to update their content, but data binding became a preferred way to update the UI layer for its autoupdate notification mechanism.

To make data binding work, both the sides of the binding must provide a change notification to the other side. The source property of a data binding can be a normal .NET CLR property or a dependency property, but the target property must be a dependency property:

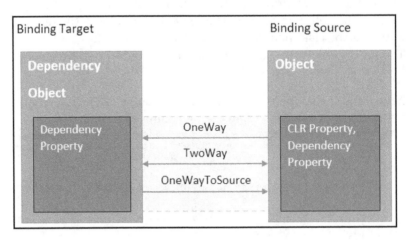

Data binding is typically done in XAML using the {Binding} markup extension. It can be unidirectional (source > target or target > source) or bidirectional (source < > target), known as **Mode** and is defined in four categories:

- **OneWay**: This type of unidirectional data binding causes the source property to automatically update the target property. The reverse is not possible here. For example, if you want to display a label/text in the UI based on some condition in the code behind or business logic, you need to use OneWay data binding as you don't need to update back the property from the UI:

    ```
    <TextBlock Text="{Binding AuthorName}"/>
    <TextBlock Text="{Binding AuthorName, Mode=OneWay}"/>
    <TextBox Text="{Binding AuthorName}"/>
    <TextBox Text="{Binding AuthorName, Mode=OneWay}"/>
    ```

- **TwoWay**: This type of binding is a bidirectional data binding, where both the source property and the target property can send update notifications. This is applicable for editable forms where the user can change the value displayed in the UI. For example, the Text property of a TextBox control supports this type of data binding:

    ```
    <TextBox Text="{Binding AuthorName, Mode=TwoWay}"/>
    ```

- **OneWay to Source**: This is another unidirectional data binding, which causes the target property to update the source property (the reverse of OneWay binding). Here, the UI sends notification to the data context and no notification is generated if the data context changes:

```
<TextBox Text="{Binding AuthorName, Mode=OneWayToSource}"/>
```

- **One time**: This causes the source property to initialize the target property. After that, no notifications will be generated. You should use this type of data binding where the source data does not change.

One way binding is the default data binding.

When you set Mode=OneWay to the Text property of a TextBox, the notification does not generate to the source property if the user updates its value in the UI.

Let's discuss it with a small and simple demonstration. First, create a new WPF project using Visual Studio 2017 and we name it Demo.WPF.DataBinding. It would have already created an XAML file named MainWindow.xaml and MainWindow.xaml.cs.

Open the MainWindow.xaml.cs file and add three dependency properties of type string named AuthorName, BookName, and PublishDate. You can use the **propdp** snippet to generate the dependency properties. After the addition of the three properties, your code will look like this:

```
namespace Demo.WPF.DataBinding
{
  public partial class MainWindow : Window
  {
    public string AuthorName
    {
      get { return (string)GetValue(AuthorNameProperty); }
      set { SetValue(AuthorNameProperty, value); }
    }

    public string BookName
    {
      get { return (string)GetValue(BookNameProperty); }
      set { SetValue(BookNameProperty, value); }
    }

    public string PublishDate
    {
      get { return (string)GetValue(PublishDateProperty); }
      set { SetValue(PublishDateProperty, value); }
```

```
        }

        public static readonly DependencyProperty AuthorNameProperty =
            DependencyProperty.Register("AuthorName", typeof(string),
            typeof(MainWindow), new PropertyMetadata("Kunal Chowdhury"));
        public static readonly DependencyProperty BookNameProperty =
            DependencyProperty.Register("BookName", typeof(string),
            typeof(MainWindow), new PropertyMetadata("Mastering Visual Studio"));
        public static readonly DependencyProperty PublishDateProperty =
            DependencyProperty.Register("PublishDate", typeof(string),
            typeof(MainWindow), new PropertyMetadata("2017"));

        public MainWindow()
        {
            InitializeComponent();
        }
    }
}
```

Now, as we have three dependency properties already defined, we can start creating the object binding. First, let's give a name `mainWindow` to the window. This is so as to easily identify the context of the code behind.

Then we need to set the data context of the grid. We can use a data binding here and will tell the grid to use the same class by assigning `mainWindow` as the element name of the context `<Grid DataContext="{Binding ElementName=mainWindow}"`.

Let's divide the `Grid` into a few rows, columns, and add few `TextBlocks` and `TextBoxes` onto it to complete the data binding steps. Here's the complete code for your reference:

```
<Window x:Class="Demo.WPF.DataBinding.MainWindow"
    xmlns="http://schemas.microsoft.com/winfx/2006/xaml/presentation"
    xmlns:x="http://schemas.microsoft.com/winfx/2006/xaml"
    x:Name="mainWindow" Title="Data Binding Demo"
    Height="350" Width="700" FontSize="12">
    <Grid DataContext="{Binding ElementName=mainWindow}" Margin="20">
        <Grid.ColumnDefinitions>
            <ColumnDefinition Width="Auto"/>
            <ColumnDefinition Width="20"/>
            <ColumnDefinition Width="*"/>
            <ColumnDefinition Width="40"/>
            <ColumnDefinition Width="Auto"/>
        </Grid.ColumnDefinitions>

        <Grid.RowDefinitions>
            <RowDefinition Height="26"/>
            <RowDefinition Height="26"/>
```

```
                <RowDefinition Height="26"/>
                <RowDefinition Height="Auto"/>
            </Grid.RowDefinitions>

            <TextBlock Text="Author Name" Grid.Row="0" Grid.Column="0"/>
            <TextBlock Text=":" Grid.Row="0" Grid.Column="1"
                HorizontalAlignment="Center"/>
            <TextBox Text="{Binding AuthorName, Mode=OneWay}" Grid.Row="0"
                Grid.Column="2"/>
            <TextBlock Text="(Mode=OneWay)" Grid.Row="0" Grid.Column="4"/>

            <TextBlock Text="Book Name" Grid.Row="1" Grid.Column="0"/>
            <TextBlock Text=":" Grid.Row="1" Grid.Column="1"
                HorizontalAlignment="Center"/>
            <TextBox Text="{Binding BookName, Mode=TwoWay}" Grid.Row="1"
                Grid.Column="2"/>
            <TextBlock Text="(Mode=TwoWay)" Grid.Row="1" Grid.Column="4"/>

            <TextBlock Text="Published" Grid.Row="2" Grid.Column="0"/>
            <TextBlock Text=":" Grid.Row="2" Grid.Column="1"
                HorizontalAlignment="Center"/>
            <TextBox Text="{Binding PublishDate, Mode=TwoWay,
                UpdateSourceTrigger=PropertyChanged}" Grid.Row="2" Grid.Column="2"/>
            <TextBlock Text="(Mode=TwoWay, UpdateSourceTrigger=PropertyChanged)"
                Grid.Row="2" Grid.Column="4"/>

            <StackPanel Grid.Row="3" Grid.Column="2" Margin="0 20 0 0">
                <TextBlock Text="You entered Author Name:" FontWeight="Bold"/>
                <TextBlock Text="{Binding AuthorName}"/>
                <TextBlock Text="You entered Book Name:" FontWeight="Bold"
                    Margin="0 10 0 0"/>
                <TextBlock Text="{Binding BookName}"/>
                <TextBlock Text="You entered Published Date:" FontWeight="Bold"
                    Margin="0 10 0 0"/>
                <TextBlock Text="{Binding PublishDate}"/>
            </StackPanel>
        </Grid>
    </Window>
```

For the first textbox, the `Text` property has been bound to `AuthorName` as a OneWay data binding, the second textbox uses a TwoWay data binding mode with the property `BookName`. The third textbox also uses a TwoWay data binding with the property `PublishDate`, but has specified `UpdateSourceTrigger=PropertyChanged`. This tells the system to notify whenever the property changes.

When you build and execute the preceding code, you will see that the following window pops up with a few textblocks and textboxes as defined in the XAML. The values in the textbox controls populate from the default value that we specified at the time of declaring the dependency properties:

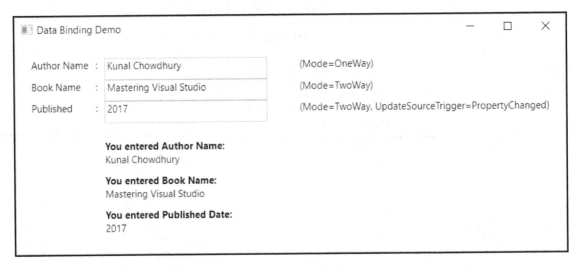

Now, modify the text of the first textbox (**Author Name**) but it will not update the label that we placed below. As it has a OneWay data binding associated with it, no update notification will be sent out even if you trigger a lost focus on that textbox control.

If you change the text of the second textbox (**Book Name**), no notification will be carried out unless you trigger a lost focus on it. **TwoWay** data binding will act here to update the associated `Textblock` automatically.

The third textbox control also has **TwoWay** data binding associated with it, but it also has a binding property that says, update the source when the property changes. So, if you start typing in the third box, you will see that the `Textblock` will immediately start getting the notification and update itself:

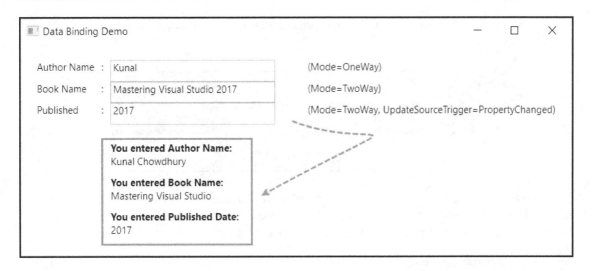

You can define four set of values to `UpdateSourceTrigger` and these are as follows:

- `Default`: When specified, it triggers based on the default association set by the target. For example, the default trigger for the `TextBox.Text` property is `LostFocus`.
- `LostFocus`: This gets triggered when the associated control loses its focus.
- `PropertyChanged`: This gets triggered when the associated property gets change notification.
- `Explicit`: This only gets triggered when the application explicitly calls `UpdateSource` of the binding.

Using Converters while data binding

In data binding, when the source object type and the target object type differs, value converters are used to manipulate data between the source and the target. This is done by writing a `Converter` class, implementing the `IValueConverter` interface. It consists of two methods:

- `Convert(...)`: This gets called when the source updates the target object.

- `ConvertBack(...)`: This gets called when the target object updates the source object:

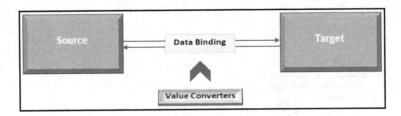

Implementation of the value converter is simple. First create a class in your project. We named it `BoolToColorConverter` and implemented it from `IValueConverter`. Implement the two methods as part of the interface.

For demonstration purpose, the class will accept a Boolean value as input and convert it to a `SolidColorBrush` object. This needs to be done in the `Convert` method. You can also add the revert conversion in the `ConvertBack` method, but for this demo, we will not implement it; rather, we will throw a `NotImplementedException`.

Here's the converter code for your reference:

```
using System;
using System.Globalization;
using System.Windows.Data;
using System.Windows.Media;

namespace Demo.WPF.Converters
{
  public class BoolToColorConverter : IValueConverter
  {
    public object Convert(object value, Type targetType, object parameter,
      CultureInfo culture)
    {
        var boolValue = value is Boolean ? bool.Parse(value.ToString()) :
false;
        return new SolidColorBrush(boolValue ? Colors.Red : Colors.Green);
    }

     public object ConvertBack(object value, Type targetType,
       object parameter, CultureInfo culture)
     {
        throw new NotImplementedException();
     }
   }
}
```

Now, we need to attach the converter class to our XAML page, load it to memory, and create the data binding. Let's first declare the `xmlns` namespace for our converter. As it is in the same project, namespace declaration will be sufficient.

Once the `xmlns` declaration is done, we need to load the converter into the window's resource and define a key for it so that it can be easily accessible:

```
<Window ...
  <Window.Resources>
    <converters:BoolToColorConverter
      x:Key="BoolToColorConverter"/>
  </Window.Resources>
    .
    .
    .
</Window>
```

The next step is to create the UI and complete the data binding. Let's first add one border and a checkbox in the XAML page. Here, instead of creating any property in the code behind, we will directly use the control properties.

As per this demonstration, the `Background` property of the border will change based on the checked status of the checkbox named `chkColor`. Let's create a data binding for the border's `Background` property. The binding path will be the `IsChecked` property of the checkbox, whose name we defined as `chkColor`. Thus, the `ElementName` will point to the name of the checkbox control, as shown in the following code:

```
<Border Background="{Binding Path=IsChecked, ElementName=chkColor}"/>
```

Now, as the `IsChecked` property returns a Boolean value and the `Background` property accepts a Brush value, we need to use the converter to the binding expression. As we have already defined the converter as a resource of the Window, we just need to reference it here as `StaticResource`. The code can now be written as:

```
<Border Background="{Binding Path=IsChecked, ElementName=chkColor,
  Converter={StaticResource BoolToColorConverter}}"
```

Here is the complete code for your easy reference:

```
<Window x:Class="Demo.WPF.Converters.MainWindow"
  xmlns="http://schemas.microsoft.com/winfx/2006/xaml/presentation"
  xmlns:x="http://schemas.microsoft.com/winfx/2006/xaml"
  xmlns:converters="clr-namespace:Demo.WPF.Converters"
  Title="Converter Demo" Height="200" Width="240">
  <Window.Resources>
    <converters:BoolToColorConverter x:Key="BoolToColorConverter"/>
  </Window.Resources>
```

```
<StackPanel Orientation="Vertical" VerticalAlignment="Top">
  <Border Background="{Binding Path=IsChecked, ElementName=chkColor,
    Converter={StaticResource BoolToColorConverter}}" Width="200"
    Height="100" Margin="10"/>
  <CheckBox x:Name="chkColor" IsChecked="True" Content="Error"
      Margin="10"/>
</StackPanel>
</Window>
```

Now, if we run the preceding sample code, it will first load the checkbox as checked because we specified the `IsChecked` property of the control as `True`. As the value is `True`, it will be passed to the converter and it will return a `Red Brush`, which will assign the background color of the border control (the following screenshot, left image).

Uncheck the checkbox to set its value as `False`, resulting the converter to return `Green Brush` and you will see that the color changes to Green (the following screenshot, right image). If you check it again, you will see it as Red.

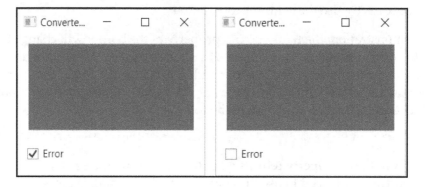

Using triggers in WPF

A trigger enables you to change property values when certain conditions are satisfied. It can also enable you to take actions based on property values by allowing you to dynamically change the appearance and/or the behavior of your control without writing additional codes in the code behind classes.

In WPF, the triggers are usually defined in a style or in the root of an element, which are applied to that specific control. There are five types of triggers:

- Property trigger
- Multi trigger

- Data trigger
- Multidata trigger
- Event trigger

Property trigger

The most common trigger is the property trigger, which can be simply defined in XAML with a `<Trigger>` element. It triggers when a specific property on the owner control changes to match a specified value:

```
<Style TargetType="{x:Type CheckBox}">
  <Style.Triggers>
    <Trigger Property="IsChecked" Value="True">
      <Setter Property="Background" Value="LightGreen"/>
    </Trigger>
    <Trigger Property="IsChecked" Value="False">
      <Setter Property="Background" Value="Red"/>
    </Trigger>
  </Style.Triggers>
</Style>
```

The preceding XAML code snippet creates a style for a checkbox control having two triggers associated with its property `IsChecked`. When the value is `True`, the background of the checkbox will be set to `LightGreen`, and when it is `False`, the background will be set to `Red`.

If we run the example, with a checkbox control in it, we will see the following results based on the checked status of it:

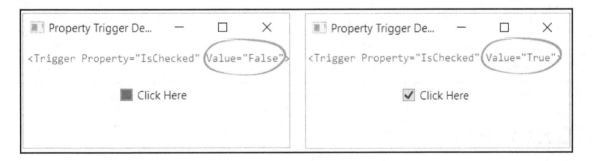

Multi trigger

This is almost like the property trigger, but here it is used to set an action on multiple property changes and will execute when all the conditions within `MulitTrigger.Conditions` are satisfied:

```xml
<Style TargetType="{x:Type CheckBox}">
  <Style.Triggers>
    <MultiTrigger>
      <MultiTrigger.Conditions>
        <Condition Property="IsEnabled" Value="True"/>
        <Condition Property="IsChecked" Value="False"/>
      </MultiTrigger.Conditions>
      <MultiTrigger.Setters>
        <Setter Property="Background" Value="Red"/>
        <Setter Property="Opacity" Value="0.5"/>
      </MultiTrigger.Setters>
    </MultiTrigger>
  </Style.Triggers>
</Style>
```

Here, in this example, we have a multi trigger associated with the checkbox control's style. When the control is enabled and unchecked, the trigger will get fired and set the background of the control to Red and opacity to 50%:

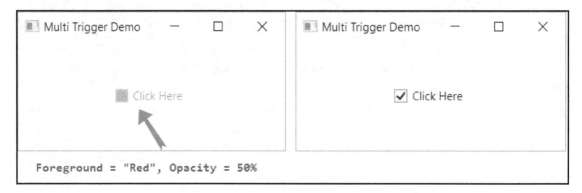

Data trigger

As the name suggests, the data trigger applies a property value to perform a set of actions on the data that has been bound to the UI element. This is represented by the `<DataTrigger>` element.

Here's an example of writing a data trigger to a UI element:

```
<StackPanel Orientation="Horizontal"
    HorizontalAlignment="Center"
    VerticalAlignment="Center">
    <CheckBox Name="chkError" Content="Error"
      VerticalAlignment="Center"/>
    <TextBlock Margin="20, 0" FontSize="50">
        <TextBlock.Style>
          <Style TargetType="TextBlock">
            <Setter Property="Text" Value="Pass" />
            <Setter Property="Foreground" Value="Green" />
            <Style.Triggers>
              <DataTrigger Binding="{Binding ElementName=chkError,
                Path=IsChecked}" Value="True">
                <Setter Property="Text" Value="Fail" />
                <Setter Property="Foreground" Value="Red" />
              </DataTrigger>
            </Style.Triggers>
          </Style>
        </TextBlock.Style>
    </TextBlock>
</StackPanel>
```

In the preceding example, we have two UI controls: a checkbox and a textblock. The
Textblock has a data trigger set to it, bound to the IsChecked property of the checkbox.
When the property value matches True, it will trigger and set the text as Fail with a
foreground color Red. In the default case (when the value matches False), the normal case
will execute and show the text Pass in Green color.

When you run the preceding example, we will see the following result based on the checked
status of the checkbox control:

Multidata trigger

This is same as the data trigger having a difference that, you can set property values based on multiple conditions defined in `MultiDataTrigger.Conditions`. Property values are defined in `MultiDataTrigger.Setters`, as shown in the following code snippet:

```
<StackPanel Orientation="Vertical" Margin="20">
  <UniformGrid>
    <CheckBox x:Name="chkOne" Content="Value 1"/>
    <CheckBox x:Name="chkTwo" Content="Value 2"/>
  </UniformGrid>
  <TextBlock Text="Mastering Visual Studio 2017" FontSize="20">
    <TextBlock.Style>
      <Style TargetType="TextBlock">
        <Style.Triggers>
          <MultiDataTrigger>
            <MultiDataTrigger.Conditions>
              <Condition Binding="{Binding ElementName=chkOne,
                Path=IsChecked}" Value="True"/>
              <Condition Binding="{Binding ElementName=chkTwo,
                Path=IsChecked}" Value="True"/>
            </MultiDataTrigger.Conditions>
            <MultiDataTrigger.Setters>
              <Setter Property="FontWeight" Value="Bold"/>
              <Setter Property="FontSize" Value="36"/>
              <Setter Property="Foreground" Value="Green"/>
            </MultiDataTrigger.Setters>
          </MultiDataTrigger>
        </Style.Triggers>
      </Style>
    </TextBlock.Style>
  </TextBlock>
</StackPanel>
```

When you run the preceding code, there will be two checkbox controls as unchecked and a text block with a font size of 20. As per the conditions mentioned in the code, you need to check both the checkboxes to trigger the same and change the font weight, font size, and foreground color of the text:

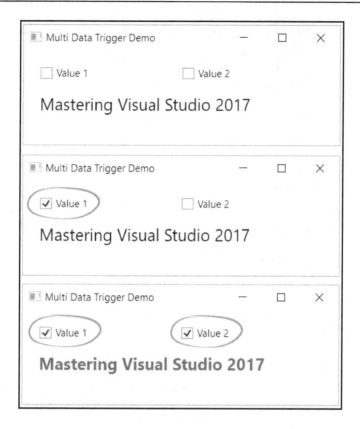

Event trigger

Event triggers are generally used to perform actions when the routed events of the associated `FrameworkElement` arises. This is mainly used in animations to control the look when a certain UI event raises.

In the following example, we have a `Textblock` control. By default, its size is set to 30 with an opacity level of 20%. It has two events, `MouseEnter` and `MouseLeave`, associated with it. Now, on mouse hover we need to specify an animation to grow the font size to 50 and the opacity to 100%. Similarly, on mouse leave, we need to bring it back to the initial state.

Here, the event trigger will help you to perform the same within the XAML page:

```xml
<TextBlock Text="Hover here" FontSize="30" Opacity="0.2"
   HorizontalAlignment="Center"
   VerticalAlignment="Center">
   <TextBlock.Style>
     <Style TargetType="TextBlock">
       <Style.Triggers>
         <EventTrigger RoutedEvent="MouseEnter">
           <EventTrigger.Actions>
             <BeginStoryboard>
               <Storyboard>
                 <DoubleAnimation Duration="0:0:0.500"
                   Storyboard.TargetProperty="FontSize" To="50" />
                 <DoubleAnimation Duration="0:0:0.500"
                   Storyboard.TargetProperty="Opacity" To="1.0"/>
               </Storyboard>
             </BeginStoryboard>
           </EventTrigger.Actions>
         </EventTrigger>
         <EventTrigger RoutedEvent="MouseLeave">
           <EventTrigger.Actions>
             <BeginStoryboard>
               <Storyboard>
                 <DoubleAnimation Duration="0:0:0.500"
                   Storyboard.TargetProperty="FontSize" To="30" />
                 <DoubleAnimation Duration="0:0:0.500"
                   Storyboard.TargetProperty="Opacity" To="0.2"/>
               </Storyboard>
             </BeginStoryboard>
           </EventTrigger.Actions>
         </EventTrigger>
       </Style.Triggers>
     </Style>
   </TextBlock.Style>
</TextBlock>
```

When you run the sample, by default, the text will be visible with a 20% opacity level. Now, if you hover the mouse on the text, you will see a smoothing animation to gradually change the size of the font and the opacity level.

When you leave your mouse out of the text, it will smoothly return to the initial state. Here, the `Duration` property of the animation has the responsibility for the smoothing effect:

Summary

In this chapter, we have learned about Windows Presentation Foundation, its architecture, XAML syntaxes, inline code, code behind, the WPF project structure, and XAML designer. We have also covered how to work with XAML markup to design a Windows application by discussing WPF controls, command-line parameters, and layout panels.

Apart from these, we discussed the new property system with an example of the dependency property, data binding and its implementation, converters, and various types of triggers.

Since we have now become familiar with XAML markups in this chapter, we can now move on to another new topic on building **Universal Windows Platform** (**UWP**) applications. Here, again, we will use XAML and C# to build applications targeting Windows 10 device families.

4
Building Applications for Windows 10 Using UWP Tools

A **Universal Windows Platform** (**UWP**) is a single API surface which is consistent across all Windows 10 devices, from your phone with a 4.5-inch screen to your phablet, tablet, laptop, PC, Xbox, a giant 84-inch Surface Hub, and all-in-ones. This guaranteed API surface enables developers to build a single app which can run on all devices that support Windows 10:

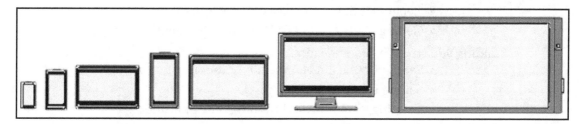

This broad range of hardware devices has been divided into multiple device families, giving the developer easy access to target one or more of them that have the same developer platform named **UWP**.

Using this single platform, with the help of a single SDK, you can build a single application which can run across all these device families, distributed via a single Windows Store:

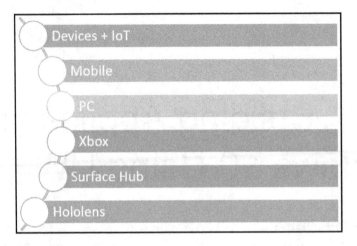

In this chapter, we are going to learn the following:

- Getting started with Universal Windows Platform (UWP):
    - Generic design principles of UWP apps
    - Getting started with UWP app development
- Building your first UWP application:
    - Setting up the development environment for first use
    - Setting up the developer mode
    - Creating, building, and running the application
    - Designing UWP applications
    - Application designing with XAML style
    - Building your own XAML control
    - Generating visual assets using the new Manifest Designer
    - Preparing UWP apps to publish to Windows Store

Getting started with Universal Windows Platform

In Windows Phone 7, the operating system was based on Windows CE, which was the operating system for small devices, but different from the OS that covers the big Windows.

When Microsoft launched Windows Phone 8, they swapped out the Windows CE operating system and based it on the Windows NT kernel. This was the same for PCs and Xbox One.

But with Windows 8.1 and Windows Phone 8.1, Microsoft delivered it on a converged developer platform with the option to build applications targeting the universal 8.1 app platform that shares a high percentage of the code.

With the launch of Windows 10, it changed again. The code has been improved further and generalized to provide a single set of APIs to create a single app which can run on all device families running the Windows 10 operating system. They named it Universal Windows Platform (UWP):

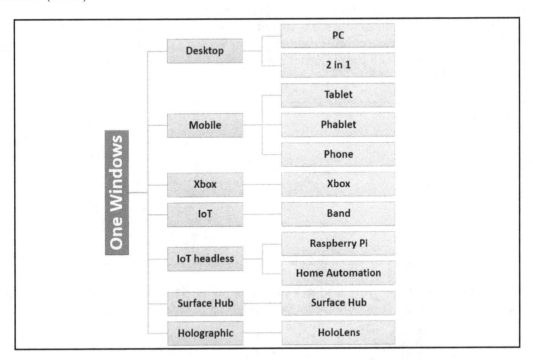

So, in the big picture, it's the **One Windows** ruling all the sets of devices under the device families.

Though they use a common shell, they still have a distinctive user experience for the end user. Each device family offers its own user experience that is appropriate for that device. There are also a small number of APIs specific to each device family that you can call to create differentiating experiences on each device.

Generic design principles of UWP apps

As UWP apps are one core, one binary app running across all devices, it is necessary for it to generalize in a way that it can smoothly run on those devices. Here are a few generic design principles that a UWP app must follow.

Effective scaling

UWP apps can automatically adjust the size of controls and fonts based on the resolution of the device where it is running. When the app runs, the system executes an algorithm to normalize the display of each control running on the screen. For example, a control having a 20 pixel font size should look proportionate on phones, tablets, desktop PCs, laptops, and/or Surface Hubs:

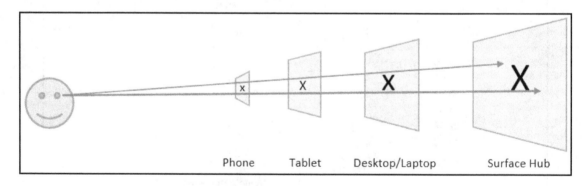

When you design your app, you need to make sure that effective scaling has been maintained for all the device families that you are going to target running the app.

Effective pixels

As you are targeting your app to scale properly in small, medium, and large resolution systems, it is necessary to take care of your design based on effective pixels instead of actual pixels.

When you place a control in the UI and the system scales the window, it does this in multiples of four. You need to make sure to snap your control to the 4x4 pixel grid to have a clear picture in a high-resolution system. If you place it in the middle of the 4x4 pixel grid, you will see a blurred image as shown in the following image:

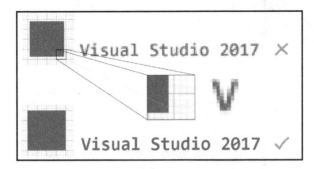

In the first example in the preceding image, you could see that the text **Visual Studio 2017** is blurred as it was not effectively placed in the 4x4 grid, but in the second example, the clarity is better as it was properly snapped to the grid block.

Universal controls

The platform provides you with a set of universal controls which you can use in all Windows devices that target UWP. This set of controls includes everything, ranging from simple buttons to the powerful **GridView** and **ListView** to display data to the user. When you use these controls, you will get the same functionalities on all device families.

Universal styles

UWP apps follow a default set of styles that automatically provide you with support for dark and light themes. You can also use the user-defined accent color or provide your custom theme. The default style also supports high contrast mode, so you can ensure that it will display properly.

Repositioning of controls

Based on the device family or the screen size, you can reposition the UI elements to get the most out of the available space. In most cases, a small device needs scrolling to display more data, but when you port it to a large screen device, you can place more controls on it to accommodate the controls in the available space. UWP app design should focus on repositioning to support the responsiveness of the UI. Consider the following screenshot:

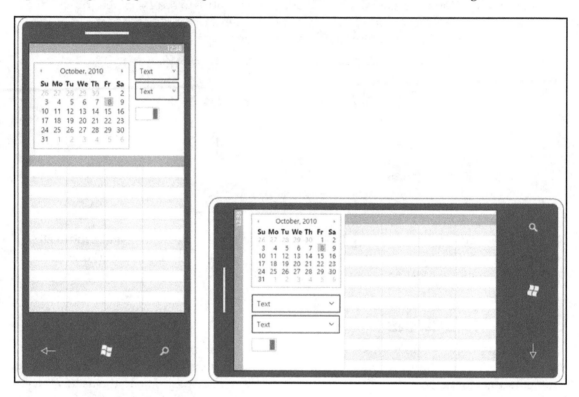

Resizing the UI

This is another UI responsiveness feature of UWP apps. Your app must be resizable based on the screen resolution. When the user changes its orientation or runs it in a higher resolution system, the app should be smart enough to utilize the available space and resize the controls accordingly to give a better reading experience. Consider the following screenshot:

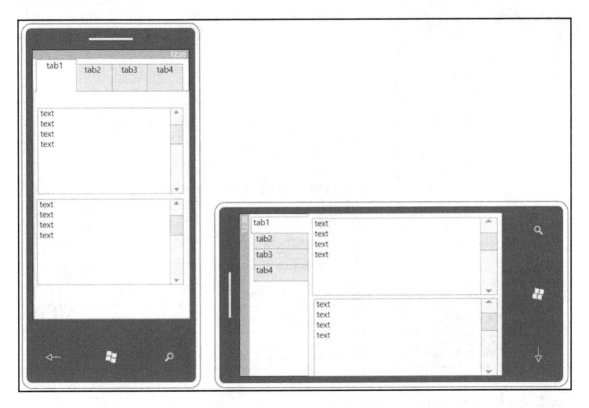

Reflowing of UI elements

Based on device and orientation, your app can offer an optimal display of content by adding more columns or reflowing the items in a different way. For example, the following design shows how it offers a two-column layout of content when the user switches from portrait to landscape mode:

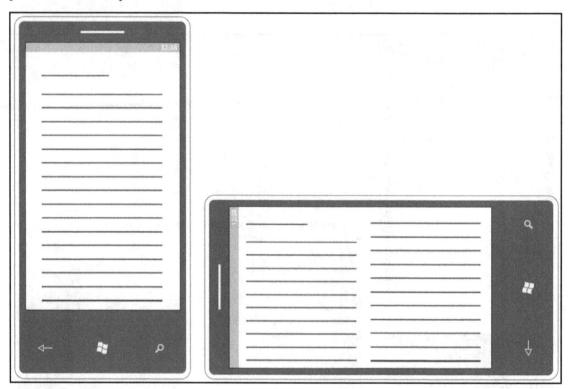

Replacing the UI Elements

It may be possible to have a better UI by providing different control sets in a different resolution or orientation of the device. This is another kind of responsive design where you are replacing the entire UI.

For example, the following design uses a calendar control and a list box in portrait view but when it changes to landscape mode, the controls have been replaced with a date picker and a set of tiles:

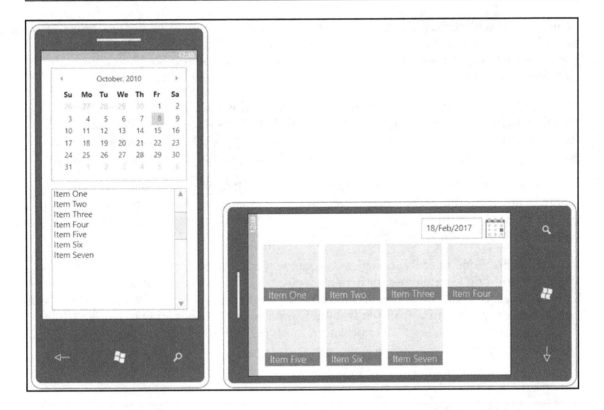

Revealing the UI elements

Sometimes, it may be possible to reveal new UI elements based on screen orientation, size, specific situations, and/or functionalities supported by the device.

For example, your app can have a map on a large display or a camera option in the lock screen if your device supports the **Windows Hello** feature.

Getting started with UWP app development

We have already discussed that the Universal Windows Platform makes it easier to build apps with a single API set, create one binary package, and distribute it to one Store to reach millions of people using Windows 10 on all their devices, such as mobile, tablet, PC, laptop, Xbox, HoloLens, Surface, and more.

To get started with the UWP app development, you need the Windows 10 operating system as the host and Visual Studio 2015 Update 3 or Visual Studio 2017 as the editor with the UWP Tools/SDK. We are going to use Visual Studio 2017 IDE in this book to go through each code example.

Let's first take a look at how we can build apps for Windows 10. You can choose the traditional Windows desktop apps (called **Classic Windows Apps**) using WinForm, WPF (which is also XAML-based), and MFC with full .NET support. You can choose between a set of programming languages such as C#, VB.NET, C++, and others to build classic apps.

Then we have the UWP, which we discussed just now. Here, you can use C#, VB.NET, or C++ to build XAML-based Universal Windows apps. If you are a JavaScript lover, you can use HTML to design the UI. This type of application can be run across all Windows 10 devices. In this chapter, we are going to focus on this topic.

In case you are from other technologies, you can still build apps for Windows 10 using the Windows bridging technologies for iOS, Android, hosted web apps, Win32, and more. These bridges for Windows allow you to convert your existing apps to UWP so that you can enhance them with the new features and publish them to Windows Store to reach all devices running Windows 10. To know more about the Windows bridging technologies, check out this page: `https://developer.microsoft.com/en-us/windows/bridges`.

Here is a diagram that demonstrates this in a simple manner:

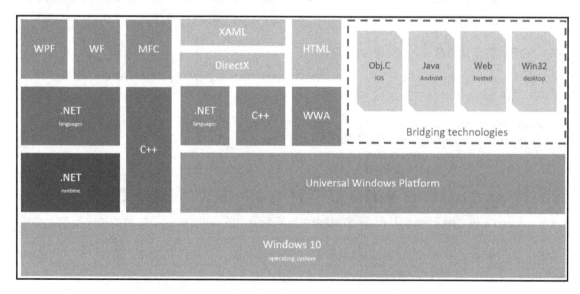

Building your first UWP application

Let us start with building our first UWP application, but before that, we need to set up the development environment for first use. Later, you can directly start with the project.

Setting up the development environment for first use

To start building apps targeting Universal Windows Platform, make sure that you have the Universal Windows Platform development workload installed on your Visual Studio 2017 dev environment.

Open the Visual Studio installer from the start screen or run the setup from the control panel and then click **Modify**, as shown in the following screenshot:

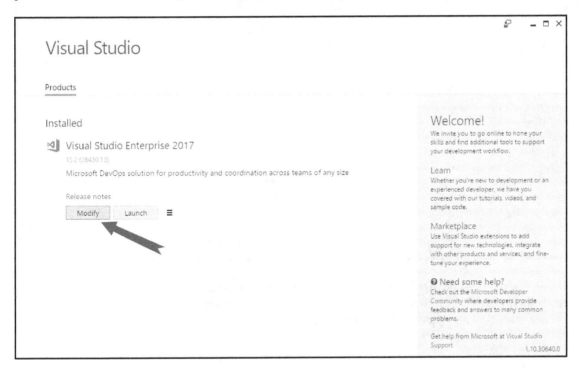

This will launch the **Workloads** screen. Check whether **Universal Windows Platform development** is checked. If it is unchecked, it means that the components related to it are not installed. Check the workload and click on **Modify** to install all the required components. It will start downloading the required packages from the Microsoft server and complete the installation:

Note that it will take around 6 GB of installation space. Make sure that you have the required internet bandwidth and available disk space.

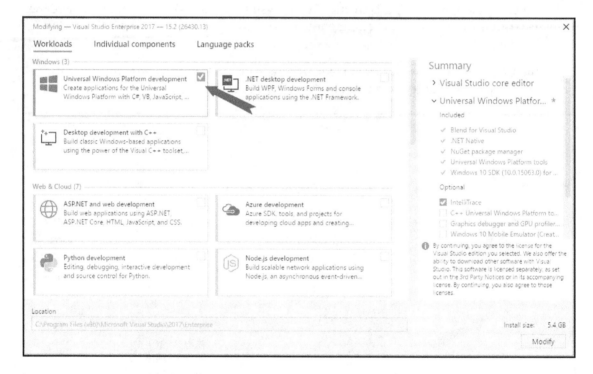

If you have already downloaded the offline installer, alternatively, you can run the installer from the installer path to save the bandwidth. If there are any new updates available in the server, the installer will auto download them.

Setting up the developer mode

To build and deploy UWP applications in your local system directly from Visual Studio, you need to set up the developer mode in the Windows developer feature set. To check and configure it, open the Windows 10 **Settings** app and click on **Update & security**.

From the left-hand side navigation panel, click on **For developers**, which will open the developer features screen in the right-hand side panel. To deploy and debug UWP apps from Visual Studio, you need to enable the **Developer mode** radio button, as shown in the following screenshot:

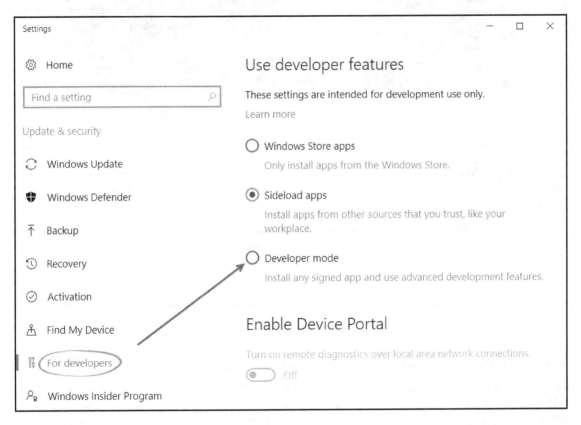

This will pop up a message box asking you to confirm whether you really want to turn on the developer mode. To continue, confirm the security risks by clicking the **Yes** button:

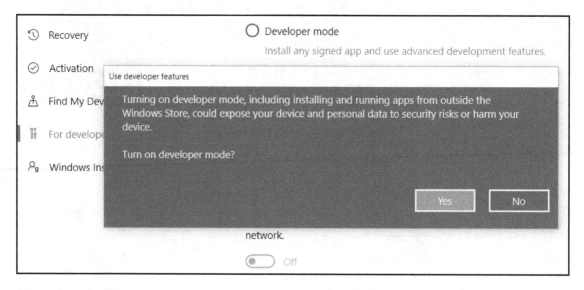

This will start downloading and installing the developer mode packages, which will not take more than a few minutes. You may have to restart your PC in order to use all the features:

Recovery	Developer mode
	Install any signed app and use advanced development features.
Activation	Installing Developer Mode package

Creating, building, and running the application

Once you have the development environment set up properly, you can start creating your UWP application project, building it, and running it on your system. To get started, open the Visual Studio 2017 IDE and create a new project either from **File** | **New** | **Project...** or from the **New Project** panel available in the start screen. When using the second approach, search for **universal** and pick up the project template type that you want to create. Alternatively, you can press *Ctrl + Shift + N* to open the new project dialog:

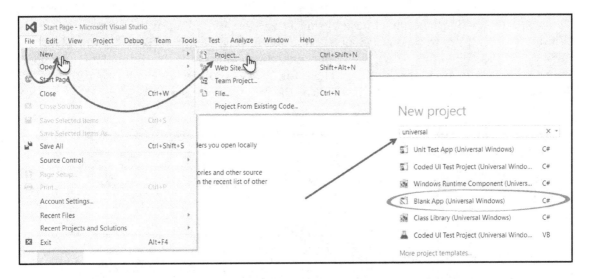

In the next screen, from the installed templates, select **Visual C# | Windows Universal** and from the right-hand side panel, select **Blank App (Universal Windows)** to create a blank basic app. Give it a name and click on **OK** to continue with the project creation:

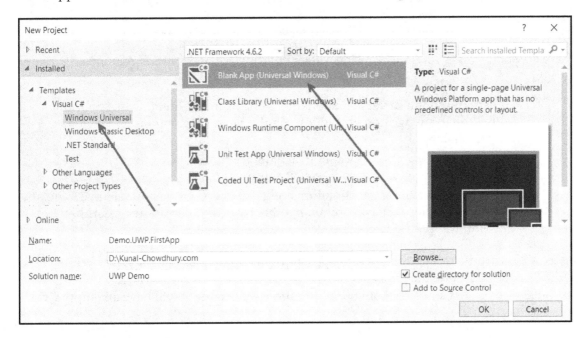

The next screen will ask you to choose the target version and minimum version of the Windows 10 platform that your universal windows app will support. Based on the SDK version installed on your system, it will populate the details in the drop-down menu. Select the one that is best suited for your app. Here, for the demo project, we will select **Build 14393** as the target version and **Build 10586** as the minimum version. Click on **OK** to continue:

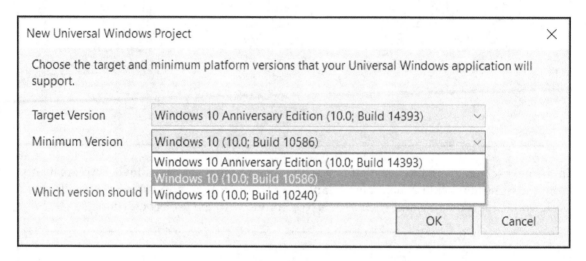

Here are some points you must consider when building applications for Windows 10, under UWP:

- When the minimum version and target version are different, your application will work in any version of Windows in the range from minimum version to target version.
- Make sure to test your application on a device running the minimum target version to ensure that the code executes properly.
- When you have the same minimum and target versions, you don't have to do any specific check for API availability. In other case, call the API that exists in the minimum supported version.

Once Visual Studio creates the selected app project, you will find the `App.xaml` and `MainPage.xaml` under the project in `Solution Explorer`. Double-click on `MainPage.xaml` to view the UI of your application. By default, it will have an empty Grid panel only:

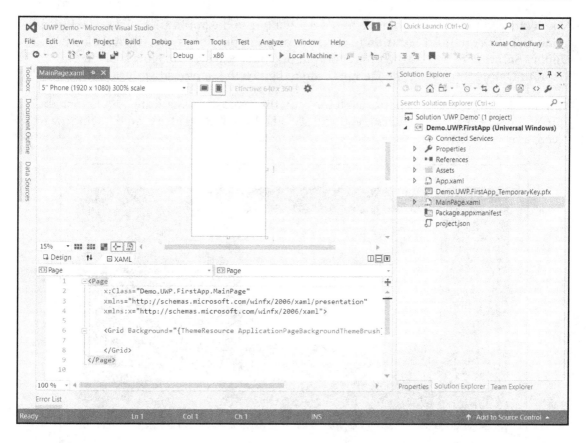

Let's add a `TextBlock` control inside the Grid panel and set its `Text`, `FontSize`, `FontWeight`, and `Foreground` properties:

```xml
<Grid Background="{ThemeResource ApplicationPageBackgroundThemeBrush}">
   <TextBlock Text="Hello UWP App!"
            FontSize="40"
            FontWeight="Bold"
            Foreground="Green"/>
</Grid>
```

Now you need to build the solution and deploy it to run the application. Go to the **Build** menu and click on **Build Solution** to check for any compilation issues. Then click on **Deploy Solution** to deploy the project output on your local system. Now click on **Start Without Debugging** under the **Debug** menu to launch the deployed application.

You can also hit *Ctrl + F5* to perform all the preceding steps automatically and launch the app on the screen. Once launched, you will see a **Hello UWP App!** text on the window in green, as specified in `MainPage.xaml`:

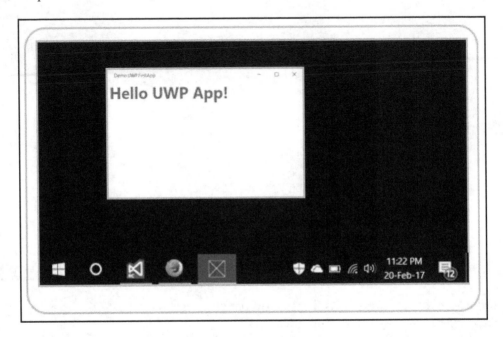

You can also deploy it to a simulator, remote machine, physical device, or emulator of your choice by clicking the arrowhead drop-down menu shown as follows. If you have any emulators installed, those will be listed here. By default, it is set to **Local Machine**. If you want to deploy it to a connected Windows Mobile device, select **Device** from the list. To deploy it in an emulator, select the one that you want to test:

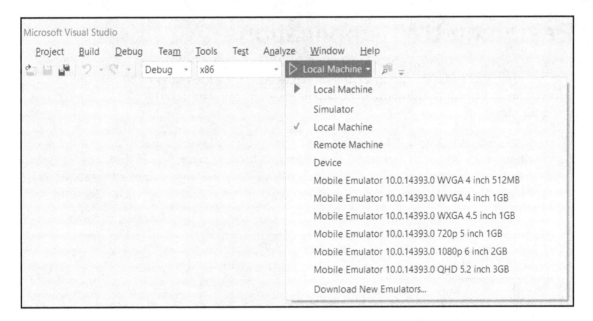

If you don't find the emulators listed here, you need to download them from the Microsoft server by clicking the **Download New Emulators...** drop-down menu entry. Find the installer and grab it out.

To work with the emulator, your device should have **Hyper-V technology/Second Level Address Translation** (**SLAT**) support. More precisely, the system should have CPU virtualization enabled.

 SLAT is a Hyper-V technology introduced in Intel and AMD processors. Intel named it **Extended Page Table** (**EPT**), introduced in processors built on the Nehalem architecture, whereas AMD named it **Rapid Virtualization Indexing** (**RVI**), introduced in their third-generation Opteron processors named Barcelona.

To check whether your system supports Hyper-V virtualization or SLAT, open **Task Manager** and navigate to **Performance** | **CPU**. At the bottom-right corner of the dialog, you will find a label titled **Virtualization**. The value of it must be **Enabled** in order to use the emulators.

Designing UWP applications

Before going into designing UWP apps, you must know that the designer window allows you to preview your UI design in various devices and in various screen orientations without building and running the app. All these can be done within the Visual Studio designer view itself.

When you open your XAML page in designer view, you will see a panel that has a drop-down menu and a few buttons inside it, as shown in the following screenshot. The dropdown lists a few devices, starting from 5-inch phone devices to tablet, desktop, Xbox, Surface Hub, IoT device, and HoloLens, each having different device sizes and screen resolution:

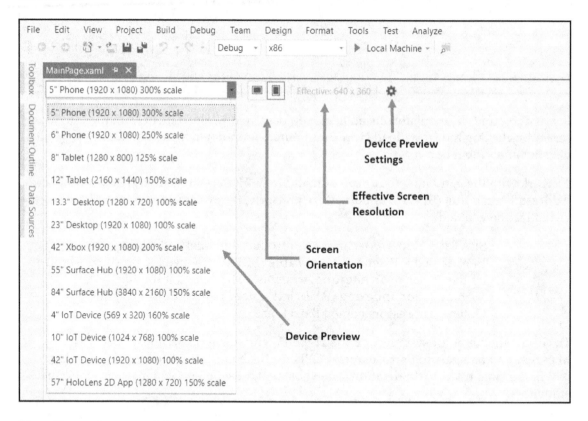

The adjacent buttons of the dropdown are used to preview your UI in different screen orientations, portrait or landscape, followed by a label that displays your effective screen resolution.

At the end of the panel, there is a small wheel to launch the **Device Preview Settings**, where you can preview your app in **High Contrast** mode and/or with a different **Theme** available by default:

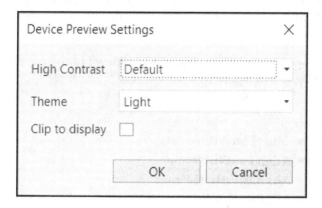

Defining XAML page layouts

In Universal Windows apps, XAML provides you with a flexible way to define your page layout by using panels, visual states, and different definitions for each device family to create good-looking, responsive UIs. We have already discussed responsive design techniques earlier in this chapter. So, let's start discussing layout patterns.

The XAML page layout pattern provides three levels of optimization techniques, which you can use to design your app screens:

- A **fluid layout** allows you to design your panels such that they can auto resize and position the children as per the available space. You can use **Grid**, **Canvas**, **StackPanel**, and **RelativePanel** to build such a fluid layout.
- An **adaptive layout** allows you to resize, reflow, reveal, or replace a part of your screen based on the window size. Visual states can be used to create an adaptive trigger to easily handle it.
- The **tailored layout** type allows you to optimize your screen for a specific device family or screen sizes. You can use a custom trigger and separate XAML files with a single or multiple code file for each device family to create a tailored layout.

In `Chapter 3`, *Building Applications for Windows Using XAML Tools*, we covered various XAML panels such as **Grid**, **Canvas**, **StackPanel**, and so on. So let's go to the next step and learn about **RelativePanel** and `VariableSizedWrapGrid`.

The relative panels

Relative panels are useful when you have nested panels in your application UI, but not in a fashion that uses a proper linear pattern to define the layout. In this type of panel, the elements are arranged in relation to the other panels described by various attached properties.

By default, an element positions itself at the top-left corner of the panel, but you can reposition it by defining relative panel alignment. There are three types of relative alignment possible in UWP applications:

- Panel alignment:
  - **AlignLeftWithPanel**
  - **AlignTopWithPanel**
  - **AlignRightWithPanel**
  - **AlignBottomWithPanel**
  - **AlignHorizontalCenterWithPanel**
  - **AlignVerticalCenterWithPanel**
- Sibling alignment:
  - **AlignLeftWith**
  - **AlignTopWith**
  - **AlignRightWith**
  - **AlignBottomWith**
  - **AlignHorizontalCenterWith**
  - **AlignVerticalCenterWith**
- Sibling position:
  - **LeftOf**
  - **Above**
  - **RightOf**
  - **Below**

To get started, let us create a UWP app project first and open `MainPage.xaml`. Now replace the **Grid** panel with a **RelativePanel** and add two border controls named **redBorder** and **greenBorder**, with background as red and green color brush respectively.

Now, select the green border (which is on top of the red border) and go to its properties. Under the **RelativePanel** category, enter the name of the control for which you want to set its relative position. In our example, we will set **redBorder** for the input box labeled **Below**. This will set a new attribute to the green border as `RelativePanel.Below="redBorder"` and immediately you will notice that the green border is placed below the red border control:

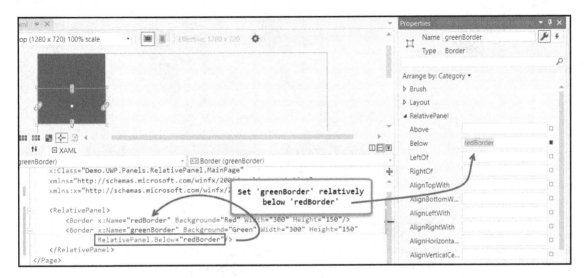

Similarly, add another border control inside the relative panel with a blue background brush and name it `blueBorder` for reference. This will be, by default, set at the top-left corner (on top of the red border control).

Now go to its properties and under the **RelativePanel** category, enter `redBorder` and `greenBorder` for the input box labeled **Below** and **RightOf**.

This will now place the blue border control adjacent to the green border. If you check the XAML code, you will notice that it has added two attributes (attached properties) to it as `RelativePanel.Below="redBorder"` and `RelativePanel.RightOf="greenBorder"`:

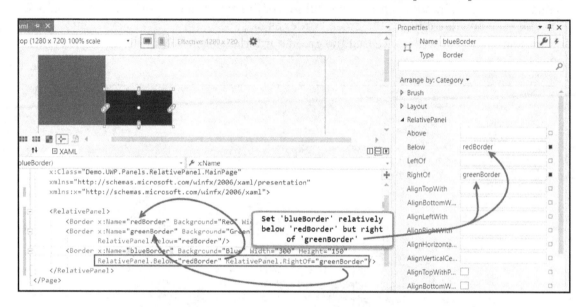

Let's add another border control with a yellow background and give it the name `yellowBorder`. We will place it next to the blue border but align it to the top of the panel. So, set **RightOf** as `blueBorder` and **AlignTopWithPanel** as checked:

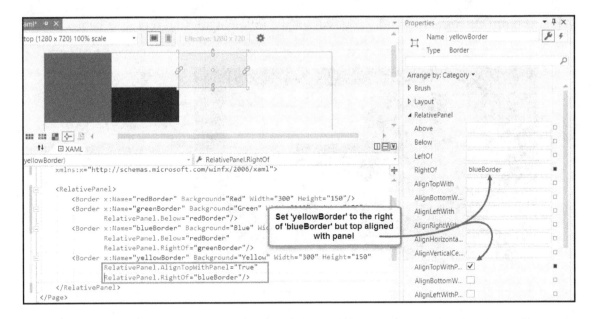

This will result in the XAML code of the yellow border control having
`RelativePanel.AlignTopWithPanel="True"` and
`RelativePanel.RightOf="blueBorder"` attached properties.

Here is the complete code for your easy reference:

```xml
<RelativePanel>
    <Border x:Name="redBorder" Background="Red"
            Width="300" Height="150"/>
    <Border x:Name="greenBorder" Background="Green"
            Width="300" Height="150"
            RelativePanel.Below="redBorder"/>
    <Border x:Name="blueBorder" Background="Blue"
            Width="300" Height="150"
            RelativePanel.Below="redBorder"
            RelativePanel.RightOf="greenBorder"/>
    <Border x:Name="yellowBorder" Background="Yellow"
            Width="300" Height="150"
            RelativePanel.AlignTopWithPanel="True"
            RelativePanel.RightOf="blueBorder"/>
</RelativePanel>
```

When you run the preceding code, you will see the following output on the screen:

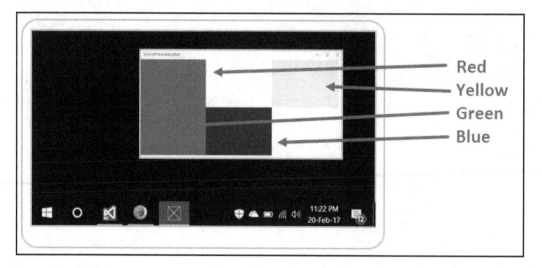

Here, the red box is placed in the top-left corner, a green box just below it, a blue box placed adjacent to the green box, and a yellow box in the top-right corner but at the same line where the red box is available.

 You will only see the **RelativePanel** category in the control's property pane if it is inside a **RelativePanel**.

The VariableSizedWrapGrid class

The `VariableSizedWrapGrid` class allows you to arrange its elements in rows and columns, wrapped to a new row or column when the maximum rows or columns defined by the `MaximumRowsOrColumns` property reaches the specified value.

You can arrange the elements from top to bottom and wrap to the next column by setting its orientation to `Vertical`. When you set it to `Horizontal`, the elements arrange themselves from left to right and then wrap to the next row.

The `RowSpan` and/or the `ColumnSpan` attached properties can be used to span the specified elements across rows and/or columns within the layout. Using this, you can create a layout just like the Windows 10 start screen having multiple small, medium, wide, and large tiles in it.

Let's see an example defining the `VariableSizedWrapGrid` layout control in action having multiple border controls in it:

```xml
<VariableSizedWrapGrid Orientation="Horizontal"
    MaximumRowsOrColumns="5">
    <Border Background="Orange" Margin="4"
            Width="100" Height="100" />
    <Border Background="Orange" Margin="4"
            Width="100" Height="100" />
    <Border Background="Orange" Margin="4"
            Width="100" Height="208"
            VariableSizedWrapGrid.RowSpan="2"/>
    <Border Background="Orange" Margin="4"
            Width="208" Height="100"
            VariableSizedWrapGrid.ColumnSpan="2"/>
    <Border Background="Orange" Margin="4"
            Width="100" Height="100" />
    <Border Background="Orange" Margin="4"
            Width="100" Height="100" />
    <Border Background="Orange" Margin="4"
            Width="100" Height="100" />
    <Border Background="Orange" Margin="4"
            Width="100" Height="100" />
</VariableSizedWrapGrid>
```

The previous example will result in the following output on the screen, having five columns of different-sized elements:

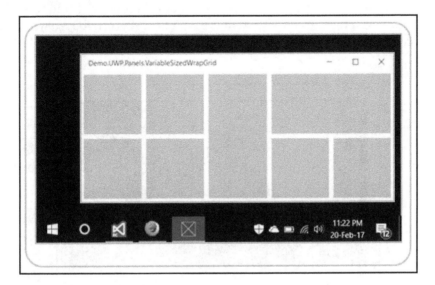

Please note the following points while using `VariableSizedWrapGrid` control:

- The content of VariableSizedWrapGrid is not virtualized
- You may see a performance impact when working with large datasets in this panel.
- VariableSizedWrapGrid can be placed inside the ItemsPanel of a GridView or ItemsControl, but cannot be placed inside an ItemsPanel of a ListView.

Data manipulation in a view

Most of the time, you will have to display and manipulate data inside your UWP applications. To do this, there are many views available as part of the SDK, among which the **GridView**, **ListView**, and **FlipView** controls are very popular and widely used. The **GridView** and **ListView** controls have the same functionalities due to their same base class, **ListViewBase**, but they display data differently.

As these are the most commonly used controls to display and manipulate data inside Universal Windows apps, let us discuss each one of them with a suitable example and code snippet.

The GridView control

The **GridView** control represents a set of scrollable items in rows and columns, stacked in a horizontal manner until they need to wrap to the next line. It is often used to display a photo/media gallery or a home page/dashboard of navigational linked items in a large display:

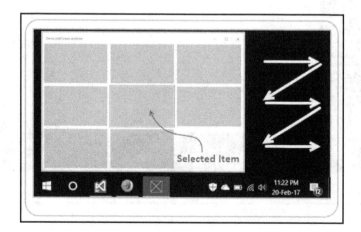

The elements can be dynamically added to its `Items` property from code behind class. You can also do a data binding of a collection of items to its `ItemsSource` property. In case you have some static data that won't change, you can directly place it in XAML inside the `GridView` tag as written in the following code to demonstrate the preceding example:

```
<GridView>
    <Rectangle Fill="Orange"
               Width="250" Height="150" Margin="4"/>
    <Rectangle Fill="Orange"
               Width="250" Height="150" Margin="4"/>
    <Rectangle Fill="Orange"
               Width="250" Height="150" Margin="4"/>
    <Rectangle Fill="Orange"
               Width="250" Height="150" Margin="4"/>
    <Rectangle Fill="Orange"
               Width="250" Height="150" Margin="4"/>
    <Rectangle Fill="Orange"
               Width="250" Height="150" Margin="4"/>
    <Rectangle Fill="Orange"
               Width="250" Height="150" Margin="4"/>
  <Rectangle Fill="Orange"
               Width="250" Height="150" Margin="4"/>
</GridView>
```

Here, we have added eight `Rectangle` controls which stack horizontally first and then move to the next row when it is unable to accommodate the next item within the same line. If you resize the window, based on the available space, the items will automatically reposition themselves in rows. When there are more items than the available space, it will add a scrollbar for a scrolling experience.

The ListView control

The **ListView** control is like what we have learned in **GridView** but with the catch that it displays the items in a stacked fashion within a single column. Like in the grid view, you can use the `Items` to add elements/data dynamically from code behind or use a data binding to its `ItemsSource` property to add a collection of items. You can also write the items in the XAML page to populate it, but in a static manner.

Let's have the same sample that we used in **GridView**, but here in a **ListView** control:

```
<ListView>
    <Rectangle Fill="Orange"
               Width="250" Height="75" Margin="4"/>
    <Rectangle Fill="Orange"
               Width="250" Height="75" Margin="4"/>
```

```
        <Rectangle Fill="Orange"
                   Width="250" Height="75" Margin="4"/>
        <Rectangle Fill="Orange"
                   Width="250" Height="75" Margin="4"/>
        <Rectangle Fill="Orange"
                   Width="250" Height="75" Margin="4"/>
        <Rectangle Fill="Orange"
                   Width="250" Height="75" Margin="4"/>
        <Rectangle Fill="Orange"
                   Width="250" Height="75" Margin="4"/>
        <Rectangle Fill="Orange"
                   Width="250" Height="75" Margin="4"/>
</ListView>
```

Here, you can see that the items are displayed in a stacked fashion in a single column though we have free space available at the right. This you can use to implement a UI with a set of data in a list manner, for example, a contact list or a list of links. When you have more items in a list view, a scrollbar will automatically appear to give you an in-built scrolling effect:

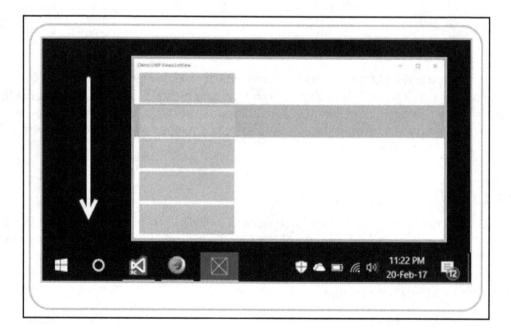

The FlipView control

The **FlipView** control is used to display a collection of images or other items in such a manner that your browsing becomes easy. The main use of this control is in a photo gallery within an app with an easy-to-navigate feature, both for touch-based and mouse-based systems. In a touch-based system, the user can swipe left/right or up/down, and in a mouse-based system, the user can navigate using the arrowheads which display on hovering the mouse.

Let us create a **FlipView** control in an XAML page by placing a few static images:

```
<FlipView>
    <Image Source="Assets/WP_001.jpg" />
    <Image Source="Assets/WP_002.jpg" />
    <Image Source="Assets/WP_003.jpg" />
    <Image Source="Assets/WP_004.jpg" />
</FlipView>
```

Alternatively, you can use the `Items` property or the `ItemsSource` property to dynamically populate a collection of items of any type. You can use horizontal (default) or vertical orientation to give left-right or top-bottom navigation controls.

If you run the preceding code (having proper images), you will see that the window will contain the following view having the images. If you hover over the control, you will see the navigational arrowheads which you can use to switch to the next or previous image (if there is one):

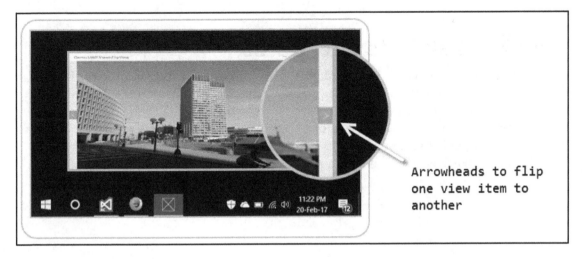

Arrowheads to flip
one view item to
another

Application designing with the XAML style

A **style** is a collection of property settings applied to one or more instances of a control to provide a better look across the application. It is possible to customize your UWP application experience by styling the XAML controls but to apply the style, the target object must be a **DependencyObject** and the target property must be a **DependencyProperty**.

You can set styles for individual controls, page-level controls, application-level controls, or shared between multiple applications running across devices.

You need to define the style under the `Resources` property. When you define the style inline to a control, it will be available only within the context of the control. When you move that style to its parent layout, it will be available within the context of the panel, for that type of control that you defined. Similarly, if you move the style to page level or application level (in `App.xaml`), it will be available for the page or application context.

When you move the style to a separate resource dictionary file as a `ResourceDictionary`, it will be available within the scope where the said resource dictionary file has been referenced. Thus, it can be shared between multiple applications. You can also merge multiple resource dictionary files into a single application and use them.

A resource defined near to the contextual structure of the control gets higher privileges and automatically overrides the resource defined in the higher level having the same key. For example, a page-level resource overrides an application-level resource.

Defining a style as a resource

A style can be defined in two ways: **implicit styling** and **explicit styling**. In implicit styling definition, you need to specify a `TargetType` for that style and all the controls defined by `TargetType` within that context will automatically use that specified style. The explicit style definition has an `x:Key` attribute along with the `TargetType` attribute and will apply it only to that target in the context which has explicitly referenced the resource as its style with the markup extension `{StaticResource}`.

Here is an implicit style definition of a button:

```
<Style TargetType="Button">
    .
    .
    .
</style>
```

Here is an explicit style definition of a button, having a key named MyButtonStyle that can be attached to a button by declaring Style="{StaticResource MyButtonStyle}" in the XAML:

```
<Style x:Key="MyButtonStyle" TargetType="Button">
    .
    .
    .
</style>
```

A TargetType property must be set in a style to avoid any exceptions.

You can use a Setter in a style to apply values to any dependency property. For example, to set the background color of a button control from style, you need to assign the Background property of the button using the Setter property value as shown in the following code snippet. You can define as many properties as you want using the Setter tag inside a style:

```
<Style TargetType="Button">
    <Setter Property="Background" Value="Orange"/>
    <Setter Property="Foreground" Value="White"/>
    <Setter Property="Height" Value="50"/>
    <Setter Property="Width" Value="100"/>
</Style>
```

Now, to use the style, you need to declare it as a resource. You can either choose it as an inline style or can place it as a page-level resource dictionary. You can go further and set it globally as an application resource.

To demonstrate, let us add it as a page-level resource which will be available only to that page context. Create a new UWP project and open the `MainPage.xaml` file. Now create the previous style under `<Page.Resources>`, which will look as follows:

```
<Page x:Class="Demo.UWP.Styles.Button.MainPage"
    xmlns="http://schemas.microsoft.com/winfx/2006/xaml/presentation"
    xmlns:x="http://schemas.microsoft.com/winfx/2006/xaml">
    <Page.Resources>
        <Style TargetType="Button">
            <Setter Property="Background" Value="Orange"/>
            <Setter Property="Foreground" Value="White"/>
            <Setter Property="Height" Value="50"/>
            <Setter Property="Width" Value="100"/>
        </Style>
    </Page.Resources>
    <Grid>
    </Grid>
</Page>
```

Now, replace the `Grid` with a `StackPanel` and add a few buttons inside it to show side by side, in a horizontal stack:

```
<StackPanel Orientation="Horizontal">
    <Button Content="Button 1" Margin="4"/>
    <Button Content="Button 2" Margin="4"/>
    <Button Content="Button 3" Margin="4"/>
    <Button Content="Button 4" Margin="4"/>
    <Button Content="Button 5" Margin="4"/>
</StackPanel>
```

As the style that we defined is an implicit style as a page resource, all the buttons within the said page will automatically apply the same. If you define an explicit style, you must set the `Style` property of the individual buttons binding the `StaticResource` key.

Let's have a look into the following UIs having two different windows. The first window has the buttons having default styles, whereas the second window has the same buttons after applying our custom style:

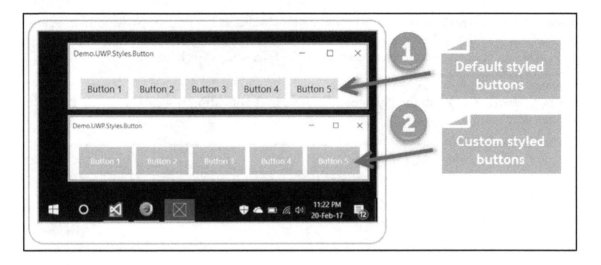

 Do note that, if you specify a value for a property both in style and on element directly, the value set on element takes higher preference than the value set on style.

You can also create/modify the style of a control using the Visual Studio editor. To get started, right-click on the control (in our case, it is a button control) in Visual designer and from the context menu, click **Edit Template | Edit a Copy...** as follows:

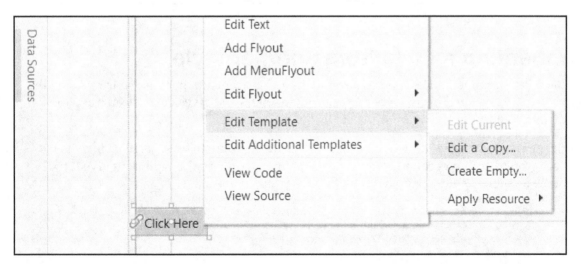

This will open a **Create Style Resource** dialog box in the screen where you need to provide the name/key of the style that you are going to generate. When you specify the name/key, it will create an explicit style. To create an implicit style, select **Apply to all**.

You can also specify where you want to create the style. By default, it will get generated in the page resource but you can change it to define in **Application** resource or create it as an inline style:

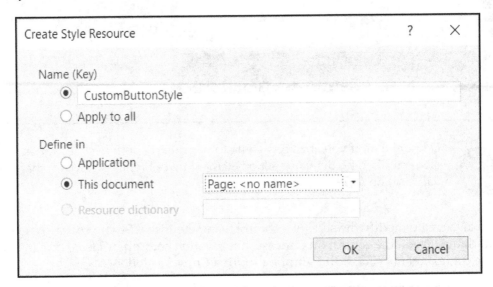

Inheriting a style from another style

Just like class inheritance, you can also inherit a style from another base style by using the property `BasedOn`. This reduces duplicate style setters and gives you a clean, easy-to-maintain code.

Let us create one base `Style` for button control having only two setters to change its background and foreground color. As we are going to inherit this style, let's give it the name `ButtonBaseStyle` by defining the `x:Key` attribute:

```
<Style x:Key="ButtonBaseStyle" TargetType="Button">
    <Setter Property="Background" Value="Orange"/>
    <Setter Property="Foreground" Value="White"/>
</Style>
```

Create another style with two more setters to define the button's height and width properties. Now inherit the first style by setting the `BasedOn` property of the second style referencing the name of the base as follows:

```
<Style TargetType="Button"
       BasedOn="{StaticResource ButtonBaseStyle}">
    <Setter Property="Height" Value="50"/>
    <Setter Property="Width" Value="100"/>
</Style>
```

Now, due to its implicit behavior, all the button controls in the page will get the second style applied. As it is referencing the first style (that is, `ButtonBaseStyle`) as a base reference, the style properties defined there will get inherited and applied to the buttons automatically.

Building your own XAML control

A custom control is a loosely coupled control defined in a class which derives from **Control**. The UI of custom control is generally defined in a resource dictionary inside the resource file. We can create themes for custom control and reuse them in various projects very easily.

Button, **CheckBox**, **TextBox**, and so on, even **ListView** and **GridView**, are nothing but custom controls. You can easily load them inside an XAML page.

It's not always possible to use only default control sets that come with the SDK. Sometimes, it is useful to create our own custom control, expose its required properties, and design the template from scratch as per our need.

A custom control generally inherits from the `System.Windows.Controls.Control` class. You may derive from a different custom control also depending on your requirement.

Custom controls are compiled into a DLL assembly and can be reused in multiple places very easily. You have total control over its code, thus giving you more flexibility to extend the behavior. Once you build and add the reference of a custom control to your project, you can find it in the toolbox and you will be able to drag and drop the control in your design view and start working with that very easily.

Let us create two **Universal Windows** projects in our solution. One will be a main application project and another will be a class library project. To get started, go to **File** | **New** | **Project**... and navigate to **Visual C#** | **Windows Universal**. First create the **Blank App (Universal Windows)** project, then follow the same steps and create the **Class Library (Universal Windows)** project:

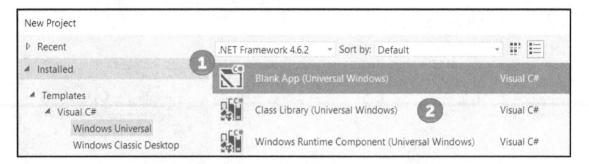

So, in your solution, there will be two projects. In the **Class Library** project, we will create the custom control and reference this assembly in the main application. Let's first add the reference in the main application. Right-click on the main application project and add a reference to the class library:

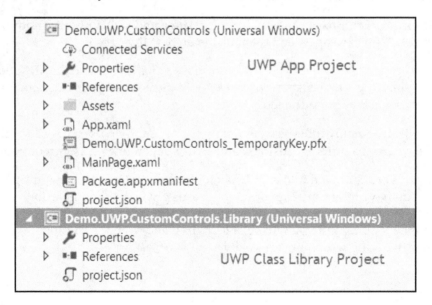

Creating the custom control

Now we will need to create our first custom control. Guess where? That will be created in the class library project. As the main application has a reference to the library already added to it, so it will automatically get the public class types or controls that we are going to create here.

So, right-click on the library project. From the context menu, click on **Add** | **New Item...** as shown in the following screenshot:

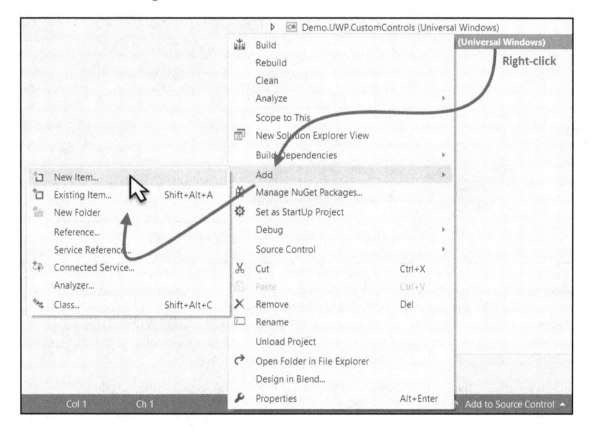

In the **Add New Item** dialog window, expand **Installed** | **Visual C#** and select the item type **Templated Control** as shown in the following screenshot. It's nothing but the type to create custom controls. Give it a good name. In our demo, we are naming it `MyCustomControl.cs`. Click on **Add** to continue:

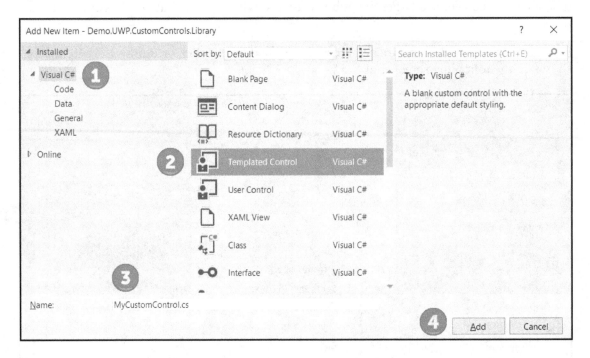

Once your first **Templated Control** (custom control) has been created in your project, you will see two files getting generated. The first one is `Generic.xaml` under a folder named **Themes**. This is the resource dictionary file that we discussed earlier in this chapter and includes the templated style of the control. The second one is the class file of the control, where you can add additional functionalities or properties of it.

If you create another custom control in the same project, the `Generic.xaml` file will get updated with the new control's template:

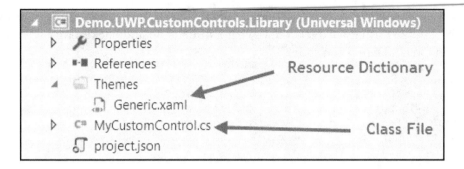

Let's see what's there in the `Generic.xaml` file. The file contains a `ResourceDictionary`, containing the templated style of the control that we have created. The setter property `Template` defines the UI of it. By default, it contains a blank `Border` control with background and border set to it from the template:

```xml
<ResourceDictionary
    xmlns="http://schemas.microsoft.com/winfx/2006/xaml/presentation"
    xmlns:x="http://schemas.microsoft.com/winfx/2006/xaml"
    xmlns:local="using:Demo.UWP.CustomControls.Library">

    <Style TargetType="local:MyCustomControl">
        <Setter Property="Template">
            <Setter.Value>
                <ControlTemplate TargetType="local:MyCustomControl">
                    <Border
                        Background="{TemplateBinding Background}"
                        BorderBrush="{TemplateBinding BorderBrush}"
                        BorderThickness="{TemplateBinding
                            BorderThickness}">
                    </Border>
                </ControlTemplate>
            </Setter.Value>
        </Setter>
    </Style>
</ResourceDictionary>
```

Now, go to the main application project and open the `MainPage.xaml` file. As we have already referenced the library project, we just need to add the XMLNS namespace of the library to the XAML page. Let's give it a prefix `controls` for easy reference.

Inside the Grid panel, add the control that we have created. You can access it from the namespace `controls` that we declared. Give it a dimension and background color to recognize in the UI. Here is the code:

```
<Page
  x:Class="Demo.UWP.CustomControls.MainPage"
  xmlns="http://schemas.microsoft.com/winfx/2006/xaml/presentation"
  xmlns:x="http://schemas.microsoft.com/winfx/2006/xaml"
  xmlns:controls="using:Demo.UWP.CustomControls.Library">

  <Grid>
    <controls:MyCustomControl Width="400" Height="35"
      Background="Orange"/>
  </Grid>
</Page>
```

Now, if you run the code, you will see the custom control that we added in the main page of the application running in the UI, which will look like this, having the control with an orange background:

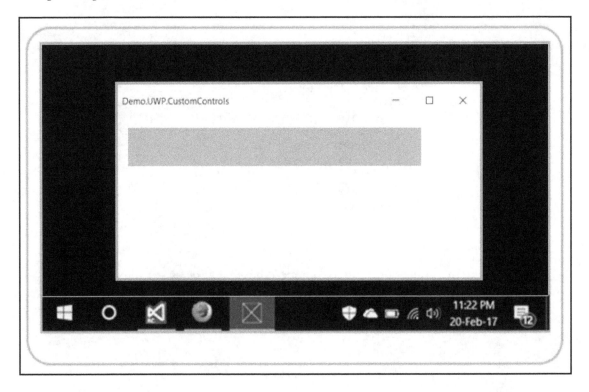

Exposing properties from a custom control

Now let us customize our control to have two properties exposed which, when filled, will show in the UI. To do this, open the MyCustomControl.cs file and create two dependency properties named FirstName and LastName. As every custom control derives from a Control having base class as DependencyObject, you can create dependency properties in it.

Here's the implementation of our class:

```
namespace Demo.UWP.CustomControls.Library
{
  public sealed class MyCustomControl : Control
  {
    public static readonly DependencyProperty FirstNameProperty =
      DependencyProperty.Register("FirstName", typeof(string),
      typeof(MyCustomControl), new PropertyMetadata(string.Empty));

    public static readonly DependencyProperty LastNameProperty =
      DependencyProperty.Register("LastName", typeof(string),
      typeof(MyCustomControl), new PropertyMetadata(string.Empty));

    public string FirstName
    {
      get { return (string)GetValue(FirstNameProperty); }
      set { SetValue(FirstNameProperty, value); }
    }

    public string LastName
    {
      get { return (string)GetValue(LastNameProperty); }
      set { SetValue(LastNameProperty, value); }
    }
    public MyCustomControl()
    {
      this.DefaultStyleKey = typeof(MyCustomControl);
    }
  }
}
```

As we have the dependency properties created, we can access them in the control's template present in the `Generic.xaml` file. Let's alter the template to have a **StackPanel** with two TextBlocks stacked in a horizontal orientation. Create the template binding to have the `Text` property of the `TextBlock` controls associated with the newly created properties. Here's the XAML template for your reference:

```
<Style TargetType="local:MyCustomControl" >
    <Setter Property="Template">
        <Setter.Value>
            <ControlTemplate TargetType="local:MyCustomControl">
                <Border
                    Background="{TemplateBinding Background}"
                    BorderBrush="{TemplateBinding BorderBrush}"
                    BorderThickness="{TemplateBinding BorderThickness}">
                    <StackPanel Orientation="Horizontal">
                        <TextBlock Text="{TemplateBinding FirstName}"
                            Margin="8 8 2 8"/>
                        <TextBlock Text="{TemplateBinding LastName}"
                            Margin="2 8 8 8"/>
                    </StackPanel>
                </Border>
            </ControlTemplate>
        </Setter.Value>
    </Setter>
</Style>
```

Now in the main page, we need to set the values to the exposed properties of our custom control. Assign the values to `FirstName` and `LastName`:

```
<Page
    x:Class="Demo.UWP.CustomControls.MainPage"
    xmlns="http://schemas.microsoft.com/winfx/2006/xaml/presentation"
    xmlns:x="http://schemas.microsoft.com/winfx/2006/xaml"
    xmlns:controls="using:Demo.UWP.CustomControls.Library">

    <Grid>
        <controls:MyCustomControl Width="400" Height="35"
            Background="Orange"
            Margin="20"
            FirstName="Kunal"
            LastName="Chowdhury"/>
    </Grid>
</Page>
```

Compile the code and run it. You will see the control updated with the first name and last name populated in the UI, which we passed from our main page to the control. The UI will look like this:

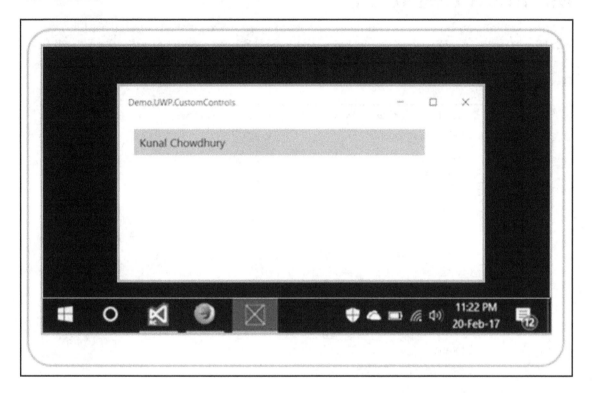

Generating visual assets using the new Manifest Designer

Every app that you build needs some basic sets of icons, logos, splash screen, and more. When you create a UWP application using the Visual Studio project template, you will find the basic set of generic images under the `Assets` folder. These include store logo, splash screen image, small tile icon, medium tile icon, wide tile icon, and lock screen logo:

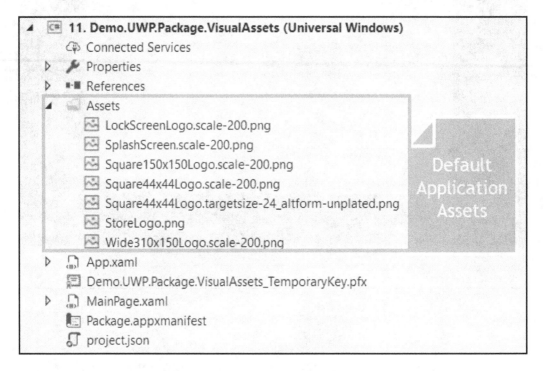

As those are generic images, you cannot build an app with those and publish to Store. It will fail immediately during the validation process. For your app, you must update those images with your app icons; create some stunning image icons to attract the user's eye.

Visual Studio 2017 allows you to easily generate these icons/images from a single image, scaling them to use on all different types of devices that your app targets.

To get started, open the `Package.appxmanifest` file present in your UWP application project. Now navigate to the **Visual Assets** tab to select an image and generate all the images that you need:

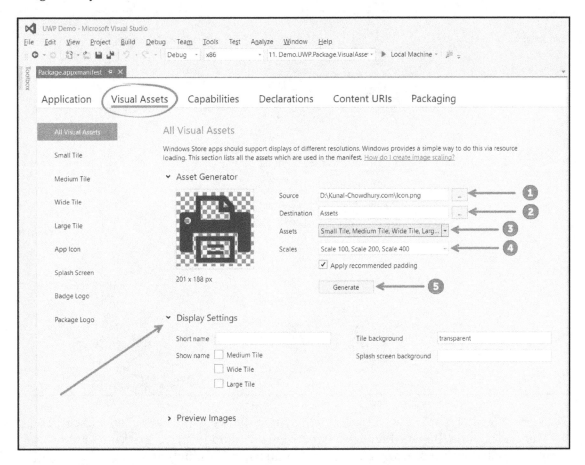

Under the **All Visual Assets** navigation entry, you will find a panel named `Asset Generator`. Select the source of the image that you want to use as a template. A preview of the selected source image will get displayed in the screen. Select the destination of the generated images. By default, it is the project's `Assets` folder.

The next step is to select the assets and various scales that you want to generate. Select the ones that your app is going to target. You can choose all of them too.

Once you have properly set these four fields, click on the **Generate** button. Visual Studio 2017 will automatically generate all the images, based on the scales and assets that you have selected:

You can also configure **Display Settings** from this screen. This will allow you to set a short name for your app tile, set the tile background color (default is transparent), the splash screen background, and the tile icons where you want to display the app name:

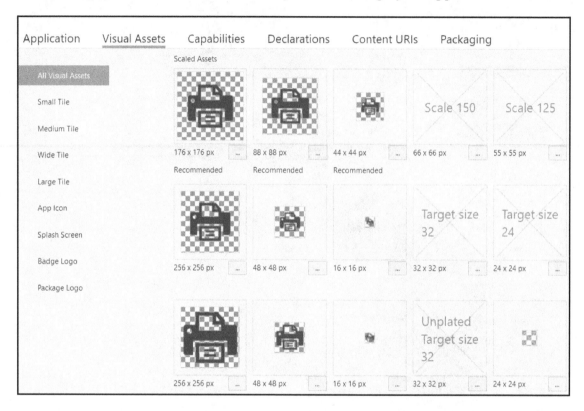

The same screen will preview all the icons/images that were generated when you clicked on the **Generate** button. Review them and if there are any modifications that you want to perform, do that before preparing your app to publish to Windows Store.

Preparing UWP apps to publish to Windows Store

When you have finished developing your Universal Windows application, have tested it properly, and are ready to publish it to Microsoft Windows Store for the people to install on their devices and use, you need to perform some basic steps in order to generate the app package and validate the bundle locally with the **Windows App Certification Kit** (**WACK**).

First, make sure that the package manifest file is correct and has all the required information updated. To do this, open the `Package.appxmanifest` file and visit all the tab details available there. In the **Application** tab, enter the **Display name** that you want for your app, select the supported orientations that your app supports, lock screen notification type, and others as shown in the following screenshot:

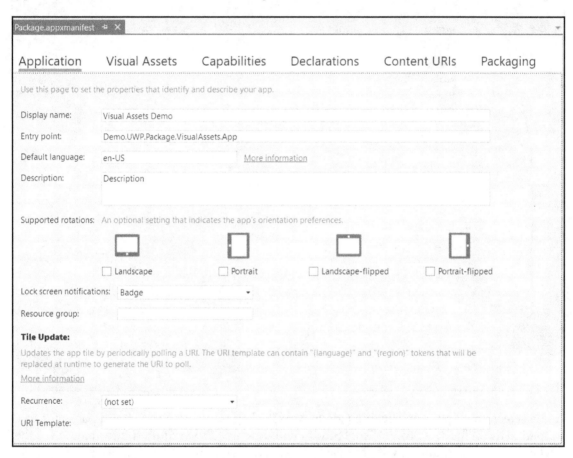

In the **Visual Assets** tab, select the images and/or generate them using the **Asset Generator** that we discussed in the previous section of this chapter. Fill in all the other details based on your app requirements and functionalities. Save the screen and build your project to make sure that there are no compilation issues.

Now navigate to the IDE menu items by navigating to **Project** | **Store** | **Create App Packages...**, as shown in the following screenshot, to start building the app packages for Windows Store using the Visual Studio wizard, which will guide you step by step:

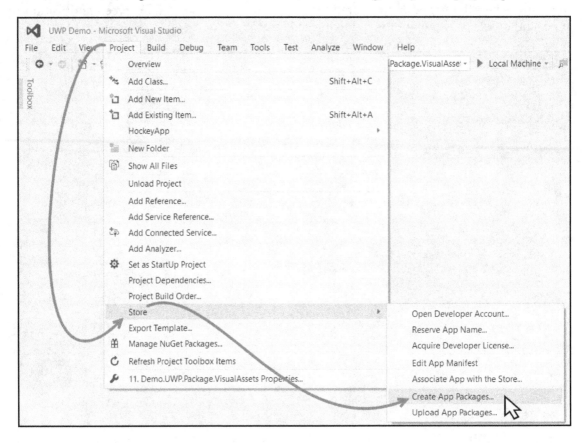

In the screen that opens on clicking **Create App Packages...**, click **Yes** to build packages to upload to the Windows Store. Visual Studio will download the required information for the packages before continuing with the package generation. You need to sign in to the Windows Store with a Microsoft Store account. If you don't have a Store account, you can create it from here: `https://developer.microsoft.com/en-us/store/register`:

It's an one-time registration (no yearly or renewal fee required) which an indie developer or an organization will have to do to publish apps to the Windows Store. The registration will cost approximately $19 USD for an individual account, and approximately $99 USD for company accounts. The exact amount may vary depending on your country/region. Once you have an account on the Store, you can publish as many apps as you want (free or paid). Microsoft won't charge any additional costs.

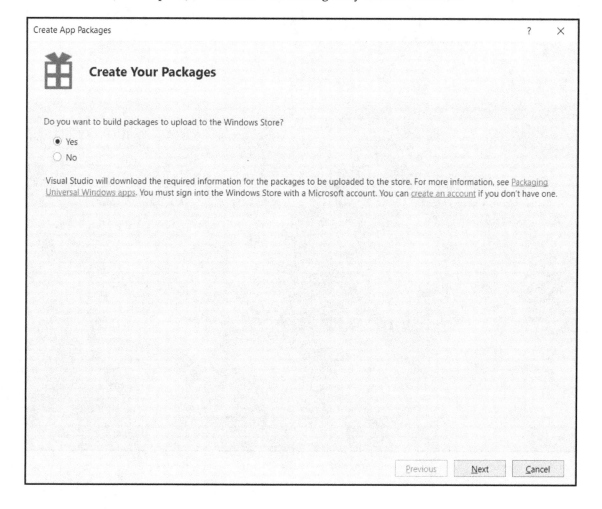

When you are signed in to your Store account, you will see the following screen with your existing apps (if any) listed in the grid. For a new app, which you have not yet published to the Store, enter a name in the input box labeled **Reserve a new app name** and click on **Reserve**. If the name is available to use in the Store, it will create the entry in your app list and enable the **Next** button to navigate to the next screen:

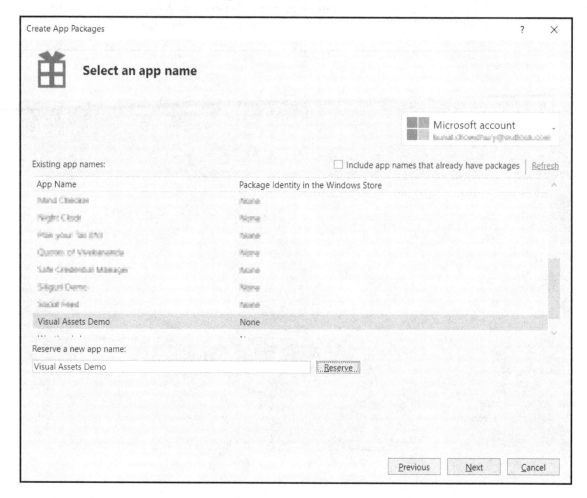

The next screen will allow you to select the output location where your app package will be generated. All the fields will be auto-populated based on the details available in the project:

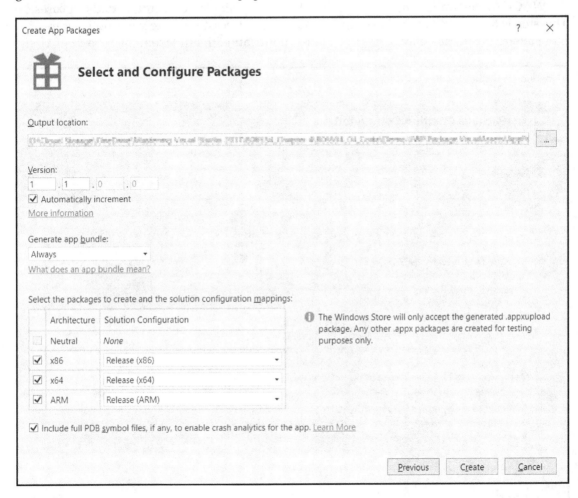

> If you want to enable the crash analytics for your app, make sure to include the full **PDB (Program Database)** symbol files. In other cases, uncheck the checkbox to have the package without debugging information.

At the end, click on **Create** to start building the app package to publish to the Store. Once the package creation is successful, you will see the following screen asking you to launch the WACK to start validating your app locally against Microsoft recommended test cases. This step is to ensure that the basic app validation is successful before you publish it to Store and to avoid the delay in getting a failed notification (if any) from the Store:

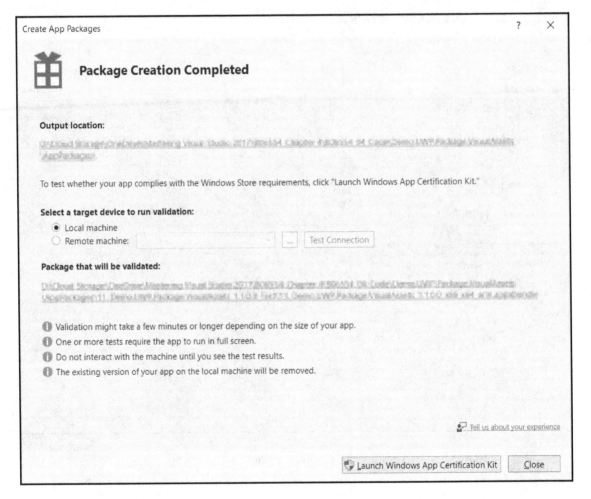

Once you click on **Launch Windows App Certification Kit**, select all the test cases which are available and execute them. It is recommended to test against all the cases before you submit the package to Store:

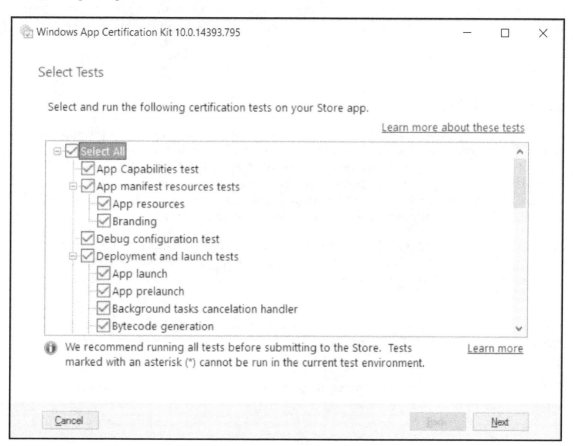

 While the validation is in progress, keep the system idle and don't interact with the device. Your app may launch multiple times automatically during this execution.

At the end of the validation, the wizard will generate a report and launch on the screen. Check whether all the tests were successful. If any of the entries say **FAILED**, you must correct that and follow the same steps again to generate the package and validate it using the WACK tool.

Once all the tests are successful, you can log in to the Windows Store developer dashboard, upload the generated package, fill in all the form entries, and submit it to Store for Microsoft testers to validate it again. If the certification gets a green signal, your app will finally publish to the Store and will be available for download. Your apps can be free, trial, or fully paid. To know more about the pricing tiers and payout options, head to the following link: `http://bit.ly/getting-paid-apps`.

Summary

In this chapter, we learnt about the platform to build Universal Windows applications which can target any device families running Windows 10. First, we learned about the generic design principles and then headed toward creating our first UWP application, after setting up the development environment. Then we learned about various XAML page layouts and data manipulation in a view to design a good-looking UWP application. We covered **GridView**, **ListView**, and **FlipView** to show data on screen.

Near to the end, we discussed how to create a style of a XAML control, assign it to a resource dictionary, and inherit a style from another base style. We then covered how to build custom controls and generate visual assets using the new Manifest Designer of Visual Studio 2017.

Finally, we have discussed how to create the app package, locally validate the package against Microsoft-specific test cases using the WACK tool, and prepare it for submission to Windows Store.

In the next chapter, we are going to learn about **.NET Core** and start building applications targeting this new .NET Framework.

Building Applications with .NET Core

5

.NET Core is an open source framework (hosted on GitHub `https://github.com/dotnet/core`), released by Microsoft and maintained by the .NET community, to build cross-platform applications for Windows, Linux, and Mac OS. You can get it from Microsoft's official .NET Core site at `https://www.microsoft.com/net/core` or GitHub. If you are using Visual Studio 2017, you can get it as part of the installer.

In this chapter, we will discuss the following core topics:

- Overview of .NET Core
- Installing .NET Core with Visual Studio 2017
- A quick lap around the .NET Core commands:
    - Creating a .NET Core console app
    - Creating a .NET Core class library
    - Creating a solution file and adding projects to it
    - Resolving dependencies in a .NET Core application
    - Building a .NET Core project or solution
    - Running a .NET Core application
    - Publishing a .NET Core application
    - Creating an ASP.NET Core application
    - Creating a unit testing project
- Creating .NET Core applications using Visual Studio

- Publishing a .NET Core application using Visual Studio 2017:
    - Framework-Dependent Deployments
    - Self-Contained Deployments
- Creating, building, and publishing a .NET Core web app to Microsoft Azure

Overview of .NET Core

.NET Core version 1.0 was first released in 2016 and now has support to work in Visual Studio 2015, update 3.3 or later, Visual Studio 2017, and Visual Studio Code only. The shared SDK component can be used to build, run, and publish applications using Visual Studio, Visual Studio Code, and the command line interface:

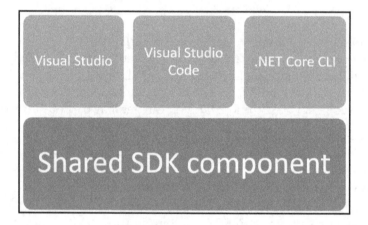

 Please note that .NET Core 2.0 is scheduled for release in Q3 of 2017 and .NET Core 2.1 is scheduled for release in Q4 of 2017 (after Microsoft releases Windows 10 Fall Creators Update).

.NET Core is a subset of the .NET Framework, and contains its core features in both runtime and libraries. The .NET Framework, which was first released in 2002, is now running version 4.6.2. Until now, it was only targeted for the Windows platform, but, as time has passed, there has been a need to target it on different platforms. Using .NET Core components, you can build apps targeting the following platforms:

- Windows:
    - Windows 7, 8, 8.1, 10
    - Windows Server 2008 R2 SP1

- Windows Server 2012 SP1, R2
- Windows Server 2016

- Mac:

  - Mac OS 10.11 or higher

- Linux:

  - Red Hat Enterprise 7.2
  - Ubuntu 14.04, 16.04, 16.10
  - Mint 17
  - Debian 8.2
  - Fedora 23, 24
  - Cent OS 7.1
  - Oracle Linux 7.1
  - Open SUSE 13.2, 42.1

It is composed of a .NET runtime, a set of framework libraries, a set of SDK tools, language compilers, and the .NET app host. Currently, you can use the C# and F# languages to build apps and libraries, and VB is on its way.

.NET Core 1.0 does not support all the app models of .NET Framework except the console and ASP.NET Core app models. It contains a smaller set of APIs from the .NET Framework as it is a subset of the other, but Microsoft is making changes to expand it further. Using .NET Core you can build apps that can execute on a device, the cloud, and on embedded/IoT devices. Following are the characteristics that best define .NET Core:

- It is an open-source platform hosted on GitHub with the MIT and Apache 2 license.
- Due to its flexible deployment nature, you can include .NET Core in your app (SCD) or install it side by side (FDD). We will discuss SCD and FDD later in this chapter.
- You can build cross-platform applications, which are currently supported by a few flavors of the Windows, Linux, and Mac operating systems.
- You can use the command-line interface to execute everything from project creation to publishing an app.
- As it is a subset of the .NET Framework it is compatible with that, along with Xamarin and Mono via the .NET Standard Library.
- Finally, it is supported by Microsoft and maintained by a vast .NET community.

Installation of .NET Core with Visual Studio 2017

To install .NET Core along with Visual Studio 2017, run the Visual Studio installer. If you have already installed Visual Studio 2017, you can modify the existing installation to install the .NET Core workload.

When the installer starts, you will see the following screen, where you can customize the workloads that you want to install. From the list, select **.NET Core cross-platform development** and click on **Install** to continue:

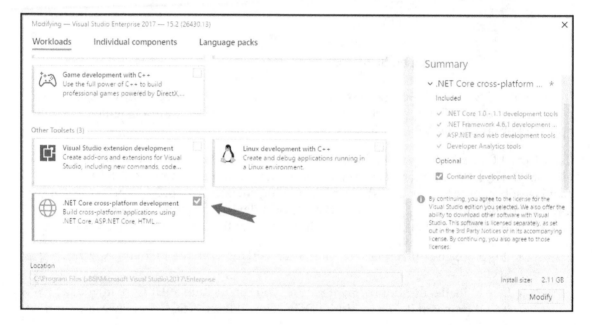

This will start the installation process. Once it completes, you may have to restart your computer for the changes to take effect.

Once the installation is successful, open a console window and type in the `dotnet new` command to populate your local .NET Core package cache, which will occur only once to improve the restore speed and enable offline access.

dotnet is the driver of .NET Core's **CLI** (**Command Line Interface**). It accepts commands followed by distinct options to run specific features.

When you use it for the first time, it will print the following output in the console window, which may take up to a minute to complete the initialization:

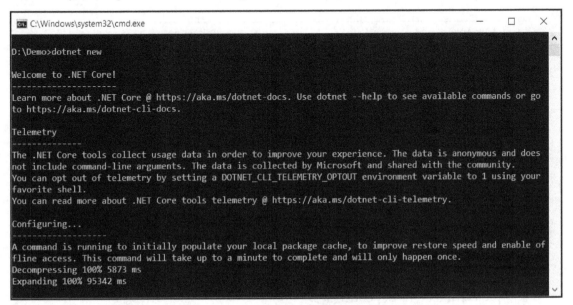

A quick lap around the .NET Core commands

The driver of the .NET Core CLI is `dotnet`. You can use this along with commands and distinct options to run specific features that it supports. Each of its features is implemented as a command, which you need to specify after the `dotnet` in the command line.

Here is the list of .NET Core commands:

- When you use `dotnet new`, it initializes new project based on the project template and language that you select. The default is C#, and, currently, C# and F# are the only programming languages supported.
- Following is the list of project templates, their short names to pass to the command, and the language type for each template, for your reference:

```
Templates                                  Short Name     Language
--------------------------------------------------------------------
Console Application                        console         [C#], F#
Class library                              classlib        [C#], F#
Unit Test Project                          mstest          [C#], F#
xUnit Test Project                         xunit           [C#], F#
Empty ASP.NET Core Web Application         web             [C#]
MVC ASP.NET Core Web Application           mvc             [C#], F#
Web API ASP.NET Core Web Application       webapi          [C#]
Solution File                              sln
```

- The `dotnet restore` command restores the dependencies and tools of a project.
- The `dotnet clean` command is used to clean the output of a project that was built earlier.
- The `dotnet build` command is used to build a .NET Core application.
- The `dotnet msbuild` command provides access to the msbuild CLI to build a project and all its dependencies.
- When you want to publish a .NET Core application as a framework-dependent or self-contained app, you should use the `dotnet publish` command.
- The `dotnet run` command is used to run the application from source.
- When you use `dotnet test`, it executes the tests using the test runner specified in the `project.json` file.
- When you want to create a NuGet package of your code, you should use the `dotnet pack` command in the CLI.
- When you specify the `dotnet sln` command, it allows you to add, remove, and list projects in a solution file.
- The `dotnet nuget delete` command deletes or unlists a project from the NuGet server.
- The `dotnet nuget locals` command is used to clear or list the local NuGet resources.

- Using the `dotnet nuget push` command, you can push a NuGet package to the server and publish it in the NuGet store.

Creating a .NET Core console app

Let's learn how to create a .NET Core console application. Here, we will discuss how to create it from the CLI using the command `dotnet new`.

As we have already seen that the short name for the command line console application template is console, we will use it to create this type of project. By default, it creates the new project in the current directory with the name of the same directory, unless you specify the name.

Let's first create a console application with all default parameters/options. Open a console window and navigate to the directory of your choice. Then enter the following command to create a console application project:

```
dotnet new console
```

This will successfully create the console application project, along with the code file as shown in the following screenshot:

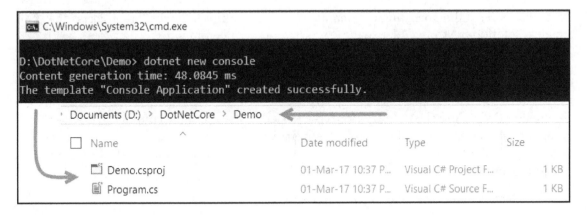

In the preceding demonstration, we have created a new folder named Demo in the `D:\DotNetCore` directory path, then navigated to that new directory (`D:\DotNetCore\Demo`) in the console window and given the command. As we have not specified any name explicitly, it will create a project in the context of the current directory. So, you will see `Demo.csproj` in that directory, with a C# file named `Program.cs`.

Let's create another project, but this time we will specify a name and the language explicitly. Navigate to the `DotNetCore` directory in the console window and enter the following command:

```
dotnet new console -lang C# -n "HelloDotNetCore"
```

This will create a new folder named `HelloDotNetCore` and a project of the same name, with a `Program.cs` code file in C#. If you want to build an F# project, specify the option as `-lang F#`:

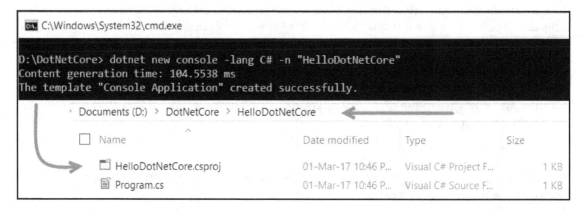

Note that none of the preceding commands create any solution file for the projects. To create a solution file from CLI, use the `dotnet new sln` command.

Creating a .NET Core class library

To create a .NET Core class library project, we need to use the same command, `dotnet new`, but with a class library type project template, whose short name is `classlib`. Let's navigate to the folder (in our case, it's `D:\DotNetCore`) in the console window and enter the following command:

```
dotnet new classlib -n "CustomLibrary" -lang C#
```

This will create a C# project named `CustomLibrary.csproj` and a C# class file, `Class1.cs`, in a directory named `CustomLibrary` under the current directory:

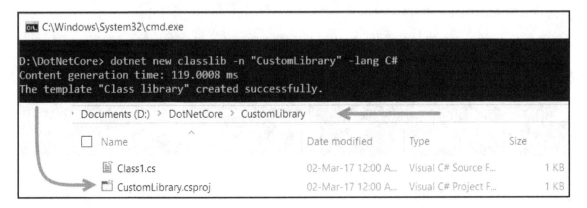

Creating a solution file and adding projects in it

Using the .NET Core CLI, you can also create a solution file and add/remove projects in it. To create a default solution file, enter the following command in the console window:

```
dotnet new sln
```

This will create a solution file named `DotNetCore.sln` in the current directory, as shown in the following screenshot:

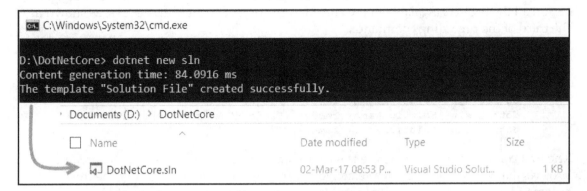

In case you want to specify a name while creating the solution file, enter the command as follows:

```
dotnet new sln -n "Demo Solution"
```

The solution file, with the specified name, will get generated in the same folder:

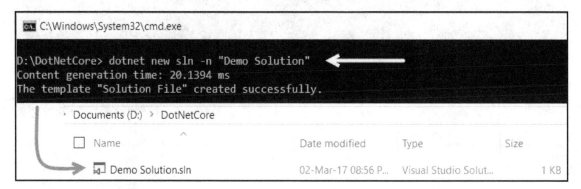

To modify the solution file from the command line to add projects in it, enter either of the following commands, providing the proper name of the solution and the project name:

```
dotnet sln <SolutionName> add <ProjectName>
dotnet sln <SolutionName> add <ProjectOneName> <ProjectTwoName>
dotnet sln <SolutionName> add **/**
```

When you want to add a single project in a solution file, use the first command. Use the second command with the names of all the projects that you want to add. When you want to add all the projects available in the current directory, you can use asterisks, as shown in the third of the preceding commands.

Similarly, you can remove any project from the solution file. You can use any of the following commands, as per your requirements:

```
dotnet sln <SolutionName> remove <ProjectName>
dotnet sln <SolutionName> remove <ProjectOneName> <ProjectTwoName>
dotnet sln <SolutionName> remove **/**
```

The first command mentioned here is used to remove a single file. When there are multiple projects that you want to remove selectively, run the second command. Use the third command when you want to remove all the projects available in the current directory from the solution file.

Let's do this in practice. We will first create two .NET Core projects of types Console App and Class Library. Then we will add them to a newly created solution file. Now, navigate to the folder where you want to create these, and work through the following steps to build our first solution file:

1. Create a console app project by entering the following command:

   ```
   dotnet new console -n "Demo App"
   ```

2. Create a class library project by entering the following command:

   ```
   dotnet new classlib -n "Custom Library"
   ```

3. Create a solution file:

   ```
   dotnet new sln -n "Demo Solution"
   ```

4. Add the projects into the solution file:

   ```
   dotnet sln "Demo Solution.sln" add "Demo App\Demo App.csproj"
       "Custom Library\Custom Library.csproj"
   ```

Here's a screenshot of the steps that we followed in the steps:

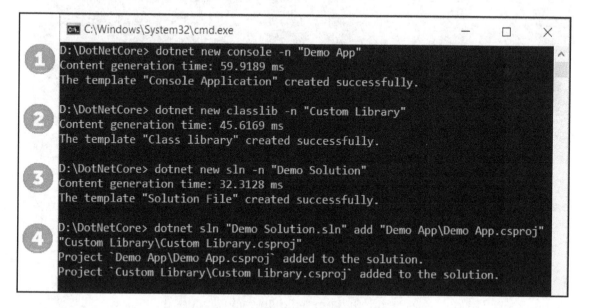

Resolving dependencies in the .NET Core application

.NET Core uses NuGet to restore dependencies and project-specific tools, which are done in parallel when you enter the command from a command line in the directory where your project/solution resides. Let's resolve the dependencies of the projects that we have just created. Enter the following command from the current directory (`D:\DotNetCore`, in our case):

```
dotnet restore
```

This will start restoring the .NET Core packages/dependencies:

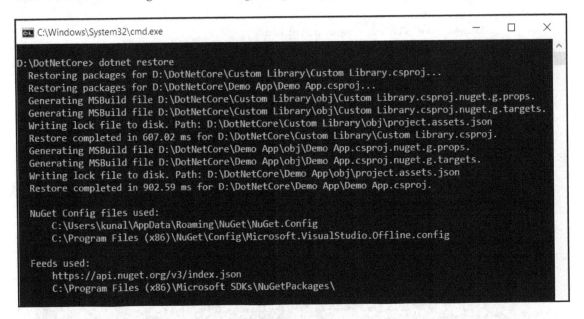

In the preceding screenshot, you can see how it executed in parallel to first restore its package dependencies and then the tool-related dependencies for MSBuild. Unless these dependencies are resolved, you cannot proceed to build and run your application.

Building a .NET Core project or solution

To build a .NET Core project from the command line, you can use the `dotnet build` command. When you specify it in a directory with multiple projects, a build will be performed for all the projects.

When there is a solution in the directory that has at least one project linked, performing the following command will build all the projects linked in the solution file:

```
dotnet build
```

Here's a screenshot of the command execution:

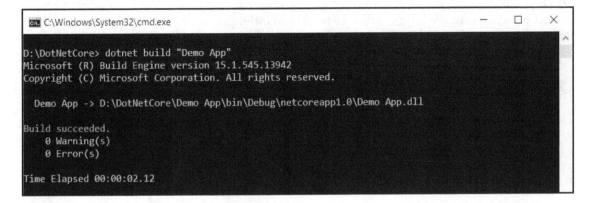

```
C:\Windows\System32\cmd.exe                                    —    □    ×

D:\DotNetCore> dotnet build
Microsoft (R) Build Engine version 15.1.545.13942
Copyright (C) Microsoft Corporation. All rights reserved.

  Custom Library -> D:\DotNetCore\Custom Library\bin\Debug\netstandard1.4\Custom Library.dll
  Demo App -> D:\DotNetCore\Demo App\bin\Debug\netcoreapp1.0\Demo App.dll

Build succeeded.
    0 Warning(s)
    0 Error(s)

Time Elapsed 00:00:02.35
```

To build a specific project or solution, provide its name or the path to it while executing the build command. Following is the command to build the Demo App project we have created (you can use either of them):

```
dotnet build "Demo App"
dotnet build "Demo App\Demo App.csproj"
```

Here's a screenshot of the execution process to build the **Demo App** application:

```
C:\Windows\System32\cmd.exe                                    —    □    ×

D:\DotNetCore> dotnet build "Demo App"
Microsoft (R) Build Engine version 15.1.545.13942
Copyright (C) Microsoft Corporation. All rights reserved.

  Demo App -> D:\DotNetCore\Demo App\bin\Debug\netcoreapp1.0\Demo App.dll

Build succeeded.
    0 Warning(s)
    0 Error(s)

Time Elapsed 00:00:02.12
```

Building a .NET Core project requires the dependencies to be resolved first. Hence, you should execute the `dotnet restore` command at least once before building your code.

The output of the build will get generated in the bin folder of the project directories. By default, it builds against the debug configuration settings, but to build the project(s) in release mode, the `--configuration Release` option needs to be specified, as follows:

```
dotnet build --configuration Release
dotnet build "Demo App" --configuration Release
```

You can also target the build for a different runtime by specifying `--runtime` followed by `<RuntimeIdentifier>`. If you want to build the project/solution against the runtime of Red Hat Enterprise Linux 7 (64-bit), enter the following commands one by one:

```
dotnet clean
dotnet resolve --runtime rhel.7-x64
dotnet build --runtime rhel.7-x64
```

The first command will clean the current workspace. The second command will build the project(s)/solution against the specified runtime (`rhel.7-x64`). The third command will build against the runtime specified.

Make sure to resolve the dependencies before retargeting to build to a different runtime.

When you build a project or a solution, the output files are written in the bin folder of the project directory. All the temporary files related to build get generated in the obj folder of the project directory, just like any other projects targeting, .NET Framework.

Running a .NET Core application

To run a .NET Core application, you can use the `dotnet run` command from the console window. As it relies on the `dotnet build` command, when you specify a project to run, it automatically builds the project and then launches the application.

To run an app in the project context, enter the following command:

```
dotnet run --project <ProjectPath>
```

If you already have a portable application DLL, you can run it directly by executing the DLL by the dotnet driver without specifying any command. For example, the following command runs the already available DLL built against .NET Core 1.0:

```
dotnet "Demo App\bin\Debug\netcoreapp1.0\Demo App.dll"
```

Please refer the following screenshot:

Publishing a .NET Core application

When you build, debug, and test your application successfully, you need to publish or deploy your app. The .NET Core provides the dotnet publish command to publish your app for deployment.

To publish a .NET Core app in the Release mode, enter the following command:

```
dotnet publish <ProjectName> -c Release
```

There are two kinds of deployment available for .NET Core applications, which are **Framework-Dependent Deployment (FDD)** and **Self-Contained Deployment (SCD)**. The first one depends on a system-wide version of .NET Core to be present before running the application, whereas the second type of deployment does not depend on any .NET Core version already installed on the system as it includes the entire .NET Core libraries and runtime, along with the resultant application files.

Let's learn more about each of the preceding deployment types with a simple demo-oriented example.

Framework-Dependent Deployments

This type of deployment model executes by default while publishing a .NET Core application. In this deployment step, only your app and any third-party dependencies get deployed, and there exists no reason to deploy .NET Core along with your app as your app will use the .NET Core version that's present on the user's system.

In this model, the output of the .NET Core application is always a `.dll` file. You won't find any `.exe` file to run.

This type of deployment has a number of benefits:

- As you don't need to deploy .NET Core along with your app, the size of your deployment package stays very small
- It reduces disk space and memory usage on the system as multiple apps can use a single .NET Core installation
- As .NET Core uses a common **Portable Executable** (**PE**) format, which the underlying operating system can understand, there's no need to define the target operating system

Let's work through the following steps to create, build, run, and publish an app using the FDD deployment model:

1. Create a directory for your solution (for example, `DotNetCore`) and navigate to it in a command window.
2. Enter the following command to create a new C# Console application:

   ```
   dotnet new console -lang C# -n "FDD Demo"
   ```

3. Create a solution file named `FDD Demo` and add the project into the solution file:

   ```
   dotnet new sln -n "FDD Demo"
   dotnet sln "FDD Demo.sln" add "FDD Demo\FDD Demo.csproj"
   ```

4. Now resolve the dependencies by entering the following command:

   ```
   dotnet restore
   ```

5. Build the solution by running the following command, which will generate the PE version of the application in the `bin\debug` folder:

```
dotnet build
```

6. If the build succeeds, the output DLL will get generated in `DotNetCore\FDD Demo\bin\Debug\netcoreapp1.0\FDD Demo.dll`. Now, enter the following command to run it:

```
dotnet "FDD Demo\bin\Debug\netcoreapp1.0\FDD Demo.dll"
```

7. Once you are ready to publish your app, enter the following command to create the release version of the project to the `DotNetCore\FDD Demo\bin\Release\netcoreapp1.0\publish` folder:

```
dotnet publish "FDD Demo\FDD Demo.csproj" -c Release
```

Here, in the FDD model, you will have only your app and its dependency files (if any), along with the PDB file and JSON configuration files, in the publish directory. No other files will get deployed there, thus keeping your deployment package very small.

Self-Contained Deployments

In this type of deployment model, .NET Core gets deployed along with your application and dependency libraries. Thus, the size of your deployment package becomes large compared to the package created by the FDD model. The version of .NET Core depends on the version of the framework that you build your app with.

In this model, the output of the .NET Core application is an `.exe` file, which loads the actual `.dll` file on execution.

The main advantages of this type of deployment are as follows:

- As you are bundling the version of .NET Core that your app needs to run, you can be assured that it will run on the target system.
- Only you can decide which version of .NET Core your app will support. You should select the target platform before you create the deployment package.
- The output is an EXE file, which loads the actual DLL.

Let's work through the following steps to create, build, run, and publish an app using the SCD model:

1. Create a directory for your solution (for example, `DotNetCore`) and navigate to it in a command window.

2. Enter the following command to create a new C# Console application:

    ```
    dotnet new console -lang C# -n "SCD Demo"
    ```

3. Create a solution file named `SCD Demo` and add the project into the solution file:

    ```
    dotnet new sln -n "SCD Demo"
    dotnet sln "SCD Demo.sln" add "SCD Demo\SCD Demo.csproj"
    ```

4. Now, open the project file `SCD Demo.csproj` in a notepad.

5. Create a `<RuntimeIdentifiers>` tag under the `<PropertyGroup>` section of your `.csproj` and define the platforms that your app targets:

    ```
    <PropertyGroup>
      <RuntimeIdentifiers>win10-x64</RuntimeIdentifiers>
    </PropertyGroup>
    ```

6. Here you can set multiple identifiers separated by semicolons.

7. Now resolve the dependencies by entering the following command:

    ```
    dotnet restore
    ```

8. Build the solution by running the following command (enter the runtime identifier that you want your app to target), which will generate the output of the application in the `bin\Debug\netcoreapp1.0` folder:

    ```
    dotnet build -r win10-x64
    ```

9. If the build succeeds, the output DLL will get generated, along with the EXE as `DotNetCore\SCD Demo\bin\Debug\netcoreapp1.0\SCD Demo.dll` and `DotNetCore\SCD Demo\bin\Debug\netcoreapp1.0\SCD Demo.exe`.

10. Now, enter the following command to run it:

    ```
    dotnet "SCD Demo\bin\Debug\netcoreapp1.0\SCD Demo.dll"
    ```

11. You can also run the EXE file directly:

    ```
    "SCD Demo\bin\Debug\netcoreapp1.0\SCD Demo.exe"
    ```

12. Once you are ready to publish your app, enter the following command to create the release version of the project to the `DotNetCore\SCD Demo\bin\Release\netcoreapp1.0\win10-x64\publish` folder:

```
dotnet publish -c Release -r win10-x64
```

If you open the published folder, you will see many other files apart from the project DLL, project EXE, JSON configs, and PDB files. You can create as many deployment packages as you want, based on your targeted RIDs. Separate folders will get generated for each RID package.

Creating an ASP.NET Core application

There are three different types of ASP.NET Core project templates available to use, which are the Empty ASP.NET Core web application (identified as `web`), MVC ASP.NET Core web application (identified as `mvc`), and Web API ASP.NET Core web application (identified as `webapi`). Among these, only the MVC web app currently has support for both the C# and F# languages.

To create an empty ASP.NET core application, enter the following command in the console window:

```
dotnet new web -n <ProjectName>
```

To create an MVC-based ASP.NET web app, enter the following command:

```
dotnet new mvc -n <ProjectName>
```

To create an ASP.NET MVC web application with no authentication, enter the following:

```
dotnet new mvc -au None -n <ProjectName>
```

To create an ASP.NET web API application, enter the following in the command line:

```
dotnet new webapi -n <ProjectName>
```

By default, ASP.NET Core web applications uses SQLite for database support. You can change it to use LocalDB instead of SQLite. To change it, append either of the `-uld` or `--use-local-db` options with a value `true`, as follows:

```
dotnet new mvc -n <ProjectName> -uld true -au none
```

Here's what happens after you enter the command, and the files/folders that it generates:

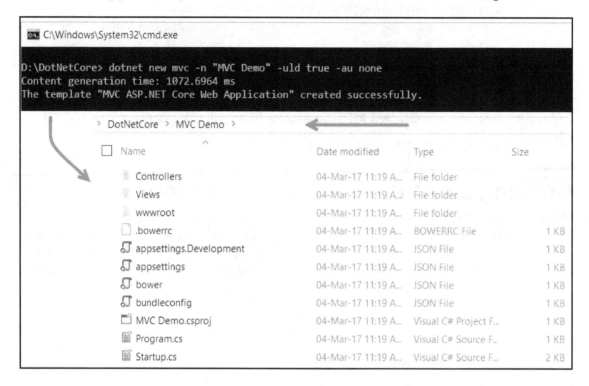

Creating a unit testing project

Unit testing projects can also be created using .NET Core. In the command line, you can specify the template code `mstest` or `xunit` to create a simple unit test project or xUnit test project, respectively.

To create a simple unit test project from the command line, enter the following:

```
dotnet new mstest -n <ProjectName>
```

To create an xUnit test project, enter the following command:

```
dotnet new xunit -n <ProjectName>
```

You can also run a unit test project from the command line. You need to execute the dotnet test command to do so. The unit testing frameworks are bundled as a NuGet package and can be restored as ordinary dependencies. You can execute either of the following commands:

```
dotnet test
dotnet test <ProjectPath>
```

Creating .NET Core applications using Visual Studio

We have discussed the .NET Core commands to create, build, run, and publish .NET Core applications. We have also covered how to create and run ASP.NET Core applications and unit testing projects.

Now, let's look at how to do it easily using Visual Studio 2017. To create a .NET Core application using Visual Studio, open the Visual Studio 2017 instance and click on **File** | **New** | **Project...** to open the New Project window (alternatively, you can press the following keyboard shortcut: *Ctrl + Shift + N*):

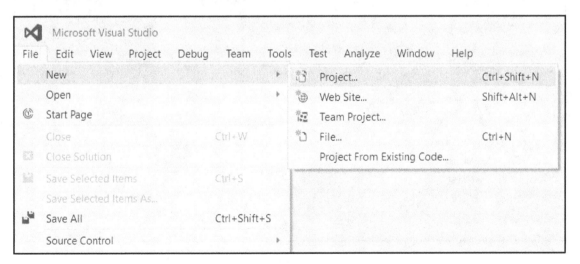

In the **New Project** dialog, navigate to **Installed** | **Templates** | **Visual C#** | **.NET Core**. Here you will see five types of template:

- Console App
- Class Library
- Unit Test Project
- xUnit Test Project
- ASP.NET Core Web Application

You can select the template you want to create. To demonstrate, let's create a console application first. From the available list of project templates, select **Console App (.NET Core)**. Provide a proper name for the project/solution file, select the location, and click on **OK** to create the project, as shown in the following screenshot:

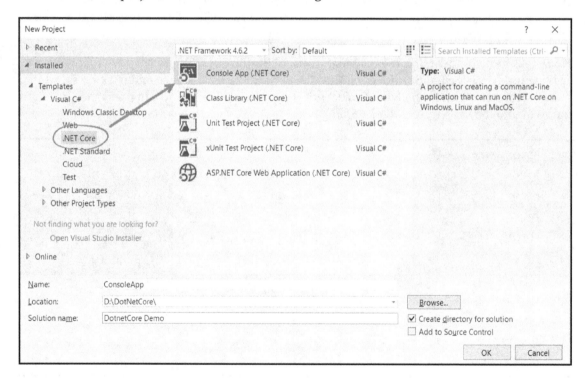

Like other project templates and unlike the CLI tools for .NET Core, this wizard will create the solution and add the project into it automatically. A class file named `Program.cs` will be available, which is the entry point to the application:

Let's build the application and run it. You will see a **Hello World** string printed on the screen. If you navigate to the `bin\debug\netcoreapp1.0` folder path of the project directory, you will see `ConsoleApp.dll`, which is our application host.

Publishing a .NET Core application using Visual Studio 2017

Visual Studio 2017 made it easy to publish a .NET Core application. While, in the CLI, it's all about commands, which you need to perform one by one to publish, but in Visual Studio it's all about a few clicks.

Similar to the command line, you can publish an application in both the FDD and SCD models from Visual Studio 2017. Let's learn how to do this with both the deployment models.

Framework-Dependent Deployments

The default deployment model that Visual Studio configures for a .NET Core application is the Framework-Dependent Deployment model. Here, when you publish an app, only the portable, executable DLL will get generated, which you need to run in a system where .NET Core is already installed.

To publish an app to create the deployment package, right-click on the project and, from the context menu that pops up on the screen, click **Publish...**, as shown in the following screenshot:

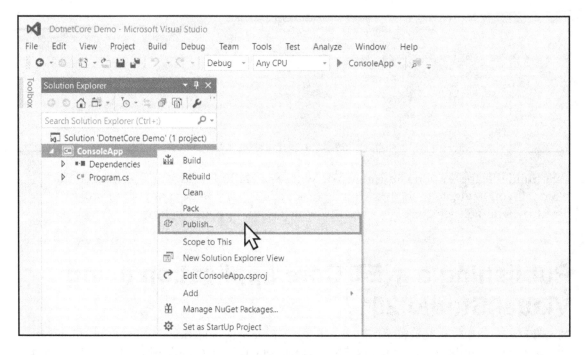

This will open the publishing wizard dialog on the screen. For a console app, the publishing target is File System. If you are publishing a web application, you can publish it to Azure App Service, Azure Virtual Machine, IIS, or FTP along with the File System:

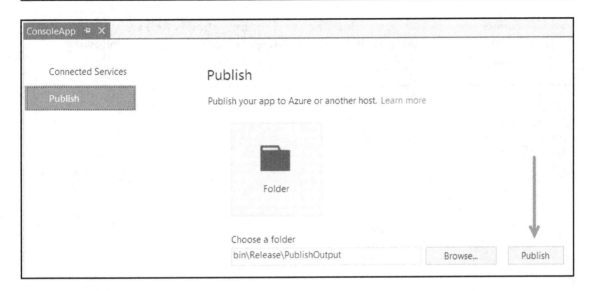

Click on the **Browse...** button to select the publish folder (the default is `bin\Release\PublishOutput`) and, when you are ready, click on the **Publish** button. This will publish the app to the selected folder and show you a summary:

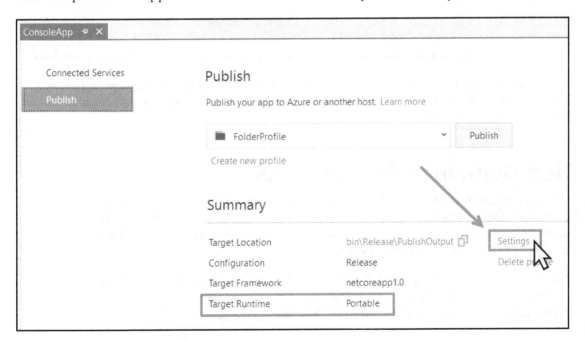

In the summary section, you can see that the build configuration is **Release** and the target runtime is **Portable**. Click on the link labeled **Settings**, which will open the following **Profile Settings** page:

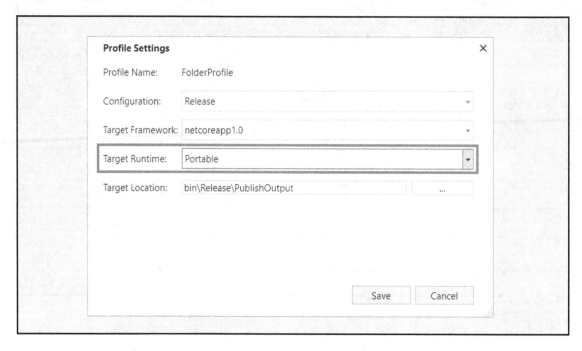

On this screen, you will be able to change the configuration, target framework, and target location. As we are publishing it as Portable Executable format (FDD model), you won't be able to change the target runtime.

Self-Contained Deployments

To do a Self-Contained Deployment for your application to run in a system without .NET Core installed, you need to first edit your project file to make some changes. In this type of deployment, the core libraries will also get copied with your application, making the deployment package larger than expected.

For SCD, first, open your project file. In Visual Studio 2017, right-click on the project in Solution Explorer and click on the menu item `Edit <AppName>.csproj`. In our case it's **Edit ConsoleApp.csproj**, as shown in the following screenshot:

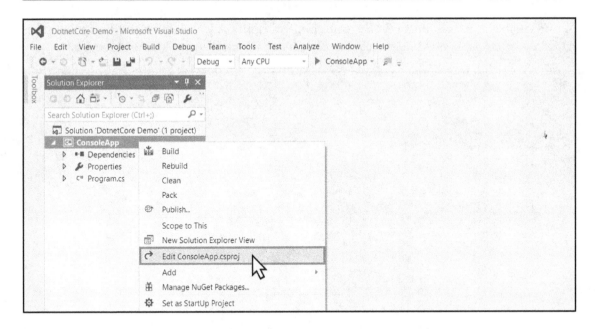

As shown in the following screenshot, enter the `<RuntimeIdentifiers>win10-x64;Ubuntu.14.04-x64</RuntimeIdentifiers>` tag inside the `<PropertyGroup>` tag as child, where `win10-x64` and `ubuntu.14.04-x64` are two different runtime identifiers that we have selected for our app's deployment. You can add more than one RID here, as a semicolon-separated values:

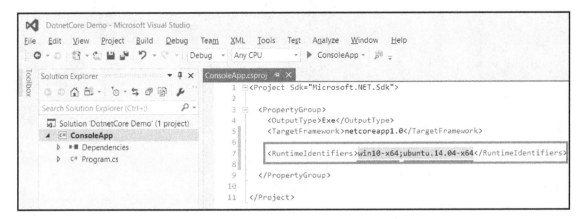

Now save the `.csproj` file, build the solution, and right-click on the project inside Solution Explorer. From the context menu, click on **Publish...** to start the deployment process:

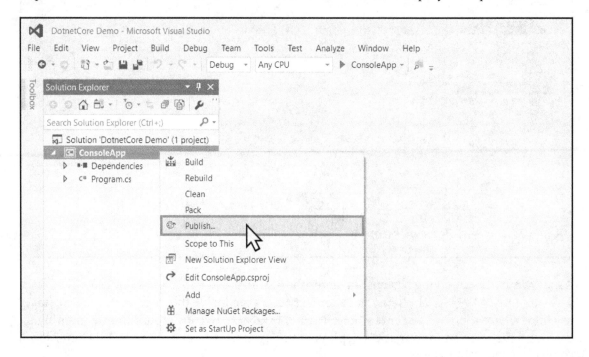

This will show the **Publish** wizard dialog, where you can set the publish target. As we are publishing a console application, we will have only one option to select and that's the File System. For a web application, you will get many options such as publishing to Azure App Service, Azure Virtual Machine, IIS, or FTP:

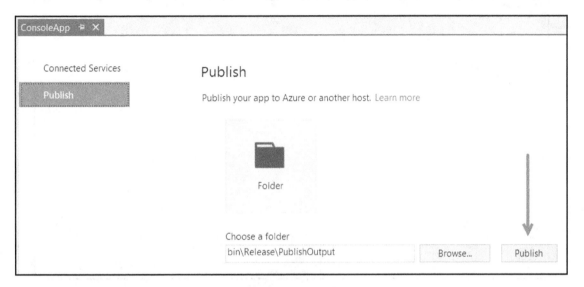

Click on the **Browse...** button and select the publish folder (the default is `bin\Release\PublishOutput`). Once you are done, click on the **Publish** button. This will publish your app to the target location and show you a summary.

Note that the configuration is by default selected as **Release** and the target runtime is set to your host system RID, which is the first entry we added as `RuntimeIdentifier` in the `.csproj` file:

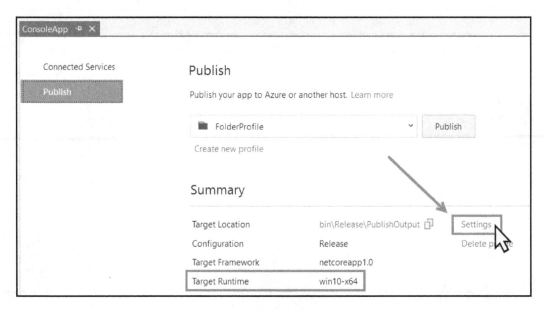

To edit the publish profile, click on **Settings**. This will open the **Profile Settings** page:

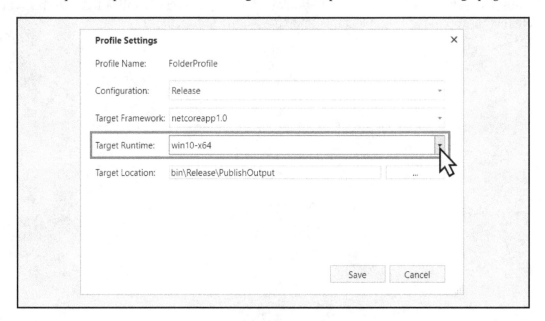

On this page, you will be allowed to change **Configuration**, **Target Framework**, **Target Runtime**, and **Target Location**. Click on the **Target Runtime** dropdown. There you will see the identifiers that we have set in the project file. In our case, it was `win10-x64` and `ubuntu.14.04-x64`. To publish the application for Ubuntu Linux, select **ubuntu.14.04-x64** from the list and click on **Save**:

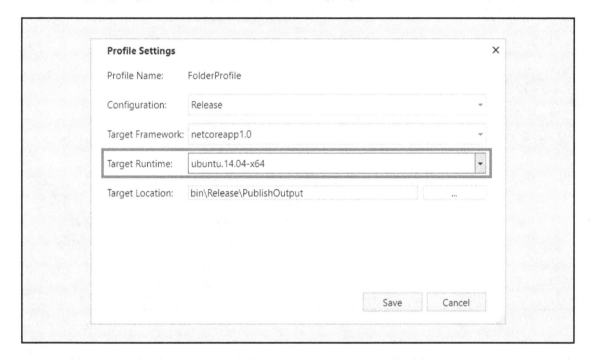

This will update the target runtime on the summary page to the Ubuntu RID. Now click on the **Publish** button to publish the application. By default, both packages will be deployed in the same publish directory. If you want to place them in separate folders, change the target location accordingly to easily identify the output:

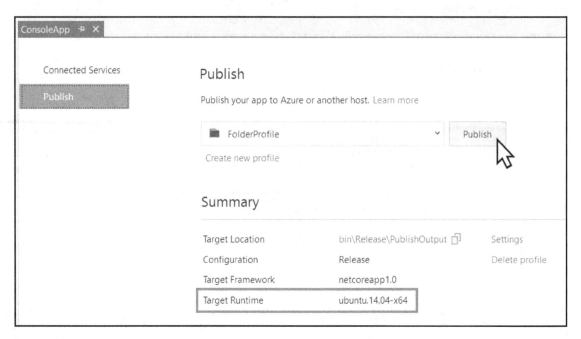

Creating, building, and publishing a .NET Core web app to Microsoft Azure

As we have already learned how to create a .NET Core console application, build and publish it using the framework-dependent and SCD models (both using CLI and from Visual Studio 2017), let us now begin with creating an ASP.NET Core MVC web application.

To begin with, click on the **File** | **New** | **Project...** menu, which will open the **New Project** dialog on the screen. You can also open it by pressing the keyboard shortcut, *Ctrl + Shift + N*.

From the available .NET Core project types, click on the **ASP.NET Core Web Application** template. Enter the project name, solution name, and location, and click on **OK** to start creating the project:

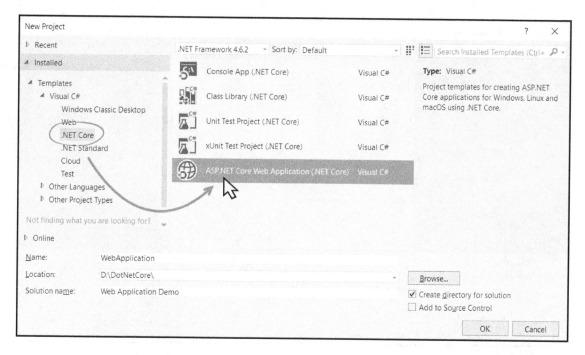

This will open another dialog on the screen asking you to select the ASP.NET Core web template. Currently, there exist three templates for you to choose from:

- Empty
- Web API
- Web Application

If you want to build a web application from scratch, select the **Empty** web template. To create an ASP.NET Core application with a RESTful HTTP service, select the **Web API** template, which will give you a sample app to start with. For a complete web application with MVC views and controllers, select the **Web Application** template:

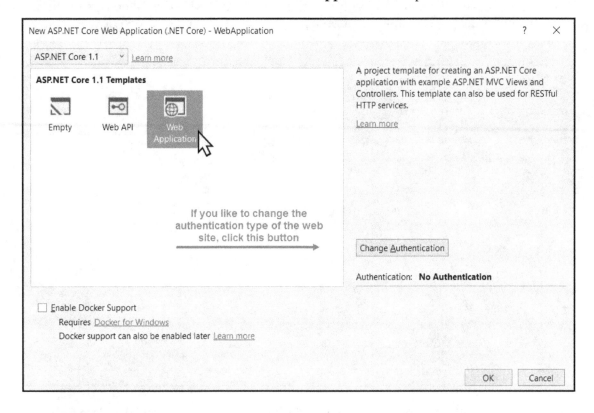

You can also set an authentication to your web app (the default is **No Authentication**) by clicking on the **Change Authentication** button:

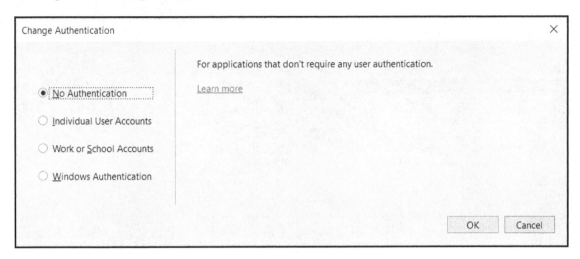

The **Change Authentication** dialog has the following four options:

- **No Authentication**: This is the default authentication type. Keep this selected if your app does not require any user authentication.
- **Individual User Accounts**: If your application will store user profiles to a SQL Server database, you need to select this option. You can also configure your signing process by using Facebook, Twitter, Google, Microsoft, or any other provider's authentication system.
- **Work or School Accounts**: To use an Active Directory or Office 365 signing process, use this type of authentication system.
- **Windows Authentication**: If you are building an intranet application that will use a Windows authentication system, select this.

Here we will use **No Authentication**, so keep it selected. Click on **OK** to continue creating the web application.

Once Visual Studio has created the project, you can build and run it. This will create a web page from the sample it has created:

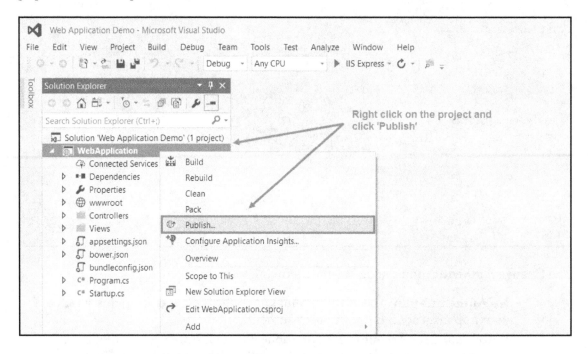

To publish the application that we have just created, right-click on the project inside Solution Explorer and click on **Publish**, as shown in the previous screenshot. This will open the app publishing wizard. Here you can select Microsoft Azure App Service, Azure Virtual Machine, File System/Folder, IIS, or FTP as the publishing target.

As we are going to publish it to Microsoft Azure, select **Microsoft Azure App Service** and click the **Publish** button:

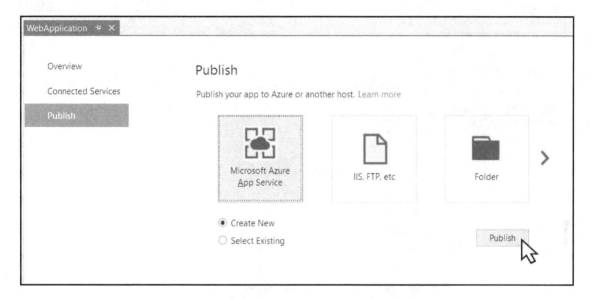

To deploy an app to Microsoft Azure, you should already have an Azure account. To create your Azure account with $200 free credit, visit the following link:
`https://azure.microsoft.com/en-us/free/`

If you already have an Azure account and are already signed in with the same MSA account in Visual Studio, the following screen will be shown asking you to provide more details on hosting your app to Azure:

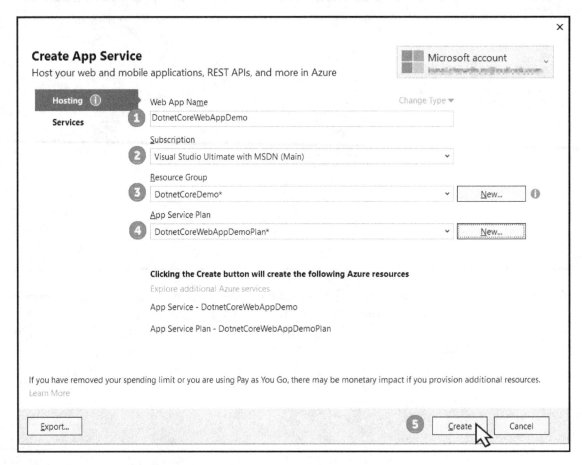

It will ask you to enter your web app name and Azure subscription details (as mentioned in the following steps) to publish it there:

1. First, enter the web application name. This should be globally unique.
2. Select the Azure subscription that you want to link with.

3. Select a **Resource Group** name. If there are no entries in the list, you need to create one by clicking the **New...** button. Fill in the required details and click **OK**.

4. Select the application service plan from the list. If the list is empty, you need to click the **New...** button to create a publishing plan by filling all the required details. Then select the plan that you have created.

5. Finally, click **Create** to start the final publishing and hosting process to Azure.

Once it starts the publishing job, it will show you the following page, with details of your application hosting. Based on the web application name that you entered earlier, it will create the **Site URL** and host to a subdomain hosted on azurewebsites.net:

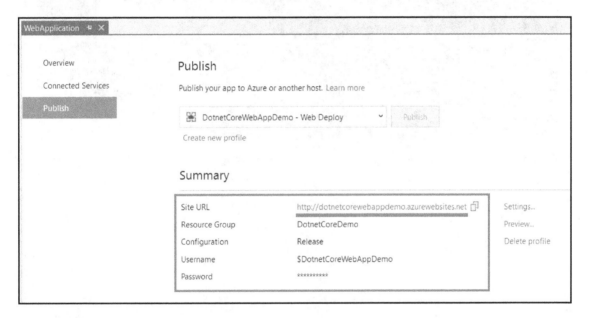

Once it successfully publishes the application to Microsoft Azure App Service, you can either click the link under **Site URL** or click on **Preview** to launch in your configured browser application.

When you launch the site on a browser, you will see the site that we created running on a public web server. As the website was created from the Visual Studio default web template, you will see the following screen:

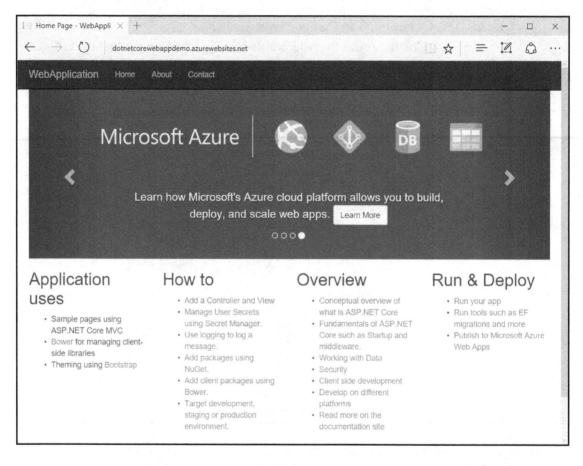

You can also view the site details by launching the Server Explorer from the Visual Studio View menu, which will look as follows:

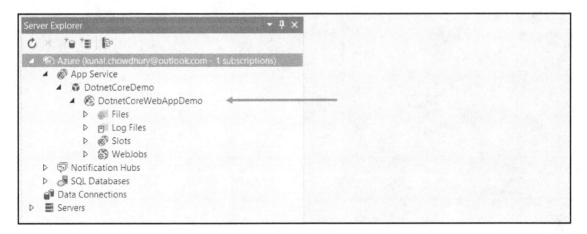

Summary

In this chapter, we have learned about the basics of .NET Core and how to install it from the Visual Studio 2017 installer. We have discussed the commands you must know to create, build, and run .NET Core applications from the CLI or console. Along with this, we have also discussed a couple of types of application deployment models, FDD and SCD.

Apart from the core commands, we also learned how to create, build, and publish .NET Core applications using the Visual Studio 2017 IDE. We also covered how to publish a web app to Microsoft Azure.

In the next chapter, we will discuss **NuGet packages** and learn how to create, publish, test, and manage them.

6
Managing NuGet Packages

NuGet is a free and open-source package manager for the Microsoft development platform. It was first introduced in 2010, and has now evolved to a larger ecosystem for the platform. Starting with Visual Studio 2012, it comes preinstalled as a Visual Studio extension.

You can create packages of your libraries and distribute them in NuGet Package gallery, http://www.nuget.org/packages, or to your local NuGet store, which, when published, can be downloaded again using NuGet Package Manager inside Visual Studio.

In this chapter, we will cover the following topics:

- Overview of NuGet Package Manager
- Creating a NuGet package library for .NET Framework:
  - Creating the metadata in a NuGet Spec file
  - Building NuGet Package
  - Building NuGet Package for multiple .NET Frameworks
  - Building NuGet Package with dependencies
- Creating a NuGet package library for .NET Standard
  - Editing the metadata of the project
  - Building the NuGet Package from Visual Studio 2017
  - Building a NuGet Package with Package References
- Testing the NuGet Package locally
- Publishing NuGet Package to NuGet Store
- Managing your NuGet packages

Overview to NuGet package manager

A NuGet package is a `.nupkg` file that contains all the required components needed to reference an external library in a project. Typically, this component is one or more DLLs and the metadata describing the package. It can consist of other components, source code, and debug symbols, but this is rare.

When you install any of the Visual Studio 2017 workloads, by default it installs the support for NuGet along with the **NuGet package manager** tool, which you can find listed under the **Individual components** tab of the installer. If you uninstall it, all the dependent workloads will automatically get uninstalled from your system:

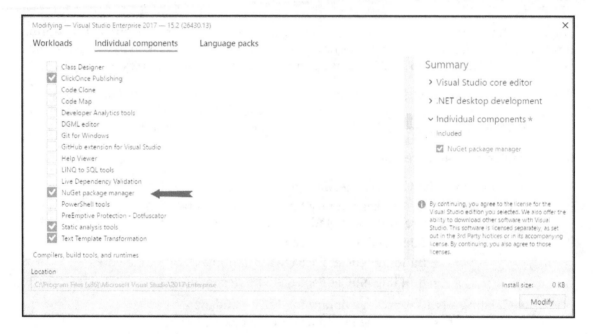

NuGet package manager comes in both console and GUI mode, integrated as part of the Visual Studio IDE. As GUI provides you with easier access to search, install, update, and uninstall a package, it is always preferable, and most of the time a developer interacts with it while using any library package through NuGet.

When you install a NuGet package, the following things happen:

1. The package that you are trying to install gets downloaded in the packages folder under your solution directory.

2. Any other NuGet packages that this package is dependent on also get downloaded automatically.

3. The references to the package content (that is, the DLL references) automatically get added to the project.

To open **NuGet package manager**, click on **Tools** | **NuGet Package Manager**, and select **Package Manager Console** for the console window or **Manage NuGet Packages for Solution...** for the GUI window. This is shown in the following screenshot:

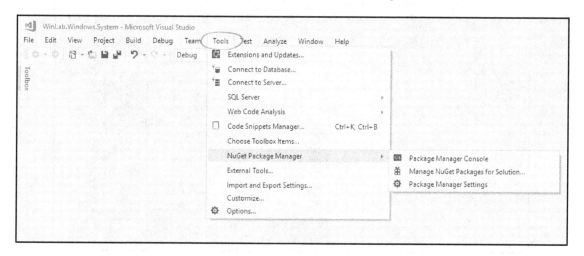

Alternatively, you can right-click on the project/solution to launch the **NuGet Package Manager** GUI from the context menu entry:

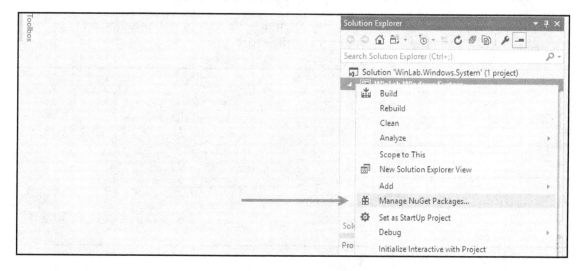

In the package manager window, search for the library that you want to install. It will give you a list of packages based on your search term. Select the one you want to install, select the suitable version, and click **Install** to continue:

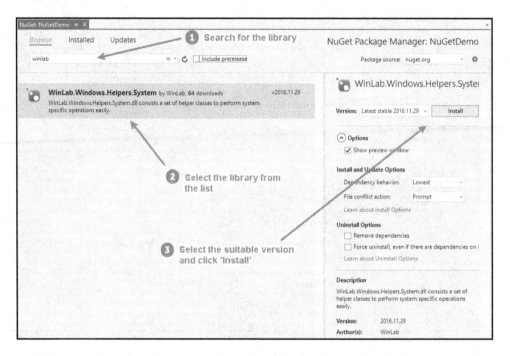

It will pop up a dialog showing you the list of packages (including dependent packages) that it's going to install. Review the changes and click on **OK** to start the download process.

Once downloaded, it will add the assembly references to your project and add an entry to the `packages.config` file under your project directory:

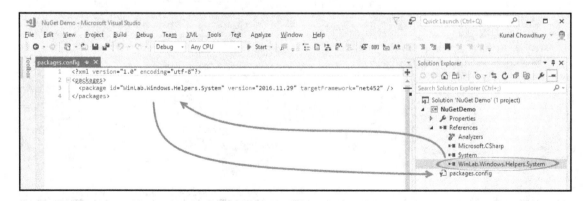

Creating a NuGet package library for .NET Framework

As we have discussed the basics of NuGet package, let's start creating our first NuGet package for libraries targeting .NET Framework. We will use the NuGet CLI to build the package for class libraries targeting .NET Framework. The NuGet CLI tool is a single `.exe` file, which you can download from the NuGet site, or directly from `https://www.nuget.org/nuget.exe`.

First, let's create a class library project, which we are going to pack later. Go to **File** | **New** | **Project...**, select the targeted .NET Framework (in our case, it's **.NET Framework 4**), and then select the **Class Library (.NET Framework)** from the available templates under **Visual C#**. Select a location for the project, give it a name, and click on **OK**:

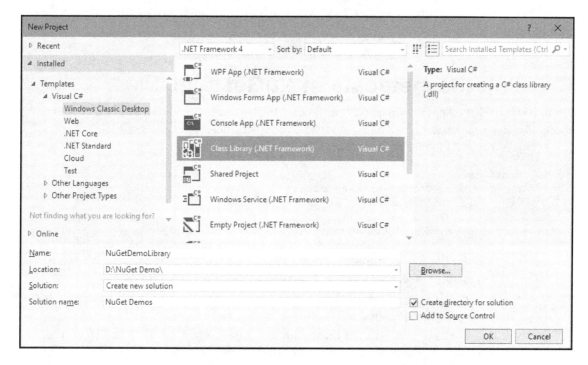

Once the project gets created, add a few classes, and some code inside them, as per your requirements. Let's add a class file called `LogHelper.cs` and add the following code inside it:

```
namespace NuGetDemoLibrary
{
  public class LogHelper
  {
    public static void Log(string message)
    {
      Console.WriteLine(message);
    }
  }
}
```

Now build the project in Release mode and ensure that there are no errors. As our demo class library (`NuGetDemoLibrary.dll`) is ready, it's time for us to create the NuGet package.

Creating the metadata in NuGet spec file

Go to the root directory of your project and copy the downloaded CLI file, `nuget.exe`, there. Open a console window, navigate to the project directory, and enter either of the following commands to create the `nuspec` file:

```
nuget spec
nuget spec NuGetDemoLibrary.csproj
nuget spec bin\Release\NuGetDemoLibrary.dll
```

For the previously mentioned NuGet commands, please note the following:

- If you use the first command `nuget spec`, it will create the `nuspec` file based on the available project files in the directory where it was executed.
- The `nuget spec <ProjectFilePath>` will create the `nuspec` file only for the project that you specified.
- If you use a specific DLL, in this fashion-- `nuget spec <DllFilePath>`, the NuGet spec file will be created based on the specified DLL. This command is mostly recommended as it creates the metadata information of the `nuspec` file from the DLL metadata.

Have a look at the following screenshot to understand it easily:

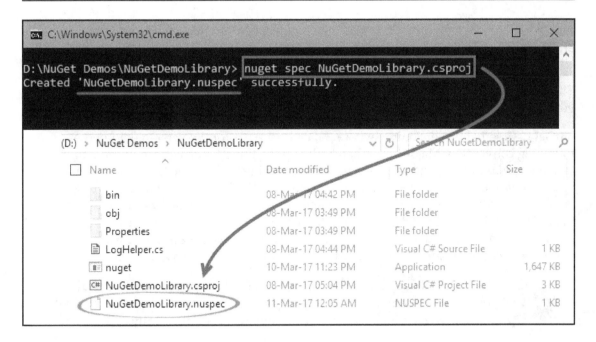

This will create the `NuGetDemoLibrary.nuspec` file with default values:

```xml
<?xml version="1.0"?>
<package >
  <metadata>
    <id>$id$</id>                              ──────────►  Must be unique, globally in NuGet Store
    <version>$version$</version>
    <title>$title$</title>
    <authors>$author$</authors>
    <owners>$author$</owners>
    <licenseUrl>http://LICENSE_URL_HERE_OR_DELETE_THIS_LINE</licenseUrl>
    <projectUrl>http://PROJECT_URL_HERE_OR_DELETE_THIS_LINE</projectUrl>   ──────► optional
    <iconUrl>http://ICON_URL_HERE_OR_DELETE_THIS_LINE</iconUrl>
    <requireLicenseAcceptance>false</requireLicenseAcceptance>
    <description>$description$</description>
    <releaseNotes>Summary of changes made in this release of the package.</releaseNotes>
    <copyright>Copyright 2017</copyright>
    <tags>Tag1 Tag2</tags>
  </metadata>
</package>
```

If you create the `nuspec` file from the DLL, most of these metadata entries will have a value picked from the generated DLL. As we have created it from the project, it has a placeholder field against most of the entries. You must replace these default values before generating the package.

The **id** field must be unique across the NuGet global store or the gallery where you are going to host the package. Generally, it gets populated from the `AssemblyName` field of the DLL. Do a check in the store or the gallery before assigning this field.

The **licenseUrl**, **projectUrl**, and **iconUrl** are optional. If you don't want to put in these links, you can remove the entire lines.

NuGet uses semantic versioning, where it has three parts for the version field in the following convention: Major.Minor.Patch, thus put a three-fields version number against it. Whenever you upload a new version to NuGet, it decides if it is the latest stable version. If you are not releasing a final version, you can inform NuGet to mark it as a pre-release version by suffixing the `-prerelease` switch or `-alpha`, `-beta`, or `-gamma` to the version field. Technically, you can add any string there but it is always preferable to put a meaningful convention. For example, if your build version is 4.5.2 and you want to set it as a pre-release beta version, change the value of the version field to `4.5.2-beta`.

 Note that NuGet prioritizes the version field in reverse chronological order. Thus, `-beta` will get higher preference than `-alpha`, and the final release version will get the highest preference automatically.

Fill all other fields mentioned under the metadata tag inside the spec file and save it. Now you need to specify the files you are going to bundle and in which folder you want to place them when downloaded from NuGet. Generally, when you download from NuGet, they are placed inside the package folder of your solution directory, categorized by package type. Here, you can also define a Framework-specific folder path, which we will discuss later in this chapter.

Let's add the output of our class library project and mark it to place under the lib folder of the target directory. Enter the following XML tag inside the package element with the path of the precompiled binary assembly:

```
<files>
    <file src="bin\Release\NuGetDemoLibrary.dll"
            target="lib\NuGetDemoLibrary.dll"/>
</files>
```

Let's update the details and save the file. The resultant output of our `.nuspec` file will look like the following block:

```
<?xml version="1.0"?>
<package >
  <metadata>
        <id>Demo.Packt.Kunal.NuGetDemoLibrary</id>
```

```
            <version>1.0.0-alpha</version>
            <title>NuGet Demo Library</title>
            <authors>Kunal Chowdhury</authors>
            <owners>WinLab</owners>
            <description>This is for demo purpose only</description>
            <releaseNotes>Change 1, Change 2, ...</releaseNotes>
            <copyright>Copyright 2017</copyright>
            <tags>Demo, Packt</tags>
        </metadata>
        <files>
            <file src="bin\Release\NuGetDemoLibrary.dll"
                target="lib\NuGetDemoLibrary.dll"/>
        </files>
    </package>
```

You can add multiple precompiled assemblies inside the package by defining them inside the `<files>...</files>` element:

```
<files>
    <file src="Assembly-1.dll" target="lib\Assembly-1.dll"/>
    <file src="Assembly-2.dll" target="lib\Assembly-2.dll"/>
    <file src="Assembly-3.dll" target="lib\Assembly-3.dll"/>
</files>
```

You can also use wildcards in the `<files>` section, as follows:

```
<files>
    <file src="*.dll" target="lib "/>
</files>
```

Building the NuGet Package

As our NuGet spec file is ready, it's time for us to create the NuGet package from the nuspec file. Use the `nuget pack` command followed by the nuspec file name to start creating the project. Enter the following command in the console window:

```
nuget pack NuGetDemoLibrary.nuspec
```

This will create a NuGet package file with the extension `.nupkg` in the same directory:

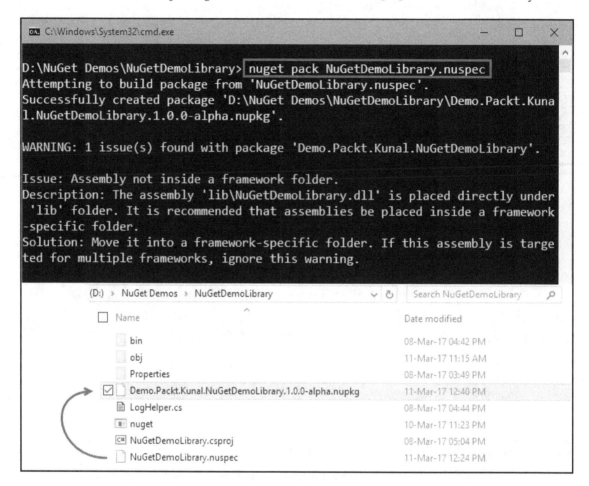

The file name will be a combination of the ID and the version that we specified in the `.nuspec` file. In our case, it generates the file `Demo.Packt.Kunal.NuGetDemoLibrary.1.0.0-alpha.nupkg`, as you can see in the preceding screenshot.

You will also see a warning message on-screen, which says one issue found as the assembly is not inside a framework folder. As we have placed the DLL under the lib folder of the target location directly, it generates this error. NuGet recommends putting the assemblies inside a framework-specific folder. You can ignore this if this assembly is targeted for multiple frameworks. But if you want to build multiple binaries for different frameworks with the same name and embed them in the same package, continue reading.

Building NuGet Package for multiple .NET Frameworks

NuGet supports multiple .NET Framework-targeting platforms. If your binary targets a specific .NET Framework, you can ask NuGet to handle it accordingly by specifying them in the `nuspec` file. For example, your binary can support only .NET Framework 3.0 or can support any version higher than .NET 3.0.

To do this, NuGet uses a proper directory structure under the lib folder, categorized by the target framework in an abbreviated format. For a .NET 2.0 targeted library, place it inside a subfolder named `net20`; for a .NET 3.5 targeted library, place it inside a subfolder named `net35`, and so on. You can get a list of supported frameworks and their abbreviated codes at `http://bit.ly/nuget-supported-frameworks`.

When you install the assembly from a NuGet package, first it checks for the target .NET Framework version of the project where you are going to install it, then selects the correct assembly version from the appropriate subfolder under the lib folder and adds it as reference:

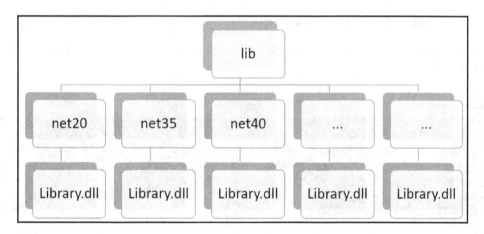

Now let's modify our existing `nuspec` file to add support for Framework-specific assemblies. As our project targets .NET 4 and above, let's specify it in the `nuspec` file. Open the existing `.nuspec` file and modify the target of our assembly file to deploy for .NET 4.0 and above. Here's the modified version of our NuGet spec file:

```xml
<?xml version="1.0"?>
<package >
  <metadata>
      <id>Demo.Packt.Kunal.NuGetDemoLibrary</id>
```

```
          <version>1.0.0-alpha</version>
          <title>NuGet Demo Library</title>
          <authors>Kunal Chowdhury</authors>
          <owners>WinLab</owners>
          <description>This is for demo purpose only</description>
          <releaseNotes>Change 1, Change 2, ...</releaseNotes>
          <copyright>Copyright 2017</copyright>
          <tags>Demo, Packt</tags>
      </metadata>
      <files>
          <file src="bin\Release\NuGetDemoLibrary.dll"
              target="lib\net40\NuGetDemoLibrary.dll"/>
      </files>
  </package>
```

Here, you will notice that the target of the assembly has been set to
`lib\net40\NuGetDemoLibrary.dll`. The subfolder `net40` under the root lib defines that
the assembly can be deployed in projects targeting .NET framework 4.0 and above.

Now open the console window in that directory and use the following `nuget pack`
command to create/update the package:

nuget pack NuGetDemoLibrary.nuspec

This time you will see that no warning messages have been generated as we have specified
the correct target framework:

You can also append a dash and add a profile name to the end of the folder to define a
target-specific framework profile. There are four profiles currently available, which NuGet
supports:

- `client` for Client Profile
- `full` for Full Profile
- `wp` for Windows Phone
- `cf` for Compact Framework

For example, to target the .NET Framework 4.0 full profile, place your assembly in a folder named `net40-full`, and to target the .NET Framework 4.0 client profile, place your assembly in `net40-client`.

Building NuGet package with dependencies

When you create a NuGet package, you can specify which dependencies your package should refer and download automatically. You can define it using the `<dependency>` tag inside the `<dependencies>` tag under `<metadata>`. When installing or reinstalling the package, NuGet downloads the exact version of the dependency specified in the `nuspec` file by default:

```xml
<?xml version="1.0"?>
<package >
   <metadata>
        <id>Demo.Packt.Kunal.NuGetDemoLibrary</id>
        <version>1.0.0-alpha</version>
        <title>NuGet Demo Library</title>
        <authors>Kunal Chowdhury</authors>
        <owners>WinLab</owners>
        <description>This is for demo purpose only</description>
        <releaseNotes>Change 1, Change 2, ...</releaseNotes>
        <copyright>Copyright 2017</copyright>
        <tags>Demo, Packt</tags>
        <dependencies>
             <dependency id="WinLab.Windows.Helpers.System"
                 version="2016.11.29"/>
        </dependencies>
   </metadata>
   <files>
        <file src="bin\Release\NuGetDemoLibrary.dll"
            target="lib\net40\NuGetDemoLibrary.dll"/>
   </files>
</package>
```

You can define dependencies to support the minimum version, maximum version, a version range, or an exact version when downloading via a package. In general, developers specify only the minimum version of a referenced dependency, but any of them are possible.

If you specify `version="1.0"` for a dependency, it marks it as the minimum required version. When you specify `version="[1.0]"`, it marks it as an exact version match. You can also define a pre-release version while defining a dependency (such as `version="1.0-prerelease"`).

Please note that a stable release version of a package cannot have a pre-release dependency.

The following table describes how you can specify a minimum version, maximum version, or a version range when defining a dependency in NuGet:

Notation	Description
1.0	Minimum version, inclusive
(1.0,)	Higher than the minimum version specified
[1.0]	Exact version
(,3.0]	Maximum version, inclusive
(,3.0)	Less than the maximum version specified
[1.0,3.0]	Version ranging between 1.0 - 3.0, inclusive
(1.0,3.0)	Version ranging higher than 1.0 but less than 3.0
[1.0,3.0)	At least version 1.0 but less than 3.0
(1.0,3.0]	Higher than version 1.0, but maximum version 3.0

Creating a NuGet package library for .NET Standard

Visual Studio 2017 provides you with an easy and comfortable way to build a NuGet package for .NET Standard libraries. **.NET Standard Library** is a formal specification of the .NET APIs, which are intended to be available on all .NET runtimes. .NET Standard Library defines a uniform set of **Base Class Library** (**BCL**) APIs for all the .NET platforms, and enables developers to produce portable class libraries that can run in all .NET runtimes.

Let's first create a .NET Standard class library. Create a new project by selecting **Class Library (.NET Standard)** under the **Visual C# | .NET Standard** templates, as shown in the following screenshot. Give it a proper name, select the location where you want to create the project, and hit **OK**:

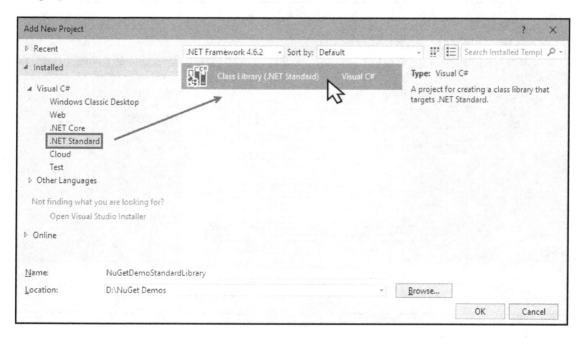

Once the project gets created, create the class files that you want to bundle with your package and write the necessary code. Build your project in Release mode to make sure there are no errors.

Editing the metadata of the project

Once your project is ready, you need to edit the metadata for the NuGet package. With NuGet 4.0 and .NET Core projects, you don't need to create any NuGet Spec (`.nuspec`) files. Instead of that, you can edit the project file itself and edit the metadata content.

To get started, right-click on the project in **Solution Explorer** and click the Edit
`<ProjectName>` menu item (in our case, it's `Edit`
`NuGetDemoStandardLibrary.csproj`), as shown in the following screenshot:

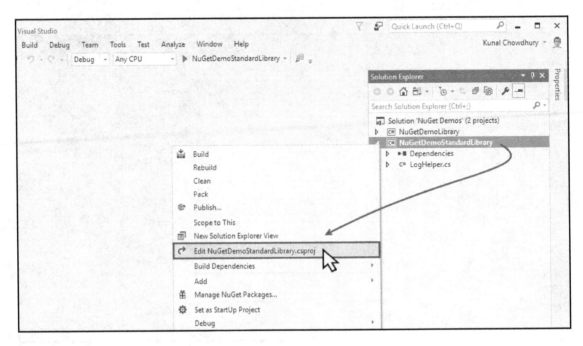

Visual Studio 2017 will open the project in an editor with the following XML content, where
the `PropertyGroup` defines the metadata information:

```
<Project Sdk="Microsoft.NET.Sdk">

  <PropertyGroup>
    <TargetFramework>netstandard1.4</TargetFramework>
  </PropertyGroup>

</Project>
```

Let's modify it to add the following package descriptions:

```
NuGetDemoStandardLibrary.csproj + X
 1  <Project Sdk="Microsoft.NET.Sdk">
 2
 3    <PropertyGroup>
 4      <TargetFramework>netstandard1.4</TargetFramework>
 5
 6      <PackageId>Demo.Packt.Kunal.NuGetDemoStandardLibrary</PackageId>
 7      <PackageVersion>1.0.0-prerelease</PackageVersion>
 8      <Authors>Kunal Chowdhury</Authors>
 9      <Description>Demo Library</Description>
10      <PackageReleaseNotes>Change 1, Change 2, ...</PackageReleaseNotes>
11      <Copyright>Copyright 2017 (c) All rights reserved.</Copyright>
12      <PackageTags>Tag1 Tag2</PackageTags>
13
14    </PropertyGroup>
15
16  </Project>
17
```

The `PackageId` must be unique across the global NuGet store, or the gallery where you want to push the package. Before assigning it, do a search on the gallery to check the status of availability. You can define the `PackageVersion` as Major.Minor.Patch. When the generated package is not a final version, you can suffix a `-prerelease` switch to it to tell NuGet that it's a pre-release version. You can also use any string to define it, but it's advisable to use a meaningful name, such as `-alpha` or `-beta`.

Once you are done modifying all the metadata values, save the project file. The following is the complete metadata for you to reference:

```
<Project Sdk="Microsoft.NET.Sdk">

  <PropertyGroup>
    <TargetFramework>netstandard1.4</TargetFramework>
    <PackageId>Demo.Packt.Kunal.NuGetDemoStandardLibrary</PackageId>
    <PackageVersion>1.0.0-prerelease</PackageVersion>
    <Authors>Kunal Chowdhury</Authors>
    <Description>Demo Library</Description>
    <PackageReleaseNotes>Change 1, Change 2 ...</PackageReleaseNotes>
    <Copyright>Copyright 2017 (c) All rights reserved</Copyright>
    <PackageTags>Tag1 Tag2</PackageTags>
  </PropertyGroup>

</Project>
```

Building the NuGet Package from Visual Studio 2017

When you are ready to create the NuGet package, change the build mode to **Release** and build it again, to make sure there are no errors. Now, right-click on the project in Visual Studio 2017 **Solution Explorer**, and from the context menu, click on the menu item **Pack**, as shown in the following screenshot:

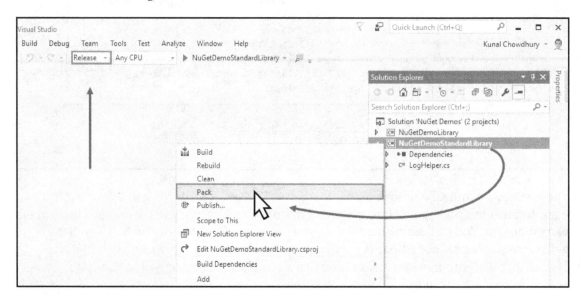

This will start the build process and create the NuGet package file (`.nupkg`) in the **bin\Release** folder of the project. The file name will construct using the `PackageId` and `PackageVersion` that we defined in the project metadata, and will generate as `<PackageId>.<PackageVersion>.nupkg` (in our case, it's `Demo.Packt.Kunal.NuGetDemoStandardLibrary.1.0.0-prerelease.nupkg`):

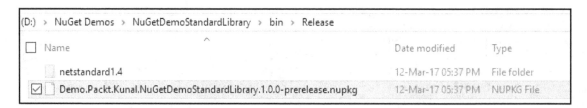

Do you know that a NuGet Package file is just a ZIP file with the extension `.nupkg`? You can rename the `.nupkg` to `.zip` and see its package content. Make sure to change it back before uploading it to nuget.org.

Building a NuGet Package with package references

You can use the XML node `PackageReference` to define the NuGet package dependencies in the .NET Core project files. You need to add an `<ItemGroup>` under the `<Project>` root to declare the package references. You can add multiple project references inside a single `ItemGroup` node. Use the `Include` attribute to assign the ID of the dependency package that you are referring, and the attribute `Version` to set the minimum, maximum, or exact version of the package:

```
<ItemGroup>
   <PackageReference Include="Newtonsoft.Json"
                     Version="9.0.1" />
</ItemGroup>
```

The NuGet package reference supports floating versions, by which you can use wildcards to tell NuGet to support only the versions within the specified build series. For example, when you say `Version="9.0.*"`, it means that the project will use the latest 9.0.x version. Similarly, `Version="9.*"` means use the latest 9.x version.

The following table shows how you can use the version notation for a dependency package to define the minimum, maximum, or a version range:

Notation	Description
1.0	Minimum version, inclusive
(1.0,)	Higher than the minimum version specified
[1.0]	Exact version
(,3.0]	Maximum version, inclusive
(,3.0)	Less than the maximum version specified
[1.0,3.0]	Version ranging between 1.0 - 3.0, inclusive
(1.0,3.0)	Version ranging higher than 1.0 but less than 3.0

[1.0,3.0)	At least version 1.0 but less than 3.0
(1.0,3.0]	Higher than version 1.0, but maximum version 3.0

In the Visual Studio 2017 NuGet package reference for .NET Core projects, you can also add a condition to control which version of the dependency package to include. This can be done with an attribute, `Condition`, within the definition of the `PackageReference` node or the `ItemGroup` node.

The following demonstrates how you can use the condition in a package reference:

```
<ItemGroup>
  <PackageReference Condition="'$(TargetFramework)'=='net452'"
                    Include="Newtonsoft.Json"
                    Version="9.0.1"/>
</ItemGroup>
```

When you have multiple library packages to target for a specific framework version, you can check the condition at the item-group level and include the package references within that. Here's how you can define it:

```
<ItemGroup Condition="'$(TargetFramework)'=='net452'">
  <PackageReference Include="Newtonsoft.Json"
                    Version="9.0.1" />
</ItemGroup>
```

Once you are done with the changes, save the file. For your reference, here's the complete code that we have used:

```
<Project Sdk="Microsoft.NET.Sdk">

  <PropertyGroup>
    <TargetFramework>netstandard1.4</TargetFramework>

    <PackageId>Demo.Packt.Kunal.NuGetDemoStandardLibrary</PackageId>
    <PackageVersion>1.0.0-prerelease</PackageVersion>
    <Authors>Kunal Chowdhury</Authors>
    <Description>Demo Library</Description>
    <PackageReleaseNotes>Change 1, Change 2</PackageReleaseNotes>
    <Copyright>Copyright 2017 (c) All rights reserved.</Copyright>
    <PackageTags>Tag1 Tag2</PackageTags>

  </PropertyGroup>

  <ItemGroup>
    <PackageReference Include="Newtonsoft.Json"
      Version="9.*"/>
```

```
    </ItemGroup>

    </Project>
```

When you are ready, build the project in Release mode to check for errors; right-click on the project in the **Solution Explorer**, and click on **Pack**. This will build the code and publish/update the NuGet package.

Testing the NuGet package locally

When you are done building your final NuGet package, you may want to push/upload it to the NuGet gallery. It could be the gallery hosted at nuget.org, a third-party gallery, or a local repository, but before that, you may want to test it locally. This you can achieve by creating a local package store.

To create the local package store, open the **NuGet Package Manager** Settings by navigating to the Visual Studio menu hierarchy, **Tools** | **NuGet Package Manager** | **Package Manager Settings**, as shown in the following screenshot:

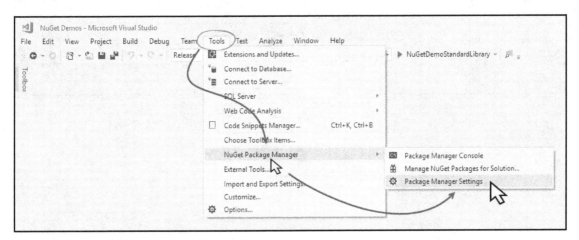

From the left-hand navigation panel, navigate to **NuGet Package Manager | Package Sources**. On the right-hand panel, it lists all the available package sources and the machine-wide package sources. Click the ✚ icon to add a new package source:

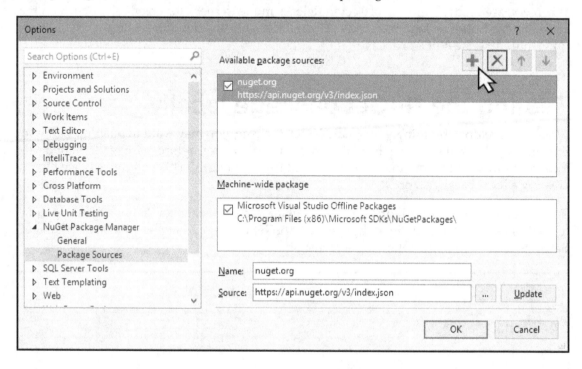

This will provide you with a field to define the new package source. Give it a name and provide the local path from where you want to read the package. Let's click the **...** (ellipsis) to browse local folders and point it to the `bin\Release` folder of our project. Click on the **Update** button to refresh the path information in the available package source that we just created. Click on **OK** to save the information:

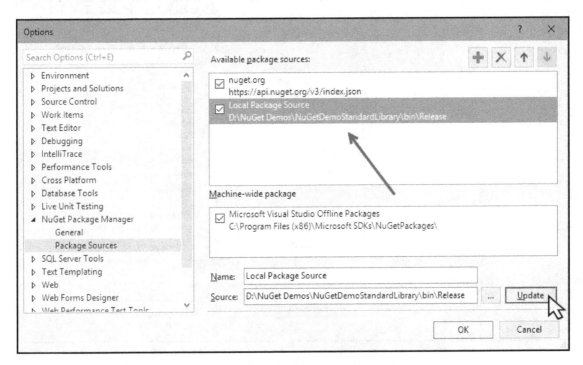

Once the package source has been defined, let's create a console application and load the dependency library from our local NuGet source. You can choose any other version, but here we will target it for .NET Core.

To create a console application in the solution, right-click on the solution file under **Solution Explorer**. From the context menu, click **Add | New Project...** to open the Visual Studio **New Project** dialog box. Select **Console App (.NET Core)** from the available list of templates, give it a name, and click on **OK** to create the console application project:

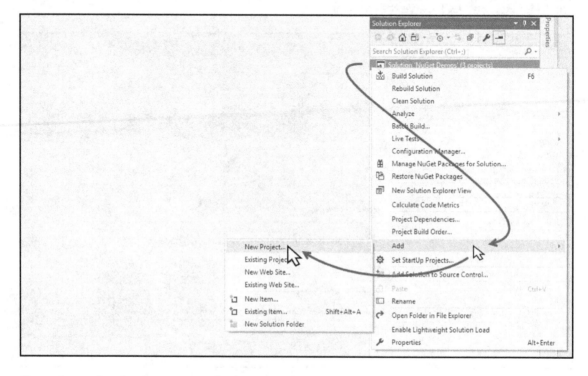

Once the project has been created, it's time to install the library from the store. As we are testing it locally before pushing it to a public store, we will install it from the local package store, and NuGet will automatically download the referenced dependencies and install them.

To do this, either right-click on the project or right-click on the **Dependencies** reference folder, as shown in the following screenshot, and from the context menu that pops up on the screen, click on **Manage NuGet Packages...** to launch the **NuGet Package Manager**:

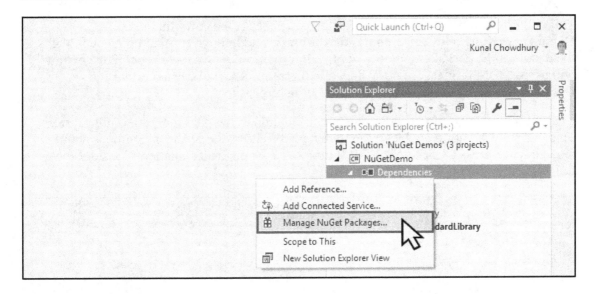

NuGet Package Manager will, by default, select the **Package source** as nuget.org. Change it to our **Local Package Source**. As in our local store, we have a pre-release version of the library; check the **Include prerelease** box:

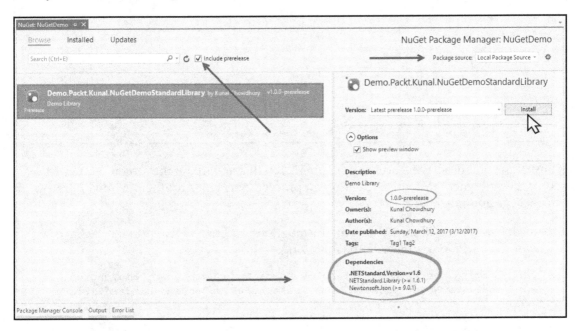

This will immediately list our library on the panel. Select the entry that says **Demo.Packt.Kunal.NuGetDemoStandardLibrary**, and in the right-hand panel you will see the details of the package from its metadata information. As we have provided, **Version** will list as **1.0.0-prerelease** and the dependent assemblies will be listed under the **Dependencies** panel, as shown in the preceding screenshot.

Click on the **Install** button to continue the installation of the package from our local store. This will show a popup on the screen to review the changes that Visual Studio is about to make in your project. Click on the **OK** button to continue the installation. Consider the following screenshot:

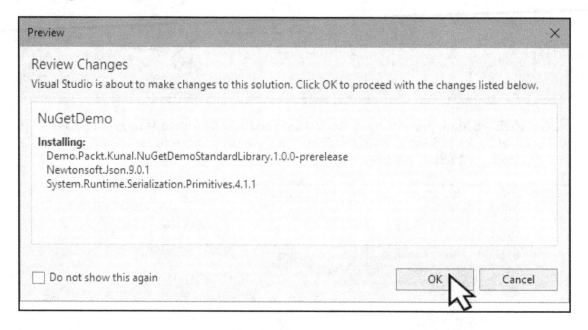

If any of the binaries have a license agreement, it will show up on the screen. You must accept the agreement to continue. Once you proceed, this will start the download process of the package and related dependencies.

The output window will trace the entire installation process and list it under Package Manager. This will look similar to the following:

```
Restoring packages for D:\NuGet Demos\NuGetDemo\NuGetDemo.csproj...
Installing NuGet package Demo.Packt.Kunal.NuGetDemoStandardLibrary
1.0.0-
    prerelease.
Committing restore...
Writing lock file to disk. Path: D:\NuGet Demos\NuGetDemo
```

```
    \obj\project.assets.json
Restore completed in 360.15 ms for D:\NuGet Demos\NuGetDemo
    \NuGetDemo.csproj.
Successfully installed 'Demo.Packt.Kunal.NuGetDemoStandardLibrary
    1.0.0-prerelease' to NuGetDemo
Successfully installed 'Newtonsoft.Json 9.0.1' to NuGetDemo
Successfully installed 'System.Runtime.Serialization.Primitives 4.1.1'
    to NuGetDemo
Executing nuget actions took 718.08 ms
Time Elapsed: 00:00:01.1269487
========== Finished ==========
Restoring NuGet packages...
Time Elapsed: 00:00:00.5185572
========== Finished ==========
```

If you now expand the **Dependencies** reference folder of the project under **Solution Explorer**, you will see a **NuGet** reference of our library package, which contains the DLL references of the binaries. Please refer to the following screenshot:

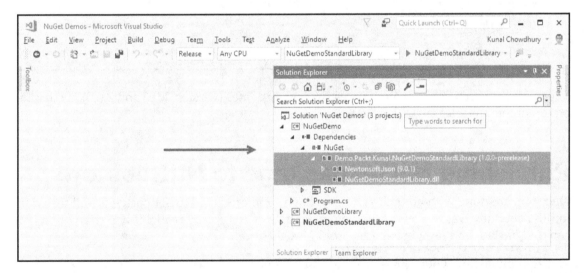

If you publish a new update of your library with a new version number, you will get an update notification, which you will find under the **Updates** tab of **NuGet Package Manager**. Select the already installed package to update to higher binaries or uninstall it from the project. Consider the following screenshot:

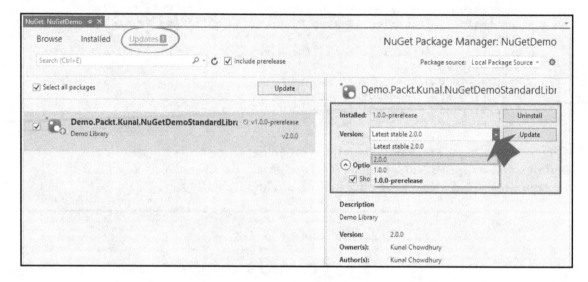

The preceding screenshot demonstrates two new updates (version 1.0.0 and 2.0.0), available on top of the pre-release version 1.0.0.

Publishing NuGet package to NuGet store

Once you are done with your class library, have generated the NuGet package, and tested it locally, you may want to push it to the NuGet gallery for public availability so that others can find, install, and use your library from NuGet Store.

To begin publishing your NuGet package, open any browser window and navigate to `https://www.nuget.org`. If you don't have an account, you need to register in the portal; otherwise, you can sign in with your account credentials. The **Register / Sign in** link is available at the top-right corner of the website:

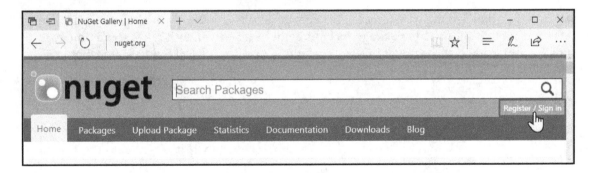

Once you are signed in to NuGet, click **Upload Package**. Under the **Choose a package...** label, click on the **Browse...** button to select the `.nupkg` file that you want to upload and publish to NuGet Store. Click the **Upload** button to continue:

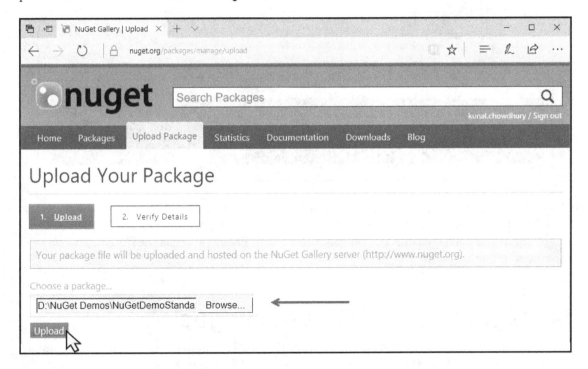

Once the package has been uploaded, verify all the details. You may want to change the metadata information from this screen. Click on **Submit** to finally publish it.

If you have uploaded any pre-release package, the site will inform you about the package. Also, a label will show **This package has not been indexed yet**, as it takes some time to index your package and show it in search results. Consider the following screenshot:

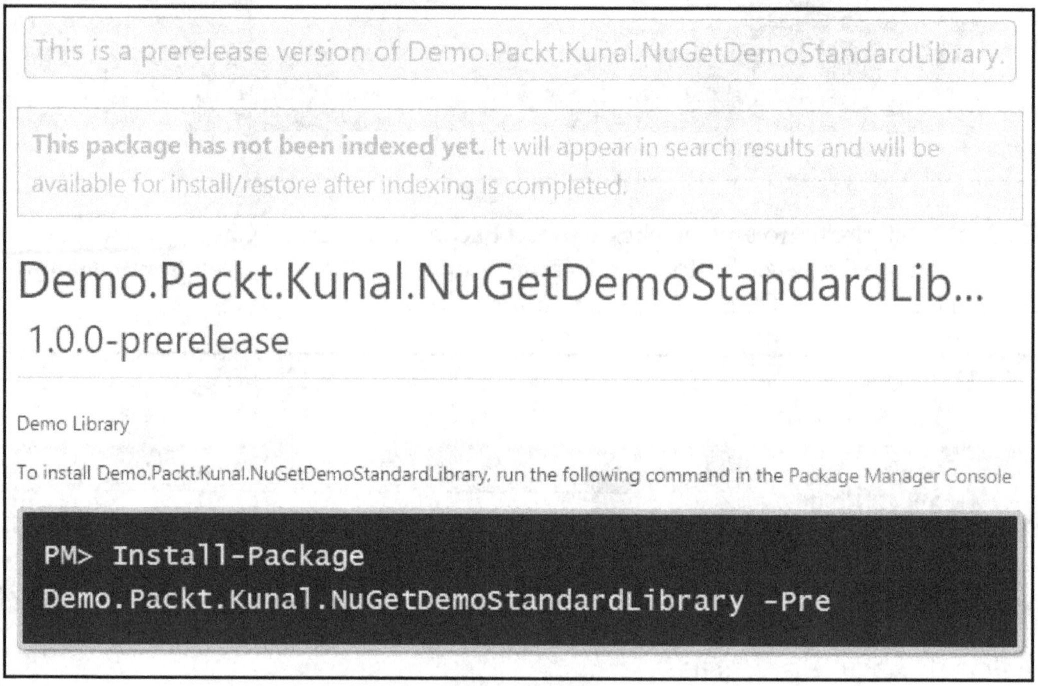

This is a prerelease version of Demo.Packt.Kunal.NuGetDemoStandardLibrary.

This package has not been indexed yet. It will appear in search results and will be available for install/restore after indexing is completed.

Demo.Packt.Kunal.NuGetDemoStandardLib...
1.0.0-prerelease

Demo Library

To install Demo.Packt.Kunal.NuGetDemoStandardLibrary, run the following command in the Package Manager Console

```
PM> Install-Package
Demo.Packt.Kunal.NuGetDemoStandardLibrary -Pre
```

Once the package has been uploaded and published, you will be able to download and install the package directly from **NuGet Package Manager**, pointing your gallery to nuget.org as the package source. You can also use the **Package Manager Console** to download it via the command line.

Managing your NuGet packages

You can manage all your NuGet packages from the **NuGet Package Manager**, which you can invoke from the Visual Studio **Tools** menu - **NuGet Package Manager** | **Manage NuGet Packages for Solution...**.

All the installed packages will get listed under the **Installed** tab, whereas the packages with new updates on the server will get listed under the **Updates** tab.

The installed packages may have overlay icons to denote the status of the package. For example, the blue arrowhead (as shown in the following screenshot for our package library) denotes that an update is available, and the green checkmark (as shown in the following screenshot for the **Newtonsoft.Json** library) denotes that the library is installed:

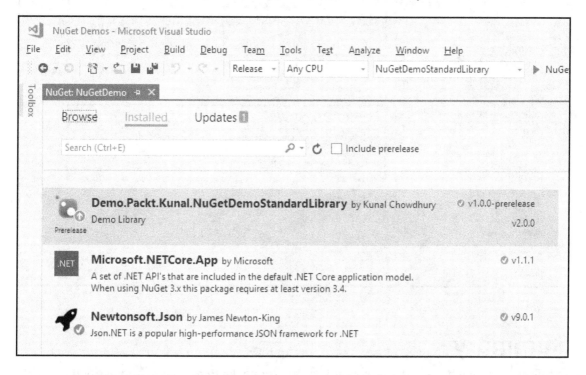

You can configure **NuGet Package Manager** to allow NuGet to automatically download the missing packages of a project/solution. You can also ask it to automatically check for any missing package during the build in Visual Studio. To enable these settings, open **NuGet Package Manager** settings.

From this screen (as shown in the following screenshot), you can also configure the default package management format to either **Packages.config** or **PackageReference**. .NET Core projects generally use the PackageReference format:

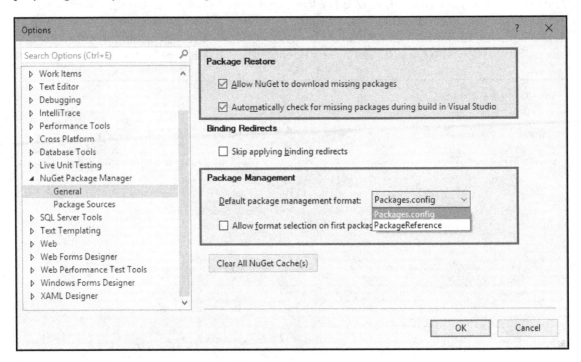

Summary

In this chapter, we have had an overview of **NuGet package manager**, and learned about its usage and the process to use it in a project/solution. We also learned how to create a NuGet package library for .NET Framework and .NET Standard. We discussed the NuGet spec file, versioning mechanism, dependencies, conditional dependencies, and the method to target NuGet package for multiple .NET Frameworks.

Finally, we discussed how to create a local package source to test a package before publishing it to a store, and how to publish it to NuGet Gallery using the nuget.org portal.

In the next chapter, we will learn the new debugging techniques available in Visual Studio 2017, along with Breakpoints, DataTips, Diagnostic Tools, and XAML UI debugging.

7
Debugging Applications with Visual Studio 2017

Debugging is the core part of any application development. It is a process that helps you to quickly look at the current state of your program by walking through the code line by line. Developers generally start debugging the application while writing code. Some developers start debugging even before writing the first line of code to know the logic and functionalities. It's a rare case scenario when a developer completes writing code without debugging the application.

Visual Studio provides us details about the running program as much as possible. It also helps to change some values while the application is already running. Thus, debugging inside Visual Studio IDE is becoming more popular day by day.

In this chapter, we are going to cover the following topics:

- Overview of Visual Studio debugger tools
- Debugging C# source code using breakpoints
    - Organizing breakpoints in code
    - Debugger execution steps
    - Adding conditions to breakpoints
    - Adding actions to breakpoints
    - Adding labels to breakpoints
    - Managing breakpoints using the Breakpoints window
    - Exporting/importing breakpoints

- Using the Data Tips while debugging
  - Pinning/unpinning Data Tips for better debugging
  - Inspecting Data Tips in various watch windows
  - Using visualizers to display complex Data Tips
  - Importing/exporting Data Tips
  - Using debugger to display debugging information
- Using the Immediate Window while debugging your code
- Using the Visual Studio Diagnostics Tools
- Using the new Run to Click feature in Visual Studio 2017
- Debugging an already running process
- Debugging the XAML application UI
  - Overview of XAML debugging
  - Inspecting XAML properties on Live Visual Tree
  - Enabling UI debugging tools for XAML

Overview of Visual Studio debugger tools

The debugger is a Visual Studio tool which works as a background process to inspect the execution of the program. Breakpoints are used to notify the debugger to pause the execution of the program when it hits at a certain line. **PDB** (**Program Data Base**) files are used to store the debugging information. It stores the line number, Data Tips information, and many other related information of the source code which are required to debug the application. Visual Studio then reads it to pause the debugging and provide more details of the execution.

 When you build the application in debug mode, the PDB file has more information than in release mode.

It is not mandatory that in all cases the debugger will work. Certain situations exist when your debugging information is invalid and in such cases the Visual Studio debugger will fail to attach to the running process: for example, if the binary version of your code is different than the actual code. This often happens when you compiled your code and attached the binary in a modified version of the original code.

When you run your application in debug mode, you will see a different layout of Visual Studio IDE. It automatically adjusts the window layout to provide you with a better environment for debugging.

In debug mode, you will not generally see the **Solution Explorer**, **Team Explorer**, Toolbox, and the Properties window. Instead, Visual Studio creates a layout with C# Interactive, Call Stack, Diagnostics Tools, IntelliTrace, Watch Window, Exception Settings, Immediate Window, and all other related information:

In this chapter, we will demonstrate some of the important tools and techniques for you to master code debugging.

Debugging C# source code using breakpoints

A **breakpoint** is a signal to tell the debugger to pause the current execution of the application at certain points defined in the code editor and wait for further commands. It does not terminate the execution, but it waits until the next instruction is set to it and then resumes at any time.

The Visual Studio code debugger provides a powerful tool to break the execution where and when you want to start the debugging process. It helps you to observe the behavior of the code in runtime and find the cause of the problem.

Organizing breakpoints in code

Let's start with placing our first breakpoint in the code and gradually move forward with code debugging. Click on the left-hand side bar of the code file in Visual Studio to place the breakpoint. Alternatively, you can press *F9* to toggle the breakpoints. Once you place a breakpoint, a red circle will be generated in the side bar and the entire code block in the line will get a dark red background:

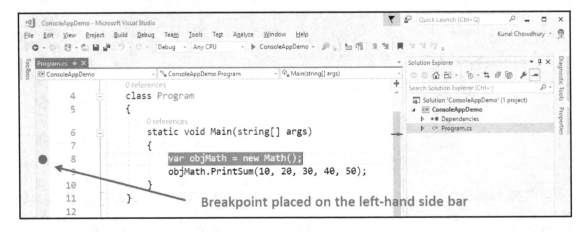

When you press *F5* or start the application in debug mode, it will break at the point where you placed it. A yellow arrow head at the left-hand side bar represents a marker of the current execution of the line, having a yellow block on the execution line. You can also drag the marker arrow up or down within the same debugging context to restart or continue the execution of the code block:

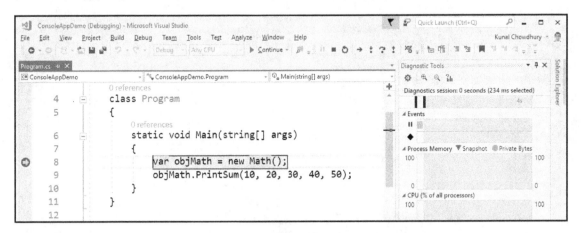

When you right click the breakpoint circle on the left-hand side bar, a context menu will pop up on the screen which allows you to delete or disable the breakpoint:

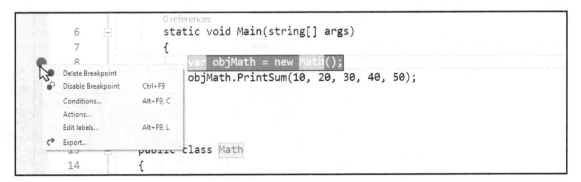

In case you want to delete or disable all the breakpoints in the currently loaded solution, you can navigate to the Visual Studio **Debug** menu and click **Delete All Breakpoints** or **Disable All Breakpoints** respectively. From this menu, you can also create a new breakpoint or toggle an existing breakpoint:

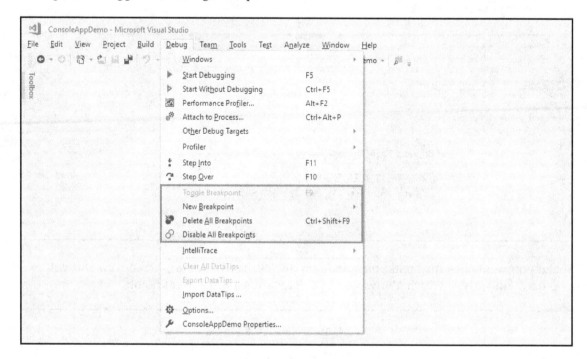

Debugger execution steps

When you are debugging a code, you may want to debug it line-by-line. Thus, you will need to execute the current line and step over to next one. Sometimes you may want to go deep into the method or property to debug the code. You can do all these things from the Visual Studio **Debug** menu:

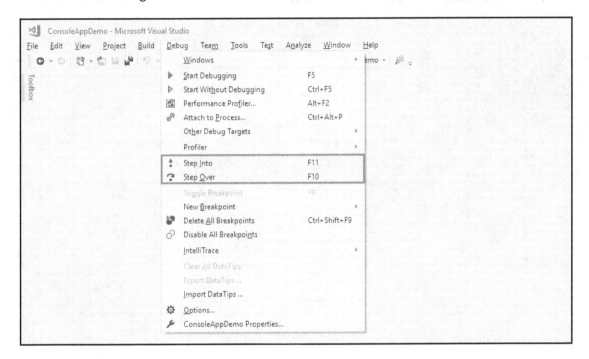

You can click the **Debug** | **Step Over** menu or press the keyboard shortcut *F10* to execute the current line and jump into the next line for execution. Click the **Debug** | **Step Into** menu item or press the *F11* key to step into any property or method for debugging. You can then continue the line by line execution by pressing *F10* or continue executing the program to the end or to the next breakpoint by pressing the *F5* key on the keyboard:

```
                        1 reference
   26          public void PrintSum(params double[] values)
   27          {
 ○ 28              var count = values.Length;   ≤ 3ms elapsed
   29              var commaSeparatedValues = string.Empty;
   30
   31              for (var i = 0; i < count; i++)
   32              {
   33                  commaSeparatedValues += values[i];
   34                  if (i != count - 1) { commaSeparatedValues += ", "; }
   35              }
   36
   37              System.Console.WriteLine
   38
   39
   40          }
   41      }
   42  }
```

💡	Quick Actions and Refactorings...	Ctrl+.
▭	Rename...	F2
	Remove and Sort Usings	Ctrl+R, Ctrl+G
▨	Peek Definition	Alt+F12
▣	Go To Definition	F12
	Go To Implementation	Ctrl+F12
	Find All References	Ctrl+K, R
🗠	View Call Hierarchy	Ctrl+K, Ctrl+T
↖	Run To Cursor	Ctrl+F10
⭲	Set Next Statement	Ctrl+Shift+F10
⊞	Go To Disassembly	Alt+G
👓	Add Watch	
👓	QuickWatch...	Ctrl+D, Q
	Execute in Interactive	Ctrl+E, Ctrl+E
	Snippet	▶
✂	Cut	Ctrl+X
⧉	Copy	Ctrl+C
🗐	Paste	Ctrl+V
	Outlining	▶

150 %

C# Interactive   Locals   Watch 1   Call Stack   Exception Settings   Immediate Window

Ready   Ln 37   Col 37   Ch 37   INS

Visual Studio also provides some smart menu entries to help you in debugging your code. When you are at any breakpoint, you can continue the execution to a specific line and break again. To do so, right click on any line within that debugging context and choose **Run to Cursor** as shown in the preceding screenshot. Alternatively, you can click the desired line and press the keyboard shortcut *Ctrl + F10* to continue the execution.

In this case, all the lines between the executing line and selected line will execute before it breaks. This is same as placing another breakpoint on that line:

```
   26        public void PrintSum(params double[] values)
   27        {
 ⊙ 28            var count = values.Length;
   29            var commaSeparatedValues = string.Empty;
   30
   31            for (var i = 0; i < count; i++)
   32            {
   33                commaSeparatedValues += values[i];
   34                if (i != count - 1) { commaSeparatedValues += ", "; }
   35            }
   36
   37            System.Console.WriteLine
   38
   39
   40        }
   41    }
   42 }
```

💡	Quick Actions and Refactorings...	Ctrl+.
	Rename...	F2
	Remove and Sort Usings	Ctrl+R, Ctrl+G
	Peek Definition	Alt+F12
	Go To Definition	F12
	Go To Implementation	Ctrl+F12
	Find All References	Ctrl+K, R
	View Call Hierarchy	Ctrl+K, Ctrl+T
	Run To Cursor	Ctrl+F10
	Set Next Statement	Ctrl+Shift+F10
	Go To Disassembly	Alt+G
	Add Watch	
	QuickWatch...	Ctrl+D, Q
	Execute in Interactive	Ctrl+E, Ctrl+E
	Snippet	▶
	Cut	Ctrl+X
	Copy	Ctrl+C
	Paste	Ctrl+V
	Outlining	▶

150 %

C# Interactive   Locals   Watch 1   Call Stack   Exception Settings   Immediate Window

Ready   Ln 37   Col 37   Ch 37   INS

You can also ask Visual Studio to jump into a specific line without executing certain lines of code. This is sometimes needed when you smell a bad code which is causing a bug to occur and you want to check without removing/commenting/changing that portion of code.

 A point to remember is that **Run To Cursor** executes lines of code in between whereas **Set Next Statement** skips code in between.

While you are at a specific breakpoint, you can right click on any line within that debugging context and select **Set Next Statement**. You can also press the keyboard shortcut *Ctrl + Shift + F10* to move the current marker of your debugger to that selected line. Alternatively, you can also drag the marker arrow of the current line to the new execution line to set it as the next statement. None of the code written within those two lines will execute during that debugging instance.

Adding conditions to breakpoints

You can add conditions to break the execution only when a certain condition is met. This is often useful when you are iterating a list and want to check the runtime value for a specific condition.

To add a condition to a breakpoint, right click on the red circle on the left-hand side bar. A context menu will pop up on the screen. Click on the menu **Conditions...** to open the inline dialog. You can also press *Alt + F9 + C* to open it:

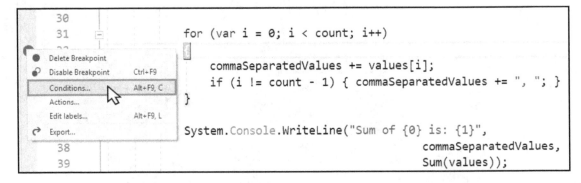

There can be three different types of conditions that you can place to a breakpoint:

- Conditional expressions
- Hit counters
- Filters

Using conditional expressions

Conditional expressions are often useful if you want to hit a breakpoint on some conditions. For example, you would like to debug a `for` statement when a specific index count is reached or when an item in a collection meets a specific value.

To add a conditional expression to a breakpoint inside Visual Studio 2017, select the **Conditions** checkbox from the **Breakpoint Settings** dialog and select the condition type as **Conditional Expression** from the dropdown. The next dropdown allows you to select the comparer (**Is true** or **When changed**). The text box next to it allows you to enter the condition. Here in this case, we entered `i == 5`:

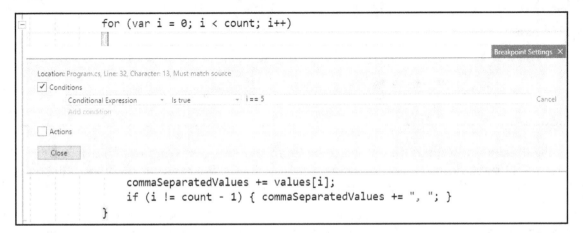

In the preceding example, the breakpoint will directly hit when the variable `i` of the `for` loop sets to `5`. You can then start your code debugging when the said conditions are met.

You can add multiple conditions by clicking the **Add condition** link which will be clubbed with the AND operator. Once a condition has been added to a breakpoint, the red breakpoint circle will show a + symbol.

Using breakpoint hit counters

A hit counter is used to determine the count of breakpoint hits on a specific line and based on that, break the debugger. This is useful in iterations where you want to stop only when the number of hits it encounters reaches a threshold value:

In the **Breakpoint settings** dialog, select the **Conditions** checkbox and from the dropdown, select **Hit Count**. From the next dropdown, select either =, **Is a multiple of**, or >= as the type of comparer and then enter the value in the text field.

When the hit count is reached, the debugger will stop at that breakpoint and wait for a further command. Like conditional expressions, you can add multiple hit counters along with other conditions with the AND operator.

Using breakpoint filters

The breakpoint filters are useful when you want to specify any additional criteria for the breakpoint. You can specify the breakpoint to hit only when a specific **MachineName**, **ProcessID**, **ProcessName**, **ThreadID**, or **ThreadName** matches.

You can select **Filter** from the first dropdown and **Is True** from the second dropdown and then specify the conditional value in the associated input box, as shown in the following screenshot:

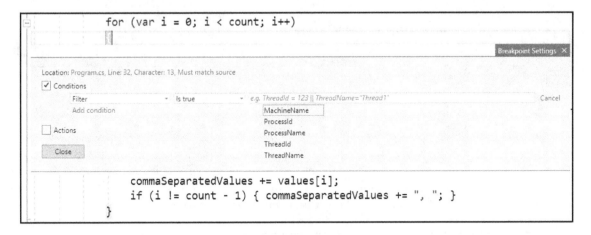

Adding actions to breakpoints

You can specify some actions to a breakpoint to log a message to the output window or run a specific function when the breakpoint reaches. This is generally done to trace an execution log and print various values at different moments of the process.

To add actions to a breakpoint, right click on the red circle on the left-hand side bar and click on **Actions...** from the context menu that pops up in the screen:

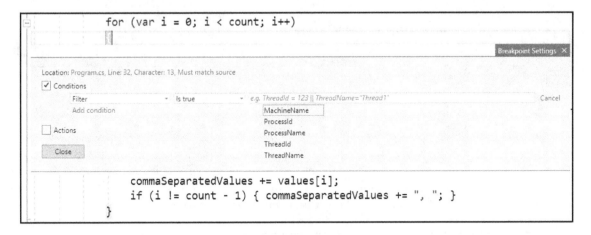

This will open the **Breakpoint settings** dialog on screen having the **Actions** checkbox as checked. In the input box, either you can enter the name of the function that you want to execute for tracing or enter the string with the variable that you want to print:

```
        for (var i = 0; i < count; i++)
        {
```

Breakpoint Settings ×

Location: Program.cs, Line: 32, Character: 13, Must match source

☐ Conditions

☑ Actions

    Log a message to Output Window: *e.g. $Function: The value of x.y is {x.y}*   ⓘ Cancel

   ☑ Continue execution

[Close]

```
            commaSeparatedValues += values[i];
            if (i != count - 1) { commaSeparatedValues += ", "; }
        }
```

You can use curly braces to print the value of a variable. For example, the following expression **The value of 'i' is {i}** will print the value of the variable i along with the text that we specified.

You can also use some special keywords, as mentioned in the following list, to print their current values:

- $ADDRESS: Current instruction
- $CALLER: Previous function name
- $CALLSTACK: Call stack
- $FUNCTION: Current function name
- $PID: Process ID
- $PNAME: Process name
- $TID: Thread ID
- $TNAME: Thread name

By default, the **Continue execution** checkbox is selected. That means the actions that we selected will be executed without stopping the code execution.

Adding labels to breakpoints

When you are working with multiple breakpoints set over multiple code files of a large project or solution, it is sometimes difficult to identify and manage them properly. Visual Studio provides a better way to organize them.

As shown in the following screenshot, right click on a specific breakpoint and click on **Edit Labels...**. Alternatively, you can press *Alt + F9 + L* to open the breakpoint labels dialog:

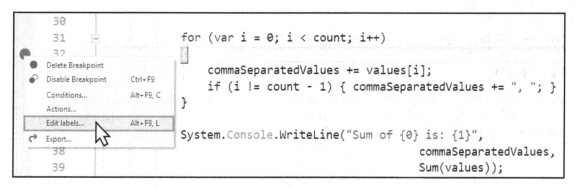

This will open the **Edit breakpoint labels** dialog window, as shown in the following screenshot:

If you have already defined any labels within the same solution, this will list all of them here. You can add a new label to your selected breakpoint or associate it with other breakpoint labels listed in this screen.

> Note that you can add multiple labels to a single breakpoint from the **Edit breakpoint labels** dialog box.

Managing breakpoints using the Breakpoints window

Visual Studio provides a straightforward way to manage all your breakpoints under a single toolbox window, which you can find by navigating to **Debug** | **Windows** | **Breakpoints** (keyboard shortcut: *Ctrl + D + B*). When you place multiple breakpoints in your code file or solution, this window helps you to navigate between them very easily.

You can add a new breakpoint, delete a breakpoint, or enable/disable it from here. This also lists the label, conditions, hit counter, filter, complete function name, process, and many other details set to each breakpoint, and is easily searchable:

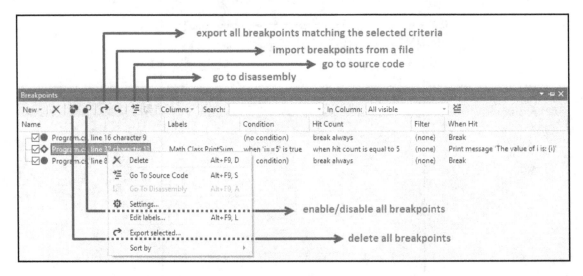

Exporting/importing breakpoints

Visual Studio allows you to export/import breakpoints. This is useful when multiple developers are working on the same code and want to debug at the same breakpoints set by other developers.

You can either export individual breakpoints by right clicking on the breakpoint circle present at the left-hand side bar or you can export all the listed breakpoints in the **Breakpoints** window by clicking the export button, as shown in the following screenshot:

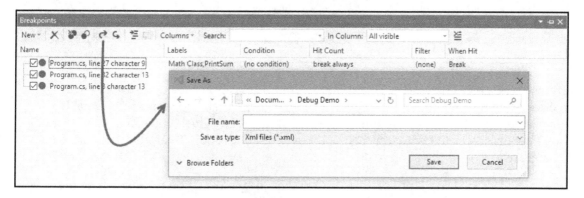

This will save the details in an XML file, which you can share with others. They need to import it by clicking the import breakpoints from the breakpoint window and all the detailed information shared by you will be automatically loaded in the editor.

Using the Data Tips while debugging

During code debugging, **Data Tips** are used to provide more information of an object/variable in the current scope of execution and work only in break mode. They use the data type information to display each value that has a type associated with it. The debugger loads the object information recursively in a hierarchical structure and displays it in the editor.

Here's an example of how the **Data Tips** load for an object:

```
      1 reference
54    public void PrintSum(params double[] values)
55    {
56        var count = values.Length;
57        var commaSeparat       values  {double[5]}     ng.Empty;
                                  [0] 10
58                                [1] 20
59        for (var i = 0; i      [2] 30  nt; i++)              Data Tips
                                  [3] 40
60        {                      [4] 50
61            commaSeparatedValues += values[i];
62            if (i != count - 1) { commaSeparatedValues += ", "; }
63        }
```

To display a **Data Tip**, place a breakpoint in your application code and run it in debug mode. When the breakpoint hits, hover over an object/variable to display the Data Tip associated with that object/variable. It is a tree of members which you can expand to get more details associated with it. When you hover out of the object/variable, the Data Tips disappear.

The Data Tips are evaluated in the current execution context where the breakpoint hits and the execution moved into suspended state. Thus, hovering over a variable in another function, which is in the current context, will show the same value in the Data Tips that are being displayed in the current execution context.

Pinning/unpinning Data Tips for better debugging

When you hover out from the variable, the **Data Tip** disappears. Thus, it is a requirement to keep it displayed. The Visual Studio editor provides a way to keep it visible. You can pin a value from a Data Tip to the editor screen and drag it to any position. To do this, just click the pin to the source icon in the tooltip (as shown in the following screenshot) and a pin icon will appear at the left-hand side on the same line where you positioned the pinned value:

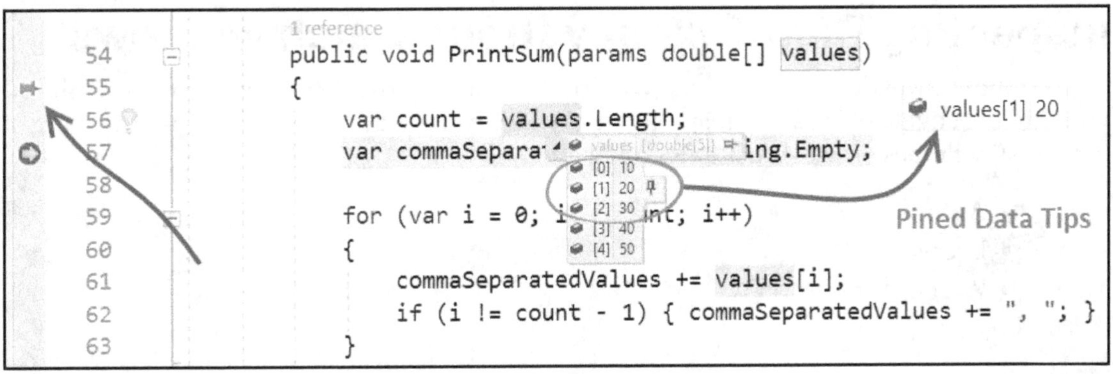

```
54      public void PrintSum(params double[] values)
55      {
56          var count = values.Length;
57          var commaSepara                ing.Empty;
                            values [double[5]]
                            [0] 10
58                          [1] 20
59          for (var i = 0;  [2] 30  nt; i++)      Pined Data Tips
                            [3] 40
60          {               [4] 50
61              commaSeparatedValues += values[i];
62              if (i != count - 1) { commaSeparatedValues += ", "; }
63          }
```

values[1] 20

You can also add a comment to a pinned data tip. Hover over the pinned value and expand the arrow head. It will provide you with a space to enter the comment, as shown in the following screenshot:

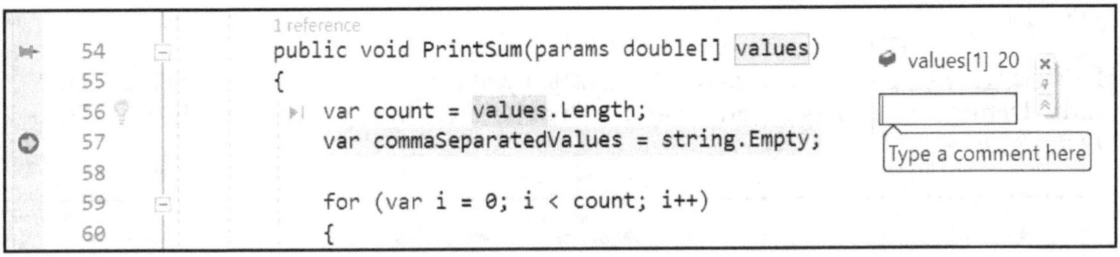

```
54      public void PrintSum(params double[] values)
55      {
56          var count = values.Length;
57          var commaSeparatedValues = string.Empty;
58
59          for (var i = 0; i < count; i++)
60          {
```

values[1] 20 ×

Type a comment here

When you are debugging your code, the value stored in the pinned entry will change as per the current context. The IDE stores the Data Tip information in a persistent storage for later use. When the debugging session is over, you can hover over the pinned icon present at the left-hand side to view the value from the last debugging session. This is often used to share the debugging details with other members of the team.

When you pin a Tata Tip's value, the icon changes to the unpin state. To unpin a Data Tip, click on unpin from source icon.

Inspecting Data Tips in various watch windows

Visual Studio provides various watch windows to simplify the debugging process, so that you can investigate objects in a fixed debugging window just like the Data Tips. There are three distinct types of watch windows available:

- Autos
- Locals
- Watch

The Autos window

The **Autos** window shows all the objects and variables information from the current executing context. This information gets loaded when the debugger hits a breakpoint. Generally, Visual Studio automatically generates this list and updates based on the context of the debugger.

Here is a screenshot of the **Autos** window, which you can manually open from the Visual Studio **Debug** | **Windows** | **Autos** menu path or by invoking the keyboard shortcut *Ctrl + D + A*:

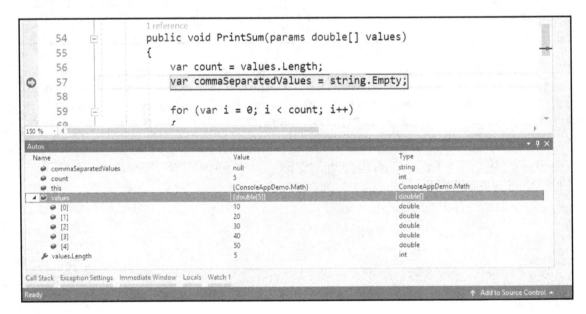

The Locals window

The **Locals** window displays the information of the local variables and objects based on the current thread execution context. You can manually invoke this window from the Visual Studio menu, **Debug** | **Windows** | **Locals**, or by pressing the keyboard shortcut *Ctrl + D + L*:

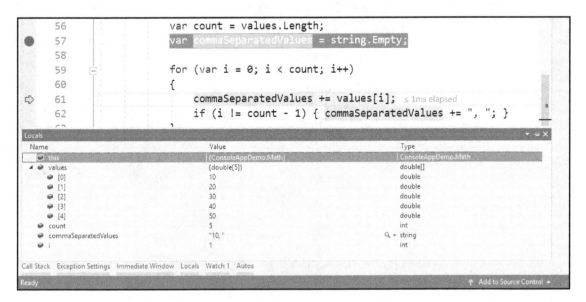

The Watch window

There can be four **Watch** windows', namely **Watch 1**, **Watch 2**, **Watch 3**, and **Watch 4**. These are customized windows which show information about objects and variables based on what you have added to them.

In general, when you add a variable in a watch window, it gets added to **Watch 1**. If you want to move it to a different watch window, you need to drag it from **Watch 1** to the other one.

 While you are in debugger break mode, you will see a blank watch window. But, you can right click on any object or variable in that context and click **Add Watch** from the context menu to add the selected variable in the watch list.

Not only objects and variables, you can also add any expression to it. Simply select an expression, right click on it and from the context menu click the **Add Watch** menu item:

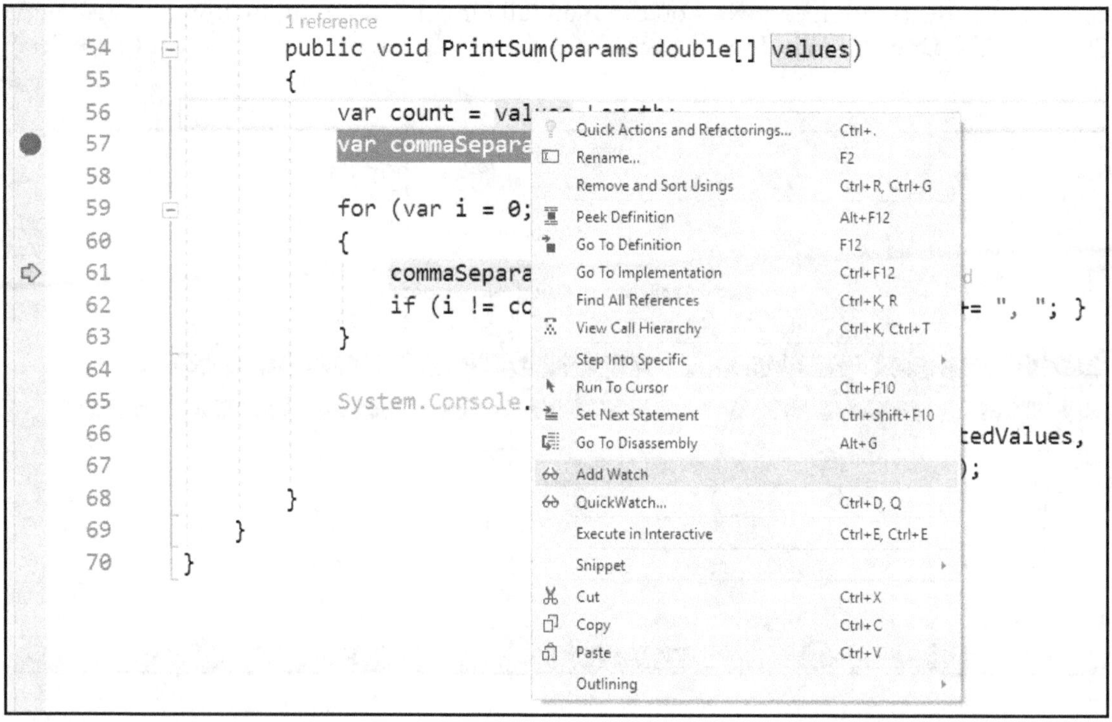

You can drag a variable, object, or an expression from the code editor to the watch window. You can also add a new item in the watch window grid by double clicking on a new grid row.

Like other windows, it also displays the data in three columns: **Name**, **Value**, and **Type**, and the tree can be expanded to get more details about a complex object, as shown in the following screenshot:

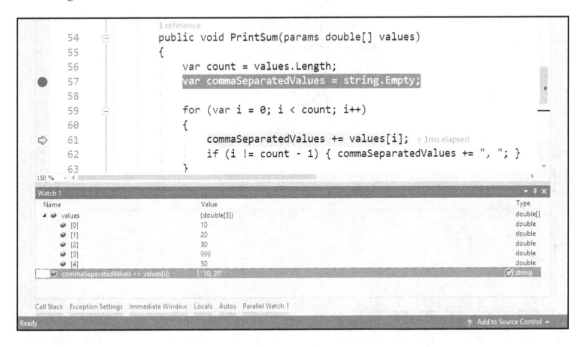

You can also add a variable, an object, or an expression to **QuickWatch** to simplify the value inspection process. From the right click context menu, click on **QuickWatch...** to add it for inspection:

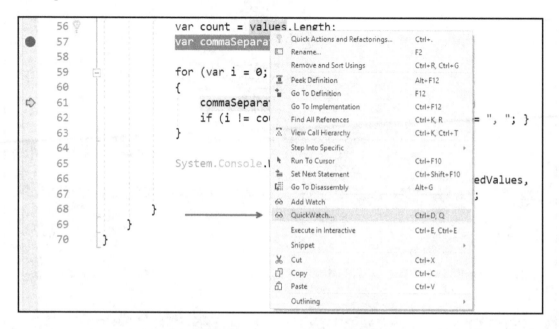

You can alternatively press the keyboard shortcut *Ctrl + D + Q* to add it to the **QuickWatch** window. You can then expand an object to display its properties or values:

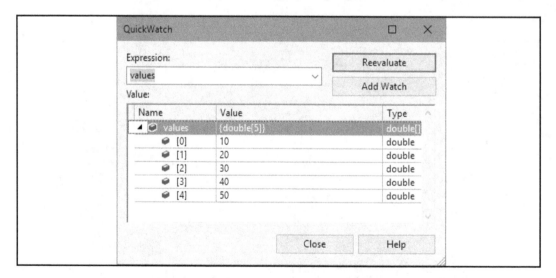

When you have a more complex object, such as an exception object, the **QuickWatch** window is useful in getting each and every detail out of the object in a single debugging tool window:

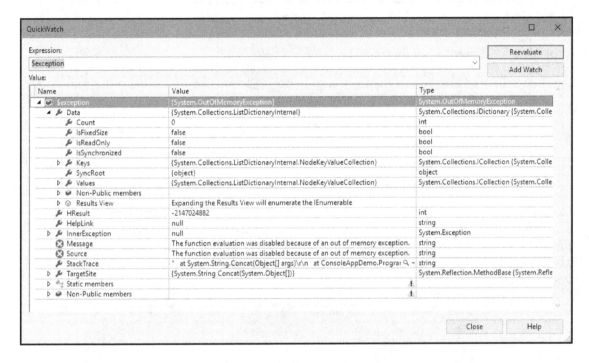

Using visualizers to display complex Data Tips

Visual Studio provides a set of visualizers to help display complex Data Tips while you debug your code. When you hover over a variable, the Data Tip can contain a find icon based on the data type associated with the debugger visualizer for that variable. Clicking on the arrow head displays a pop up menu with the list of visualizers for that debugging instance.

For example, check the following screenshot where we have four visualizers, **Text Visualizer, XML Visualizer, HTML Visualizer,** and **JSON Visualizer**:

```
for (var i = 0; i < count; i++)
{
    commaSeparatedValues += values[i];
    if (i != cou    commaSeparatedValues  Q ▾  "10, 20, 30, 40"      lues += ", "; }
}                    ✓  Text Visualizer
                        XML Visualizer
                        HTML Visualizer
System.Console.W        JSON Visualizer          {0} is: {1}",
                                                 commaSeparatedValues,
                                                 Sum(values));
```

Here, if you click on **Text Visualizer**, a dialog box will appear showing the text representation of the debugging value. The text visualizer shows it in text format, whereas the XML, HTML, or JSON visualizer shows it in the respective format based on the associated data type. Based on the content of the variable, you should use the respective visualizer:

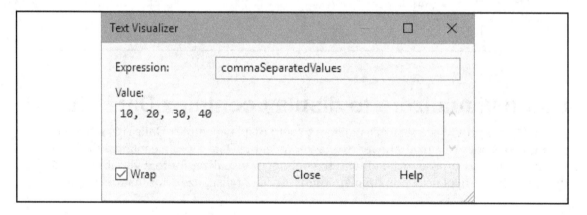

Here's an example of how the Visual Studio **XML Visualizer** represents the content of an XML document:

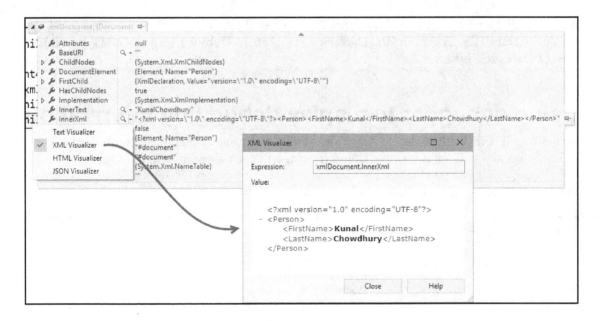

Importing/exporting Data Tips

Like breakpoints, you can also export Data Tips to an XML file which you can share with your team. Others can import it to the same source and debug it further. To export the Data Tips, go to the Visual Studio menu, **Debug | Export DataTips...**, which will open the **Export DataTips** dialog. Select the folder where you want to save the XML file, give the file a name, and click **Save**. It will produce an XML which will look like the one shown in the following screenshot (at the right side):

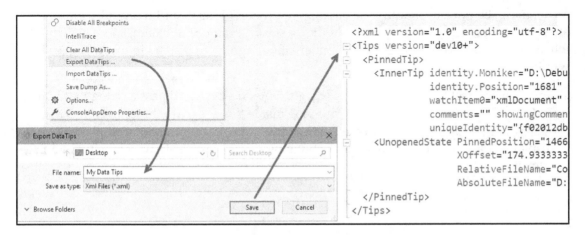

It is a SOAP-based XML file and includes all the related information that you need to reload the entire Data Tips. To import the Data Tips, navigate to **Debug** | **Import DataTips...** and select the desired file.

Using debugger to display debugging information

Sometimes it is difficult to debug a complex data type value. For example, with a collection of Employees, if you see it inside a Data Tip, you will see that each item of the list displays the object by default. To view each property, you need to expand it, which becomes difficult in some scenarios when you have a lot of data:

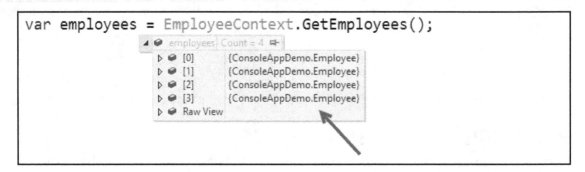

As shown in the preceding screenshot, we are expanding the object to check the property values of each object. As it's a simple object, we may find it easy but think about a scenario having multiple properties and variables inside it. Debugging that becomes very difficult; that you already know.

So, what can be done to simplify the debugging process? Visual Studio provides an attribute, `DebuggerDisplay`, present in the `System.Diagnostics` namespace, which when set to a class, controls how the member value is going to display in the debugger window.

To implement it, set the `DebuggerDisplay` attribute to a class and pass a string that you want to display as an argument to it. The value inside the { } (curly braces) defines the property that you want to show in the **Debugger** window. You can add multiple properties to display in the Data Tips for an easier debugging experience, as shown in the following screenshot:

```
[DebuggerDisplay("FirstName={FirstName}, LastName={LastName}, Designation={Designation}")]
public class Employee
{
    public string FirstName { get; set; }
    public string LastName { get; set; }
    public string Designation { get; set; }
}
```

Now, when your debugger hits and you hover over to see the Data Tip, you will see that the string that you passed as an argument to the DebuggerDisplay attribute (along with the property details in curly braces) gets printed in the Data Tips instead of the object representation. Here's a screenshot of how it will look in our example that we have just used:

```
var employees = EmployeeContext.GetEmployees();
```
```
    ⊿ ● employees  Count = 4  ◘·
        ▷ ● [0]        FirstName="Kunal", LastName="Chowdhury", Designation="Technical Lead"
        ▷ ● [1]        FirstName="Rajat", LastName="Sharma", Designation="Software Developer"
        ▷ ● [2]        FirstName="Suresh", LastName="Yadav", Designation="Software Developer"
        ▷ ● [3]        FirstName="Rahul", LastName="Pradhan", Designation="Test Engineer"
        ▷ ● Raw View
```

In C#, you can also use an expression inside the curly braces which has implicit access to the member variable of the current instance of the target type.

Using the Immediate Window while debugging your code

Immediate Window, which is present under the Visual Studio menu, **Debug** | **Windows** | **Immediate**, and can also be invoked using keyboard shortcut *Ctrl* + *D* + *I*, is used while debugging an application. You will find it useful while executing statements, evaluating expressions, and/or printing any values present within the debugging context.

For example, let's take the preceding example to populate the `employees` object. Once your debugging context has evaluated the said object, you can perform an operation on that object within the **Immediate Window**.

In general, entering the object name `employees` will print the object information available in that collection. When **DebuggerDisplay** is set to the model class, entering the same `employees` will print the entire details of the object in a formatted string as defined in the debugger display attribute.

You can also evaluate an expression by defining it in the **Immediate Window**, if the same is available within the same debugging context:

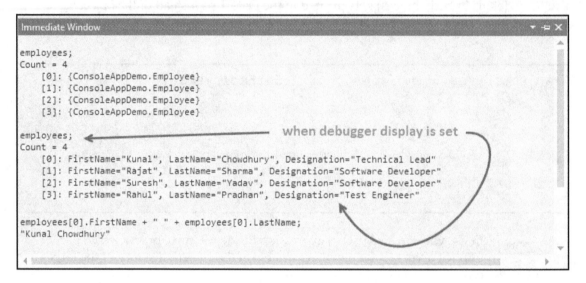

Using the Visual Studio Diagnostics Tools

The Diagnostics Tools feature of Visual Studio provides you with historical information about your application in a debugging session. Along with Visual Studio 2013, Microsoft first introduced the Performance and Diagnostics hub feature which changed over time and was relaunched as Diagnostics Tools in Visual Studio 2015 with more limited options than the version currently available in Visual Studio 2017.

When you start a debugging session, the **Diagnostics Tools** window will automatically launch and show side-by-side of your code window. In case it is unavailable, you can launch it from the Visual Studio **Debug** | **Windows** | **Show Diagnostics Tools** menu or alternatively you can press the keyboard shortcut *Ctrl + Alt + F2*:

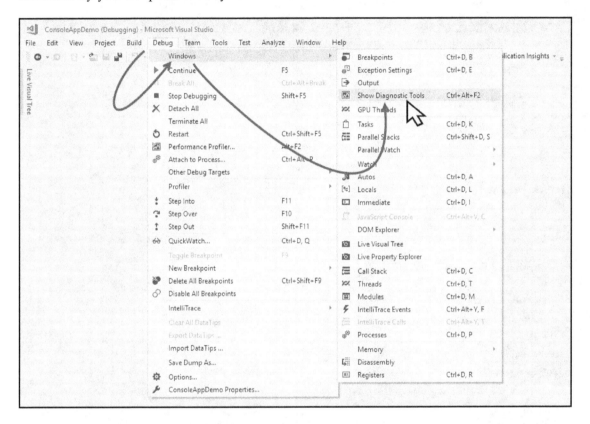

The window shows you detailed historical information about your application, **PerfTips**, in the events graph and events table. It also allows you to correlate execution time with the Memory and CPU utilization graph. You can take snapshots of the current memory utilization and enable/disable the CPU profiling in this screen:

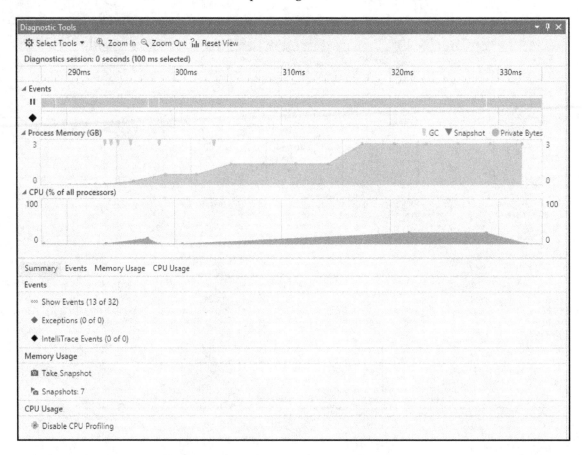

In the preceding screenshot, check how the memory was utilized over time. The yellow arrow head means the time when the **garbage collector** was called, either automatically by the system or forcefully from the code:

Summary Events Memory Usage CPU Usage			
			▼ Filter ▾ Search Events 🔎 ▾
Event	Time	Duration	Thread
Breakpoint: PrintSum, Program.cs line 110	0.25s	1ms	[388] Main Thread
Step: PrintSum, Program.cs line 113	0.27s	14ms	[388] Main Thread
Step: Main, Program.cs line 13	0.27s	1ms	[388] Main Thread
Step: Main, Program.cs line 16	0.27s	1ms	[388] Main Thread
Step: Main, Program.cs line 17	0.27s	7ms	[388] Main Thread
Step: Main, Program.cs line 32	0.28s	4ms	[388] Main Thread
Step: Main, Program.cs line 34	0.28s	3ms	[388] Main Thread
Step: Main, Program.cs line 37	0.28s	5ms	[388] Main Thread
Step: Main, Program.cs line 38	0.29s	9ms	[388] Main Thread
Step: Main, Program.cs line 39	0.29s	1ms	[388] Main Thread
Step: Main, Program.cs line 42	0.32s	31ms	[388] Main Thread
Step: Main, Program.cs line 43	0.35s	25ms	[388] Main Thread
⇨ **Step:** Main, Program.cs line 45	0.35s	3ms	[388] Main Thread

To view all the events performed while debugging the context, switch to the **Events** tab. It gives you a new IntelliTrace experience in Visual Studio and saves you valuable debugging time. It captures additional events and useful information about the execution of your application, thus allowing you to identify the potential root causes of any issues. When an exception happens, it also maintains the history of the events where they occurred.

When you want to know more about a specific event, click the item from the list and activate **Historical Debugging** to set the debug window back to a time when the event occurred. You can then see the call stack, the values of local variables, and other important information available at the time when the event occurred:

Summary Events Memory Usage CPU Usage					
📷 Take Snapshot	🔎 View Heap	✕ Delete			
Time	Objects (Diff)		Heap Size (Diff)		
1	0.24s	250	(n/a)	49.19 KB	(n/a)
3	0.25s	278	(+28 ↑)	50.38 KB	(+1.20 KB ↑)
4	0.25s	280	(+2 ↑)	50.45 KB	(+0.06 KB ↑)
5	0.25s	281	(+1 ↑)	50.49 KB	(+0.05 KB ↑)
6	0.27s	342	(+61 ↑)	54.30 KB	(+3.81 KB ↑)
7	0.32s	390	(+48 ↑)	57.36 KB	(+3.05 KB ↑)
⮞ 8	0.35s	403	(+13 ↑)	124.59 KB	(+67.23 KB ↑)
⮞ 9	0.35s	403	(+0)	124.59 KB	(+0.00 KB)

To know more about the memory utilization, navigate to the **Memory Usage** tab. Here you need to first take snapshots of the current memory usage by clicking the **Take Snapshot** button, as shown in the preceding screenshot.

Using this tab, you can monitor the memory usage (increased/decreased) and identify the memory issues while you are debugging your code. Clicking on the individual links in each item will give you more details about the snapshot and heap objects, as shown in the following screenshot:

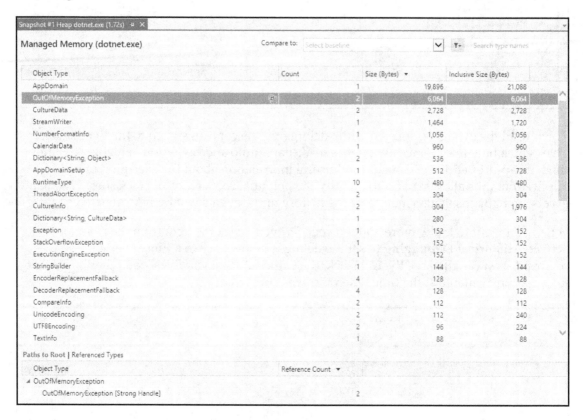

The **CPU Usage** tab provides you details about the CPU utilization and tells you how many CPU resources were used by your code. You can correlate this information with the CPU usage graph shown in the tools window and find out the spike where a higher utilization took place, as shown in the following screenshot:

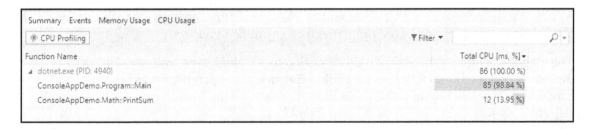

 You should start **CPU Profiling** to grab this information about CPU utilization by the program currently in the debugging context.

If you spot a potential issue when debugging, you can check this tab to get the per-function breakdown to identify the problem. Double clicking any item will give you details about the call tree, as shown in the following screenshot:

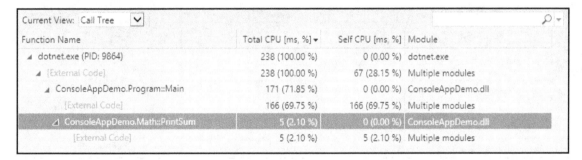

This provides the following details about each function that is available in the call tree:

- **Total CPU %**: This provides you the CPU activity in the selected function and functions it called. The information is provided in percentage value.
- **Self CPU %**: This provides the percentage of CPU activity in the selected function but not in the functions where it has been called.
- **Module**: This provides the name of the module where the call has been made.

By investigating these column values, you can easily identify the code block where the CPU utilization was higher and based on that you can optimize your code.

The diagnostic tool provides you with an option to enable/disable native profiling (the default is: disabled). Click the **Select Tools I Settings...** to open the diagnostic tools property pages, where you will be able to enable native heap profiling or native corruption detection, as shown in the following screenshot:

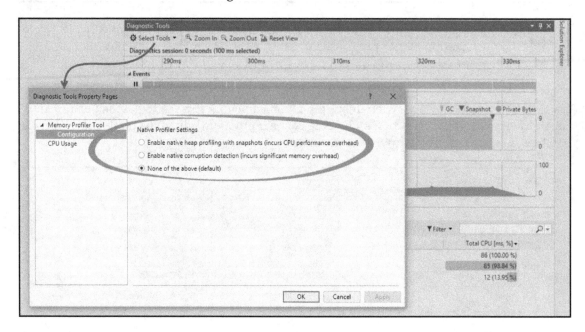

Using the new Run to Click feature in Visual Studio 2017

Visual Studio 2017 provides a new feature, named **Run to Click**, which makes the debugging steps easy. Whenever you are in a debugging context, you can mouse hover on any line to let the IDE show you a green icon near to the line. You can then click on that icon to instruct the debugger to execute to that line and break for the next instruction. This is similar to the menu item, **Run to Cursor**, but with easier steps to execute:

```
18
19    XmlDocument xmlDocument = new XmlDocument();
20
21    XmlDeclaration xmlDeclaration = xmlDocument.CreateXmlDeclaration("1.0", "UTF-8", null);
22    XmlElement root = xmlDocument.DocumentElement;
23    xmlDocument.InsertBefore(xmlDeclaration, root);
24
25    XmlElement element1 = xmlDocument.CreateElement(string.Empty, "Person", string.Empty);
26    xmlDocument.AppendChild(element1);
27
28    XmlElement element2 = xmlDocument.CreateElement(string.Empty, "FirstName", string.Empty);
29    element2.AppendChild(xmlDocument.CreateTextNode("Kunal"));
30    element1.AppendChild(element2);
31
32    XmlElement element3 = xmlDocument.CreateElement(string.Empty, "LastName", string.Empty);
33    XmlText text1 = xmlDocument.CreateTextNode("Chowdhury");
34    element3.AppendChild(text1);
35    element1.AppendChild(element3);
36
```

It is often useful to debug from one line of a code block to another by clicking just the icon, instead of placing breakpoints on each line. This option is enabled by default, but you can disable/enable it any time from Visual Studio **Options** | **Debugging** | **General**, as shown in the following screenshot:

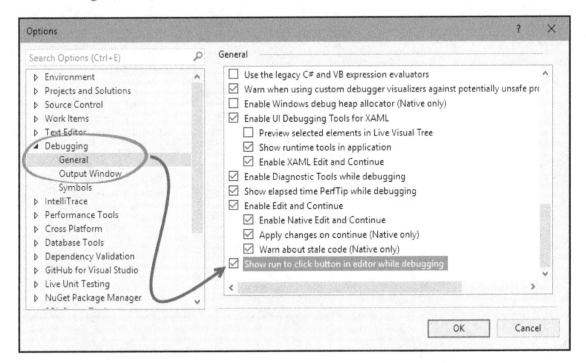

Debugging an already running process

It is often necessary to debug an already running process. It could be a service, an existing process, or a website running on a local or remote system. Visual Studio provides us with an option to debug a running process. When you are debugging a remote process, you will need the Microsoft Visual Studio Remote Debugging Monitor service running.

To get started, you will need to open the exact code that was used to build the process. If there is a change in the code, the debugging information will not be loaded. Once you open the solution, go to the **Debug** | **Attach to Process...** menu, which will open a dialog window, **Attach to Process**, on the screen. Alternatively, you can press *Ctrl + Alt + P* to invoke the window:

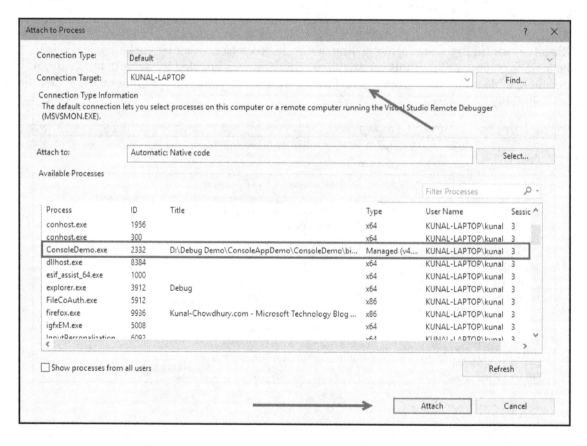

From the **Connection Type** dropdown, select the type of the connection that you want to attach. To attach a local process, keep the selection to **Default**. Based on your requirement, you can either select **Remote (no authentication)**, **SSH**, or **WebKit websocket (no authentication)** as a connection type.

Select the **Connection Target** entry, which is the local system by default and then from the **Available Processes** list, you can select the process that you want to debug, if the same code has been loaded inside Visual Studio. You can also choose the **Show processes from all users** checkbox to get a list of processes running by other users in the same system.

At the end, click the **Attach** button to attach the process with Visual Studio. If everything goes fine, the process will get attached with the solution loaded inside the Visual Studio IDE.

While debugging an already running process, you should keep in mind that:

- To debug the process properly, the debug version of the application must be used. A release build can also work but with reduced debugging functionalities.
- The debugging information should be present (PDB File) and mapped with the process.

When the debugging information gets loaded, the breakpoint will hit by the debugger and you will debug the application as-is, as you did when you started the application from Visual Studio in debug mode.

In case you want to debug a remote application, you should run the MSVSMON.exe file, which comes along with Visual Studio, to start the remote debugging session.

Visual Studio 2017 provides a new feature which allows you to reattach to a process that you last attached in the Visual Studio current context. This saves time as you don't have find the process in the process list again and attach to it. Just navigate to the Visual Studio menu **Debug** | **Reattach to Process...** or press *Shift + Alt + P* to automatically attach with the previous selected process:

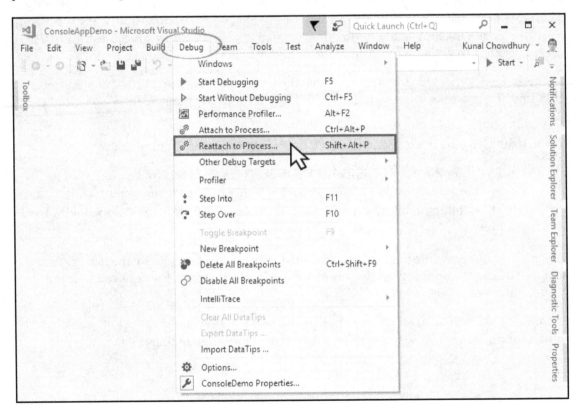

Debugging XAML application UI

Visual Studio 2017 provides a very good feature to make the XAML app development easier. You can now edit your XAML code of a WPF or UWP application, when the application is running in debug mode. You don't have to recompile your project to view the changes. You will automatically see it in the live application as and when you are modifying the markup.

Just as with *F12* - **Developer Tools** of browser applications, you can now navigate to the **Visual Tree of XAML** page when the application is running in debug mode and attached with the Visual Studio 2017 debugger tool.

Overview of XAML debugging

Live Visual Tree and **Live Property Explorer** are two tool windows which will help you to perform XAML debugging more easily. You can now inspect the XAML at runtime and visualize the layout to show alignments and space for UI elements. If you have lots of data bindings, you can use **Live Visual Tree** and **Live Property Explorer** to change properties in runtime and see how it affects the design of the running application. You can invoke the tool windows by navigating to the Visual Studio menus, **Debug | Windows | Live Visual Tree** and **Debug | Windows | Live Property Explorer**, respectively:

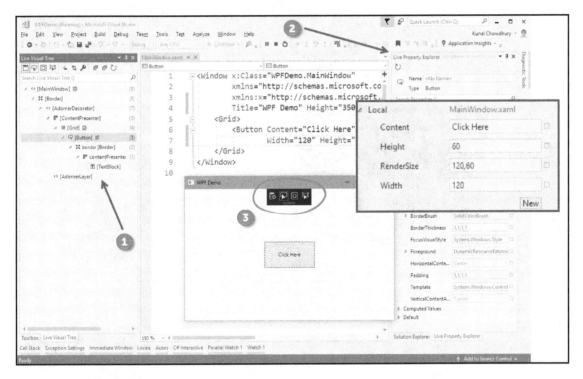

When you run an XAML application from Visual Studio and the debugger is attached, you will notice the following, as shown in the preceding screenshot:

- The **Live Visual Tree** window (highlighted as **1** in the screenshot) gives you a tree view of the UI elements of your running XAML application and provides information about the number of XAML elements inside each container. If the interface changes from one state to another, Live Visual Tree also changes in runtime.
- The **Live Property Explorer** window (highlighted as **2**) provides you with default values of the properties for the visual element that you have selected. By default, these fields are in disabled mode. But you can add a new entry to **Local** by clicking the **New** button and overriding the existing value. When you stop the debugging instance, the local changes will get lost.
- You will also notice a floating toolbar (highlighted as **3**) on your application, which is only available in debug mode. This allows you to easily select the element in the running instance of the application and inspect its Visual Element in the Live Visual Tree. The floating toolbar contains four buttons: **Go to Live Visual Tree**, **Enable Selection**, **Display layout adorners**, and **Track focused element**, as shown in the following screenshot:

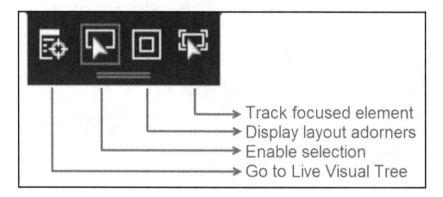

Inspecting XAML properties on Live Visual Tree

Let's start by creating a new WPF project. Go to **File** | **New** | **Project...** and from the available project templates under **Visual C#** | **Windows Classic Desktop**, select the **WPF App (.NET Framework)** template. Give it a name and click **OK** to create the project.

This will create a blank project with a `MainWindow.xaml` page which will have a blank `<Grid/>` layout inside the `<Window/>` tag, as shown in the following screenshot. Run the application in debug mode to launch the **Live Visual Tree** explorer. If the tool window does not come up automatically, navigate to the Visual Studio 2017 menu **Debug** | **Windows** | **Live Visual Tree**:

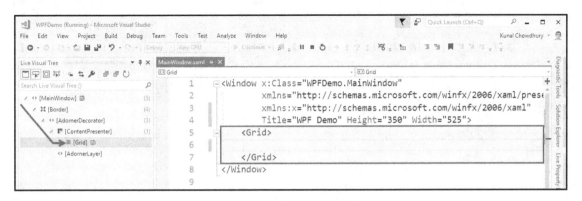

When you run the app, it will have a blank window in the screen as we have not added any control in the UI. But, in the **Live Visual Tree** explorer, you can see that there are many other items in between `MainWindow` and `Grid`, which generally renders by the Presentation Framework automatically. It's called the visual representation of the XAML UI.

As Visual Studio 2017 supports XAML modifications while the application is running in debug mode, let's add a `ListBox` control inside the `Grid` tag and add some static strings as `ListBoxItem`, without closing the running app:

```
<Grid>
  <ListBox>
    <ListBoxItem>Item 1</ListBoxItem>
    <ListBoxItem>Item 2</ListBoxItem>
    <ListBoxItem>Item 3</ListBoxItem>
    <ListBoxItem>Item 4</ListBoxItem>
  </ListBox>
</Grid>
```

Once you add the preceding XAML code in the XAML editor of Visual Studio, the application UI will automatically refresh and show you a list box with the added strings. The **Live Visual Tree** explorer will also get an update to reflect the added control:

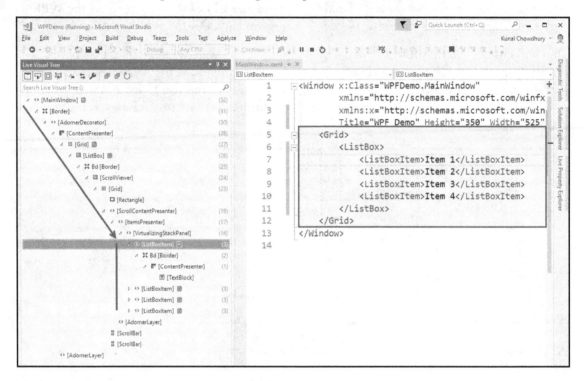

As shown in the preceding screenshot, the `ListBox` control will get placed in the Grid but the items inside the `ListBox` control (named as `ListBoxItem`) will be placed multiple layers down in the Visual Tree accompanied by `Border`, `ScrollViewer`, `Grid`, and other layout panels.

This is how the XAML controls actually render in the UI. The more levels of elements you have in a Visual Tree, the more performance issues it may hit. Detecting and eliminating unnecessary elements in the Visual Tree is just one of the major advantages of the **Live Visual Tree** debugger window.

You can also inspect the Visual Tree representation of any control from the UI by using the **Enable Selection** control. Switch to your application UI and, as shown in the following screenshot, click the second icon (**Enable Selection**) of the XAML debugger toolbox.

Now, hover over the application UI to see a dotted adorner on the controls that you are hovering on. Click the one that you want to see in the **Live Visual Tree** explorer and it will directly navigate you to the selected item, as shown in the following screenshot:

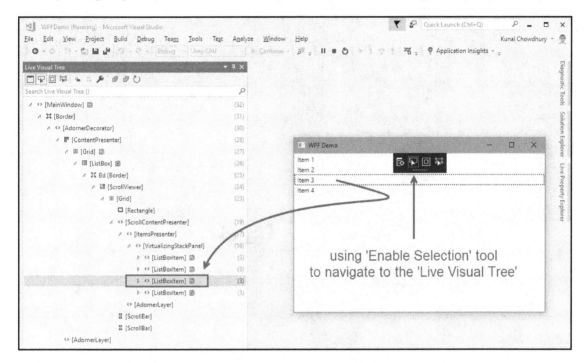

Visual Studio 2017 also supports modification of the selected element in the **Live Visual Tree** window. This you can do in the **Live Property Explorer** window. In case it does not show up automatically, you can invoke it by navigating to the Visual Studio menu **Debug | Windows | Live Property Explorer**.

As shown in the following screenshot, select the third `ListBox` item and change its text by modifying the content property at runtime. You will see that the value that you entered in the **Live Property Explorer** window gets automatically updated in the UI:

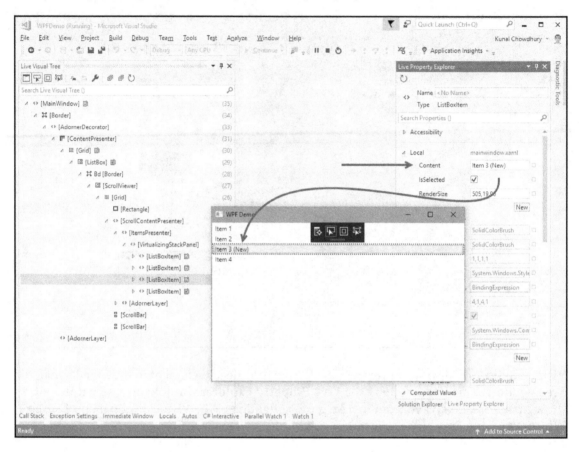

In the **Live Property Explorer** window you will find most of the properties disabled. This is because those are either inherited from implicit/explicit styles or have default values. To experiment with the UI element properties, you should modify the properties inside the **Local** panel.

To override an existing property value of the selected element from the Live Visual Tree, click the **New** button present in the **Local** panel:

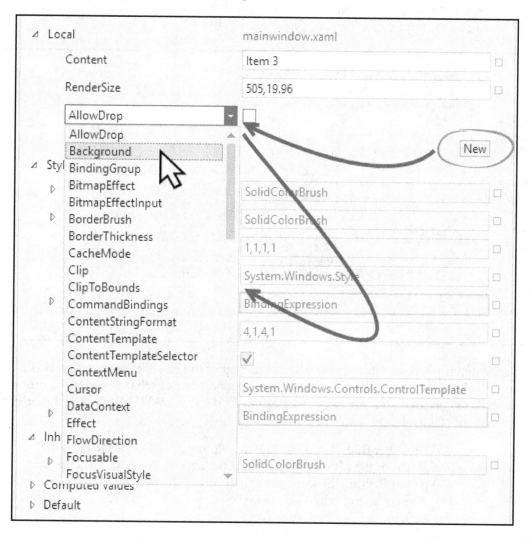

This will add a dropdown list in the panel, where you will be able to select the property that you want to change. When you select the property, the panel will get populated with the appropriate property boxes to fill it.

Let's add a **Background** property to the third `ListBox` item and set the color as Red (**#FFFF0000**) to it. You will see that it will get **SolidColorBrush** with the color value that you have entered. Activate the application window to see the visual representation of the property live in the application window, as shown in the following screenshot:

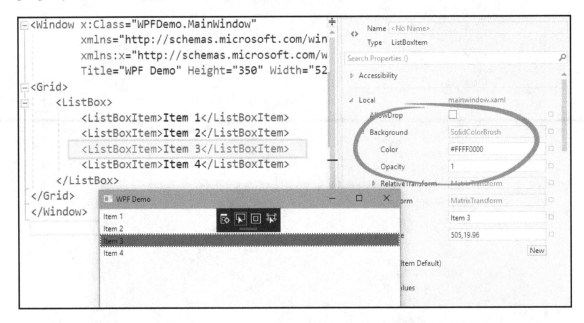

Do notice that the actual element in the XAML designer did not get the changes. This is because the Live Property Explorer only gives you a preview of what you want to modify in runtime. Based on that, you can change the original UI in the XAML view or designer view for permanent changes.

> Do remember that, if you end the debugging session, the changes that you performed in the **Live Property Explorer** window will get lost and when you restart it, you will see fresh values as per the default.
>
> This is often useful when you want to see the changes live at runtime for any element inside the Visual Tree.

To permanently set the properties of any UI element while the application is running in debug mode, either use the XAML code view or the XAML designer view. The running application will automatically get the update of the style changes as shown in the following screenshot:

Enabling UI debugging tools for XAML

In case you could not see the UI debugging tools on the application while running in debug mode, this could be because the **Enable UI Debugging Tools for XAML** option is turned off. When this is disabled, you will not be able to view the **Live Visual Tree** and **Live Properties** window.

To enable the XAML debugging tools, go to the Visual Studio options from the **Tools |
Options...** menu. Now, from the **Debugging | General** section of the **Options** window,
select the checkbox, **Enable UI Debugging Tools for XAML**, as shown in the following
screenshot:

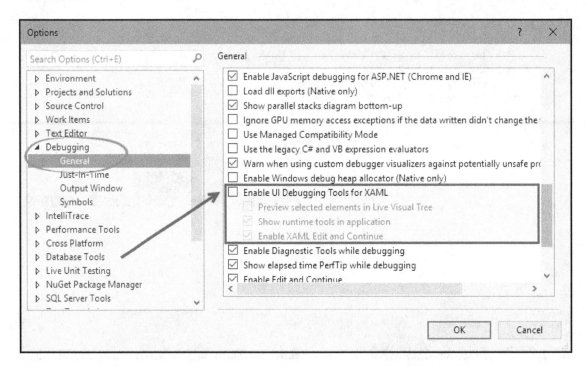

To be able to change the XAML elements and their properties when the application is
already running in debug mode, check the **Enable XAML Edit and Continue** option. If you
modify this option, you need to restart the debugging process for the changes to take effect.

Summary

In this chapter, we learned about the debugger execution steps and how to debug C# code using breakpoints. Here we covered organizing breakpoints, setting conditional breakpoints, hit counters, breakpoint filters, actions, and labels. We also covered how to manage breakpoints in code using the **Breakpoints** window of the Visual Studio debugger tools and discussed how to import/export them.

Apart from this, we discussed Data Tips in detail. We discussed pinning/unpinning Data Tips and the various watch windows, visualizers, importing/exporting Data Tips, and the usages of the debugger display attribute.

At the end, we discussed **Immediate Window**, **Visual Studio Diagnostics Tools**, the all new Run to Click feature, debugging an existing process, and debugging the UI of an XAML application. The XAML debugging covered the **Live Visual Tree**, and **Live Property Explorer** window, and how to edit an XAML page while the application is running in debug mode.

In the next chapter, we will cover testing applications using Visual Studio 2017. There we will discuss how to use the new **Live Unit Testing** feature to automatically run the impacted unit tests to visualize the result and code coverage in the background, as and when you are editing the code.

8
Live Unit Testing with Visual Studio 2017

In computer programming, **Unit Testing** is a software development and testing process by which the smallest testable parts of source code, called **units**, are tested to determine whether they are performing as per the design. Unit testing is generally part of an automation process, but you can run it manually too.

Visual Studio 2017 has a new productivity feature called **Live Unit Testing**, which is currently available in the Enterprise edition and only for C#/VB.NET projects that target the Microsoft .NET Framework.

Keeping a baseline on an understanding of the basics of the Unit Testing process, in this chapter, we are going to discuss only the new feature Live Unit Testing and will cover the following points:

- Overview of Live Unit Testing in Visual Studio 2017
    - Unit testing framework support
    - Understanding the coverage information shown in the editor
    - Integration of Live Unit Testing in **Test Explorer**
- Configuring Visual Studio 2017 for Live Unit Testing
    - Installing the Live Unit Testing component
    - General settings of Live Unit Testing in Visual Studio
    - Starting/pausing the Live Unit Testing
    - Including and excluding test methods/projects

- Unit testing with Visual Studio 2017
    - Getting started with configuring the testing project
    - Understanding the package config
    - Live Unit Testing with an example
- Navigating to failed tests

Overview of Live Unit Testing in Visual Studio 2017

The new Live Unit Testing feature in Visual Studio 2017 allows us to quickly see the code coverage details and the unit test case execution result, without leaving the code editor window. The Live Unit Testing automatically runs the impacted unit tests in the background as we edit the source code, and in real time it visualizes the unit testing result and coverage within the editor.

It currently supports C#/VB.NET projects targeting the .NET Framework, but only in Visual Studio 2017 Enterprise edition. When enabled, the unit test results and visualization of the code coverage results appear on a line-by-line basis in the editor, as shown in the following screenshot:

```
2 references
public class Math
{
    3 references | ❸ 1/2 passing
    public int Divide(int val1, int val2)
    {
        if (val2 == 0) { throw new ArgumentException(); }

        return val1 / val2;
    }
}
```

The live feedback notifies us in real time of the change that has broken the program. This way it helps you to maintain the quality of code by ensuring that the tests are always being passed as you make the changes to a new feature or a bug fix.

In the preceding screenshot, check the left-hand side bar, which has green ✓ marks and red ✗ icons. This provides live notification of the unit test results.

Unit testing framework support

At present, the Live Unit Testing in Visual Studio 2017 Enterprise edition supports only three popular unit testing frameworks, namely xUnit, NUnit, and MSTest. But there are a few supportive version specifications that you must meet for Visual Studio unit testing adapter and unit testing framework, as mentioned here:

- **xUnit**: Framework version 2.0 or higher, adapter version 2.2.0 or higher
- **NUnit**: Framework version 3.5.0 or higher, NUnit3Test adapter version 3.5.1 or higher
- **MSTest**: Framework version 1.0.5 or higher, MSTest test adapter version 1.1.4 or higher

In case you have an older version of the test framework references and/or adapter version in your existing projects, make sure that you remove those and add the new references for Live Unit Testing.

Understanding the coverage information shown in editor

When you enable Live Unit Testing, the Visual Studio code editor provides you sufficient information to notify of the changes that you are working on in the code coverage. It also provides you with real-time unit test results by displaying icons in the left-hand side bar. It's known as **coverage visualization**, and you can visualize it on a line-by-line basis in the editor:

- The blue dash (▬) indicates that the line of executable code does not have any test coverage.
- The green check mark (✓) indicates that the line of executable code is covered by passing unit test cases.
- The red cross mark (✗) indicates that the line was executed, but at least one unit test case was failed.
- When you see a blue dash with a clock icon (⏱), it indicates that the line of executable code does not have any test coverage at this moment, but it is processing the changes that have been made and is going to update the visualization with refreshed data.
- When a green check mark comes with a clock icon (✓⏱), it indicates that the data is not up to date for the test case that passed earlier.

- The red cross mark with a clock icon (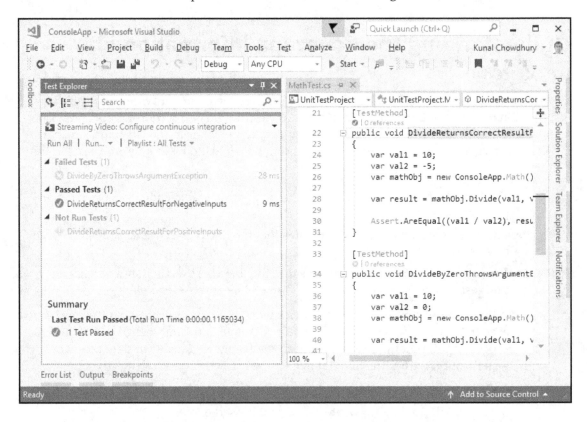) denotes a failed test case for which the data is not yet up-to-date. When processing the changes, the visualization will update automatically with new data.

Integration of Live Unit Testing in Test Explorer

Visual Studio 2017 provides a seamless coding and testing environment. The Live Unit Testing and the **Test Explorer** inside Visual Studio are synchronized to give a proficient coverage over the unit test execution throughout the project/solution.

While you are modifying the existing code, the Live Unit Testing executes in the background for the impacted test cases for which you are changing the code, and based on that, it lists the result in the **Test Explorer** automatically, and in well-defined text.

When there are some non-impacted test cases available, those get listed as dimmed:

Configuring Visual Studio 2017 for Live Unit Testing

The component Live Unit Testing comes with Visual Studio 2017 Enterprise edition only. To use it, you must first install the component from the Visual Studio installer and configure it as an optional setting.

You can start/pause/stop using the Live Unit Testing module at any point of time. You can also include/exclude unit test cases to run as part of Live Unit Testing.

In this section, we are going to discuss all of these topics. Let's first start with the installation of the component.

Installing Live Unit Testing component

To install the Live Unit Testing component in an existing installation of Visual Studio 2017 Enterprise edition, run the installer and modify the existing installation. Now navigate to the **Individual components** tab. Scroll down to the section marked **Development activities** and select the **Live Unit Testing** component as shown in the following screenshot. If it is already checked, that means the component is already installed:

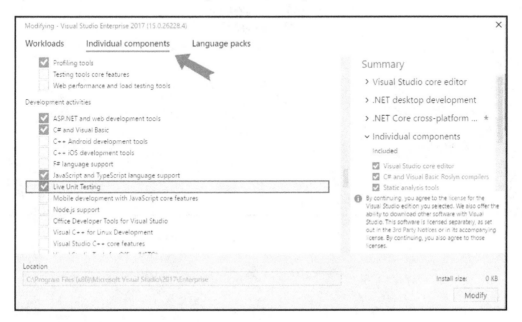

Based on your selection, click on the button **Modify** or OK. The component will not take more than 3 MB of installation space.

General settings of Live Unit Testing in Visual Studio

There are a few configurable options available for Live Unit Testing, which you can modify if you want to. To do so, navigate to **Options** from the **Tools** menu. Now, from the left pane, select **Live Unit Testing | General**.

In the right pane, there are a couple of settings available, as shown in the following screenshot:

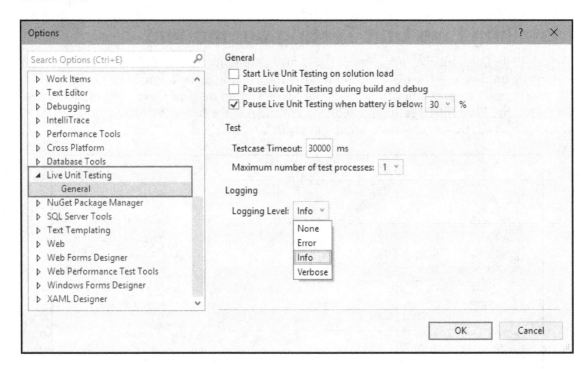

The first option enables you to control whether the Live Unit Testing runs automatically on solution load. The second option enables you to control whether the Live Unit Testing will pause while building and/or debugging is in progress. The third option will let you pause the automatic test execution when the battery power falls below a threshold value. By default, it is set to **30%**.

In this screen, you can also control the **Testcase Timeout** in milliseconds, which is **30000 ms** (30 secs) by default. You can also set the number of test processes that the Live Unit Testing will create.

Aside from these, you can set the logging level of Live Unit Testing. When it is set to **None**, there won't be any automatic logging performed; when it is set to **Error** or **Info**, only error messages or informational messages will get logged based on the selection. Set it to **Verbose**, if you want to log every detail. The default logging level is **Info**.

Starting/pausing the Live Unit Testing

To enable the Live Unit Testing to work, navigate to the **Test** | **Live Unit Testing** menu and click on **Start**, as shown in the following screenshot:

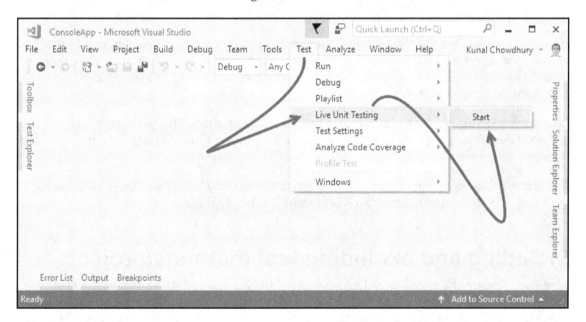

There exist some cases where you want to pause or stop the automatic execution of the Live Unit Testing process. Visual Studio 2017 allows you to temporarily pause or stop it. You can even restart the process. To invoke any of these commands, navigate to the **Test | Live Unit Testing** menu and click on the respective menu items as per your need:

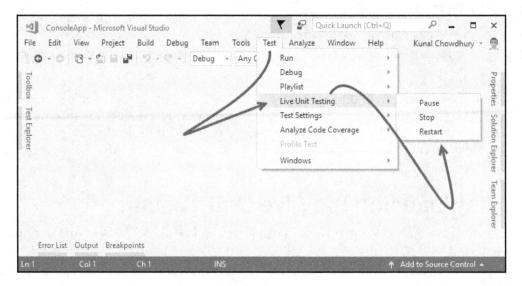

When you pause the Live Unit Testing, there won't be any coverage visualization in the Visual Studio editor as the process will go into a temporary suspended state. When you want to resume, click on **Continue**, and it will do the necessary work to update the visualization as soon as it can.

To completely stop the Live Unit Testing process, click on **Stop**. This will remove all the collected data from the process. When you start the process again, it takes longer to load the data and update the visualization.

Restarting is like stopping the process and starting it again. Thus, it also loses all the loaded data and reloads it, making it take longer to update the glyphs.

Including and excluding test methods/projects

Live Unit Testing always runs in the background to give you real-time data of the unit testing result and code coverage. But there exist some cases where you don't want to run all the cases. This may be because of some projects, classes, or methods in a solution that you don't modify for a prolonged period. Unnecessarily running all those cases is just an overhead.

Visual Studio 2017 provides you with an option to include/exclude a specific method, class, or a test project selectively. You can right-click inside a method, select **Live Tests** from the context menu, and then **Include** or **Exclude**. This will internally mark the selected method to be included or excluded from Live Unit Testing as per your choice and save the information in the user settings. When you reopen the solution, the same information will be remembered by Visual Studio:

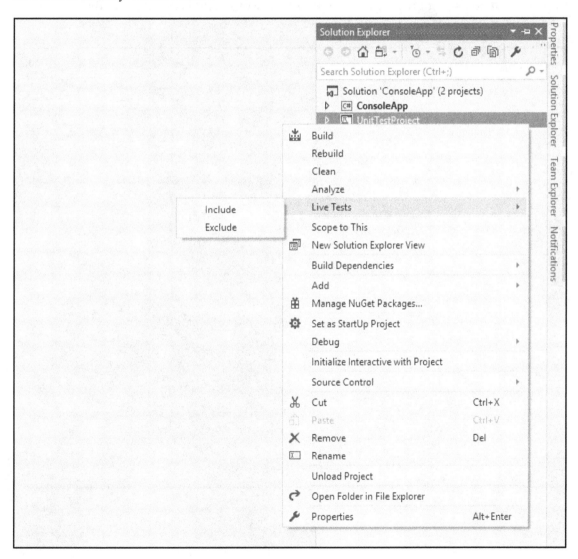

If you want to include/exclude a specific class, do these same steps by right-clicking inside a class but outside a method. To include/exclude an entire file, right-click outside the class but within the file. All test cases in that file will be either included or excluded, based on your choice.

You can also individually include/exclude a test project. Right-click on that project and from the context menu select **Live Tests** and then **Include** or **Exclude**, as shown in the following screenshot:

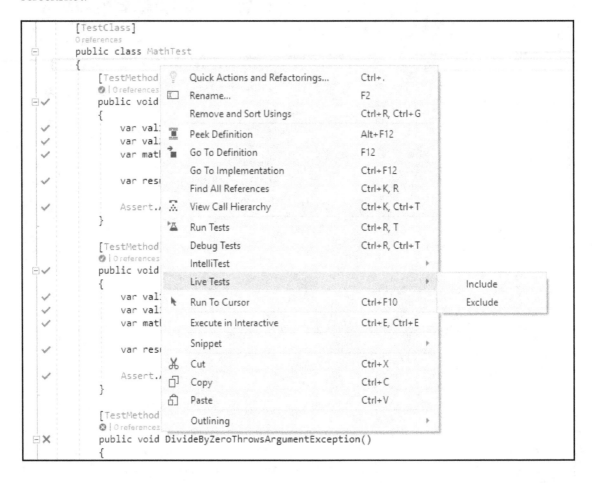

Unit testing with Visual Studio 2017

As we have already discussed this new feature, its configuration settings, and the way to start and stop live unit testing, let's begin demonstrating with a live example. Let's first create a console application for a demo.

Getting started with configuring the testing project

Open your Visual Studio 2017 IDE, go to **File | New | Project| Console App (.NET Framework)** as the project template. Create the project by giving it a name (in this example, we are naming it `ConsoleApp`).

Now, create a class named `Person` and inherit it from the `ICloneable` interface (just for this demonstration). Implement the interface to generate a `Clone()` method, which will by default throw `NotImplementedException`. Leave it as it is; we are going to revisit this method later. Add few string properties named `ID`, `Name`, and `Address`. Here's the implementation of the class, for reference:

```
public class Person : ICloneable
{
  public string ID { get; set; }

  public string Name { get; set; }

  public string Address { get; set; }

  public object Clone()
  {
    throw new NotImplementedException();
  }
}
```

As we have our `Person` class in our application project, let us create the unit testing project for testing and code coverage. Right-click on the solution file in **Solution Explorer** and navigate to **Add | New Project...** from the Visual Studio context menu. This will open the **Add New Project** dialog on the screen. Select the project type **Unit Test Project (.NET Framework)** from the **Test** category, give it a name (for example, `TestConsoleApp`) and click **OK** to create the unit testing project in the same solution:

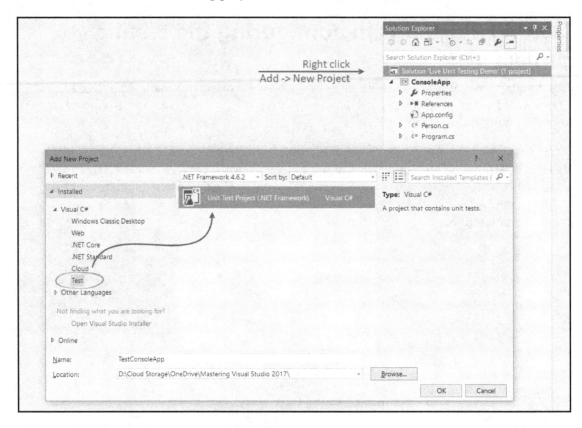

Once the unit testing project gets created in the solution, add the assembly reference of the main project into it to refer the classes available there. Right-click on the unit testing project and, from the context menu, select **Add | Reference**. From the **Reference Manager** dialog window, navigate to **Projects | Solution** and then select the projects that you want to add as references. Finally, click on **OK** to continue.

Understanding the package config

Once you add the project reference to the unit testing project, the IDE adds a few additional assemblies into the testing project. These are used to add support to the testing framework:

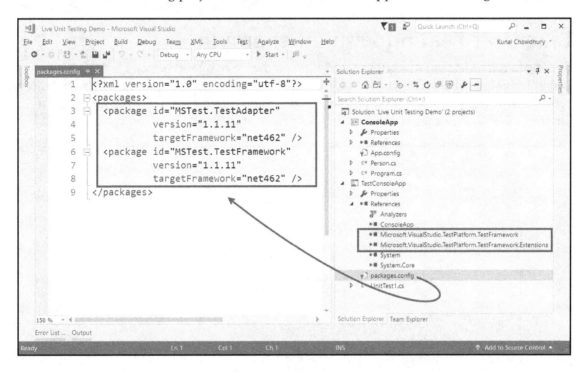

If you expand the `References` folder of the **TestConsoleApp** project, you will see two assembly references **Microsoft.VisualStudio.TestPlatform.TestFramework** and **Microsoft.VisualStudio.TestPlatform.TestFramework.Extensions**, along with the reference of our main project. These two DLL references are the core files that are needed for the unit testing project to function.

In the same project, you will find a file named `packages.config`, which defines the packages required for the unit testing to create the test adapter with the referenced project. The file content will look like the following XML content, with `MSTest.TestAdapter` and `MSTest.TestFramework` defined in it:

```
<?xml version="1.0" encoding="utf-8"?>
<packages>
  <package id="MSTest.TestAdapter"
        version="1.1.11"
        targetFramework="net462" />
```

```
<package id="MSTest.TestFramework"
        version="1.1.11"
        targetFramework="net462" />
</packages>
```

Live Unit Testing with an example

Let's open the `UnitTest1.cs` file and add the following two test methods in it. The first one will create two instances of the `Person` class and check to ensure that both the instances are different. The second method will create one instance of the `Person` class, assign it to another variable, and check to ensure that both the instances are equal:

```
6        [TestClass]
         0 references
7        public class UnitTest1
8        {
9            [TestMethod]
             ● | 0 references
10           public void TestTwoInstanceOfPersonInstancesAreNotEqual()
11           {
12               var person1 = new Person();
13               var person2 = new Person();
14
15               var status = person1 == person2;
16
17               Assert.IsFalse(status);
18           }
19
20           [TestMethod]
             ● | 0 references
21           public void TestAssigningOneObjectToAnotherReferencesSameObject()
22           {
23               var person1 = new Person();
24               var person2 = person1;
25
26               var status = person1 == person2;
27
28               Assert.IsTrue(status);
29           }
```

When you start writing the code line-by-line, you will see that the Live Unit Testing will run in the background and provide the status of the code coverage and test results at the left-hand side bar. Here, in the preceding screenshot, every line generates a green check mark (✔) indicating that the written test cases have passed and all the lines have been covered.

In case you are unable to see the live unit test working, refer to the *Configuring Visual Studio 2017 for Live Unit Testing* section of this chapter.

When you have any unit test method fail, the icon will change to a red cross mark (✘) at the line where it failed. Refer to the *Overview to Live Unit Testing in Visual Studio 2017* and *Understanding the coverage information shown in editor* sections of this chapter for more details about the various icons shown in the editor.

Let's create another two test methods that will call the `Clone()` method of the class. Here, the live unit test will break at the same line where the method has been called and indicate it with a red cross mark, as you can see in the following screenshot:

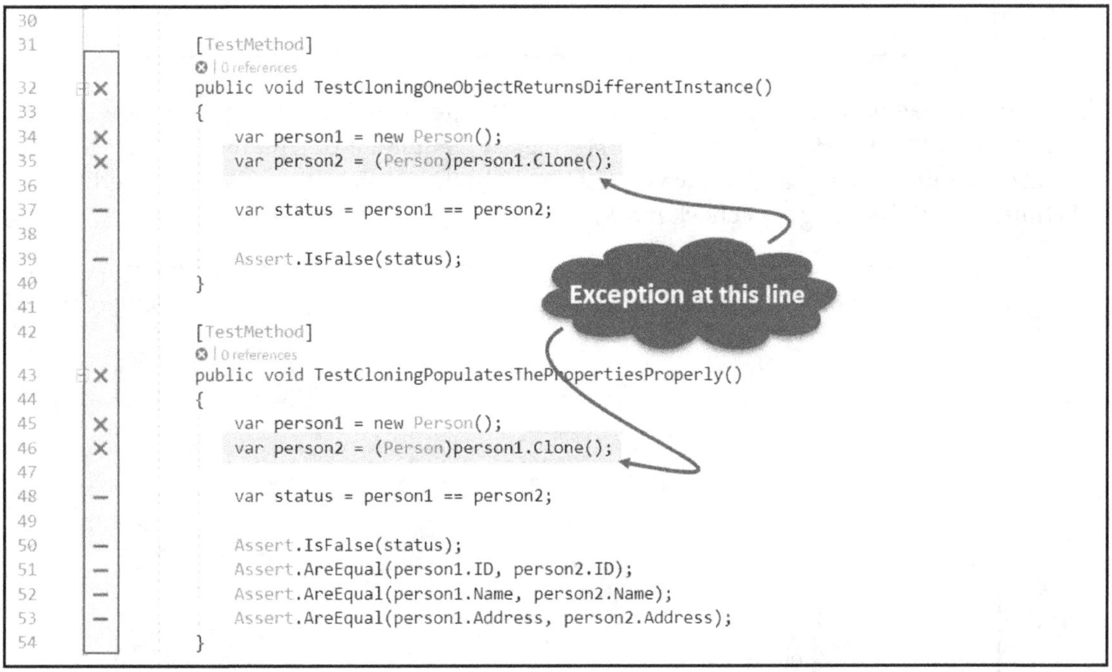

```
30
31            [TestMethod]
              ❸ | 0 references
32    ✘       public void TestCloningOneObjectReturnsDifferentInstance()
33            {
34    ✘           var person1 = new Person();
35    ✘           var person2 = (Person)person1.Clone();
36
37    ─           var status = person1 == person2;
38
39    ─           Assert.IsFalse(status);              Exception at this line
40            }
41
42            [TestMethod]
              ❸ | 0 references
43    ✘       public void TestCloningPopulatesThePropertiesProperly()
44            {
45    ✘           var person1 = new Person();
46    ✘           var person2 = (Person)person1.Clone();
47
48    ─           var status = person1 == person2;
49
50    ─           Assert.IsFalse(status);
51    ─           Assert.AreEqual(person1.ID, person2.ID);
52    ─           Assert.AreEqual(person1.Name, person2.Name);
53    ─           Assert.AreEqual(person1.Address, person2.Address);
54            }
```

In the preceding example, the `Clone()` method call breaks as it throws a `NotImplementedException`. The rest of the lines of the said test methods will be decorated with a blue dash mark (─) as these are all unreachable codes.

Let's revisit the `Person` class, where you will see the following status notification from the Live Unit Testing framework:

```
7 references
public class Person : ICloneable
{
    2 references | ✗ 0/1 passing
    public string ID { get; set; }

    2 references | ✗ 0/1 passing
    public string Name { get; set; }

    2 references | ✗ 0/1 passing
    public string Address { get; set; }

    2 references | ✗ 0/2 passing
    public object Clone()
    {
        throw new NotImplementedException();
    }
}
```

Now, move ahead and implement the body of the `Clone()` method, which will now return an object by calling the `MemberwiseClone()` method. After a moment, the live unit test will execute automatically and show you the status in the left-hand side bar of the editor. This time, all will have a green check mark:

```
7 references
public class Person : ICloneable
{
    2 references | 1/1 passing
    public string ID { get; set; }

    2 references | 1/1 passing
    public string Name { get; set; }

    2 references | 1/1 passing
    public string Address { get; set; }

    2 references | 2/2 passing
    public object Clone()
    {
        return MemberwiseClone();
    }
}
```

Let's navigate to the test class. You will see that the code coverage is now 100% for those two methods. You will also see that all the test methods have passed. This way, the framework ensures that the cases execute while you write the code, and give you live feedback of the changes that you performed, thus reducing the extra effort of executing the test cases manually:

```
31          [TestMethod]
            ⊘ | 0 references
32          public void TestCloningOneObjectReturnsDifferentInstance()
33          {
34              var person1 = new Person();
35              var person2 = (Person)person1.Clone();
36
37              var status = person1 == person2;
38
39              Assert.IsFalse(status);
40          }
41
42          [TestMethod]
            ⊘ | 0 references
43          public void TestCloningPopulatesThePropertiesProperly()
44          {
45              var person1 = new Person();
46              var person2 = (Person)person1.Clone();
47
48              var status = person1 == person2;
49
50              Assert.IsFalse(status);
51              Assert.AreEqual(person1.ID, person2.ID);
52              Assert.AreEqual(person1.Name, person2.Name);
53              Assert.AreEqual(person1.Address, person2.Address);
54          }
```

Navigating to failed tests

Visual Studio 2017 allows you to quickly navigate to the failed tests and gain an understanding of their failings. You can click on (✓) or (✗) to see how many tests were being hit by the given line that you clicked:

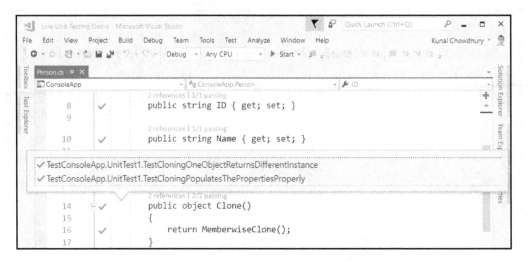

When you hover over a failed test in the tooltip, it provides additional information with `StackTrace` to provide you more with more insight of the failure:

Summary

In this chapter, we learned about the new Live Unit Testing feature of Visual Studio 2017. Here we discussed the supported unit testing framework and adapters to run Live Unit Testing inside the IDE. We also discussed the coverage information shown in the editor and the integration in **Test Explorer**.

Then we learned how to configure Visual Studio for Live Unit Testing. There we discussed how to install the component by running the installer, and how to use the general settings. We also discussed how to start/stop/pause the Live Unit Testing and how to include any specific test methods/projects to show the real-time unit testing status and code coverage.

Later in this chapter, we demonstrated how to create a unit testing project, configure the unit testing framework, and use it in real time with a simple example. At the end, we discussed the ways to navigate to failed tests and grab more details out of them.

In the next chapter, we will discuss **Microsoft Azure** and learn how to accelerate cloud development with it to build and manage Azure websites and Azure app services.

9

Accelerate Cloud Development with Microsoft Azure

Microsoft Azure is an open, flexible, enterprise-grade cloud computing platform from Microsoft which was first released as **Windows Azure** on February 1, 2010 and then got renamed as **Microsoft Azure** on March 25, 2014. You can build, deploy, and manage applications and services using the Azure portal, globally available through the Microsoft data centers.

It basically delivers **IaaS (Infrastructure as a Service)**, **PaaS (Platform as a Service)**, and **SaaS (Software as a Service)** and supports different programming languages, tools, and frameworks to build and manage applications/services.

In this chapter, we will discuss the following topics:

- Understanding the cloud computing basics
  - Infrastructure as a Service
  - Platform as a Service
  - Software as a Service
- Creating your free Azure account
- Configuring Visual Studio 2017 for Azure development
- Creating an Azure website from the portal
  - Creating a web application
  - Creating an App Service Plan
- Managing Azure websites (web apps) from the portal

- Creating an Azure website from Visual Studio
    - Creating an ASP.NET web application
    - Publishing the web application to cloud
- Updating an existing Azure website from Visual Studio
- Building a Mobile App Service
    - Creating an Azure mobile app
    - Preparing an Azure mobile app for data connectivity
    - Adding a SQL data connection
    - Creating a SQL database
- Integrating a Mobile App Service in a Windows application
    - Creating the model and service client
    - Integrating the API call
- Scaling an App Service Plan

Understanding the cloud computing basics

Cloud computing is a very broad concept. When you or your business need to consider cloud services for your infrastructure or application deployment, you should understand the basics of it. Generally, there are three types of cloud computing models:

- Infrastructure as a Service
- Platform as a Service
- Software as a Service

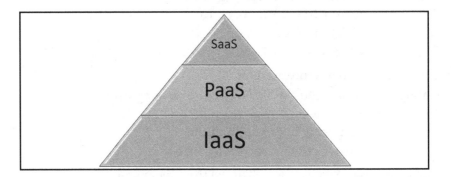

Infrastructure as a Service creates the main building blocks, **Platform as a Service** comes on top of it, giving you another platform to use **Software as a Service**. Software as a Service stays at the highest block of the cloud computing system. Let's discuss all these basic service blocks in detail with the following diagram:

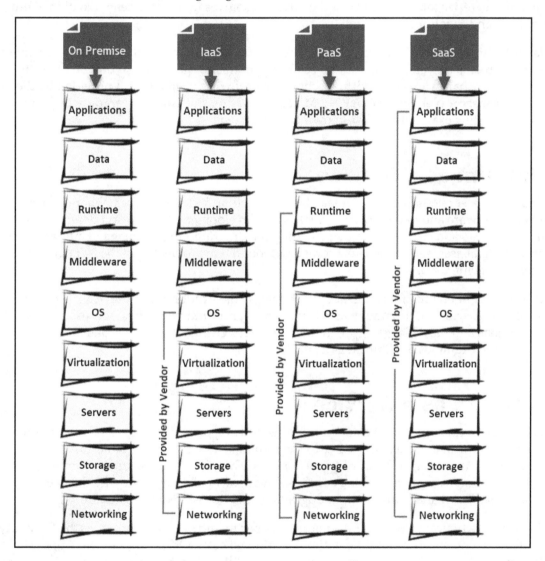

Infrastructure as a Service

In the fundamental building blocks of cloud computing resources, IaaS takes the physical computer hardware to build a virtual infrastructure to utilize the resources. You can create, reconfigure, resize, or remove any of the virtual resources in the data centers within a few moments and monitor them remotely.

IaaS is the most flexible cloud computing model and allows you to automate deployment of servers, process power, storage, and networking. In this service model, you don't have to purchase any hardware as the virtual ecosystem is already available and provided by the vendor. **Amazon Web Service (AWS)**, **Microsoft Azure**, and **Google Compute Engine (GCE)** are a few examples of well-known IaaS providers.

Platform as a Service

PaaS comes just one step above the IaaS block, which provides a platform where you can develop software and deploy them. It makes the development, testing, and deployment simpler, faster, and cost effective by providing the programming language to interact with services, databases, servers, and/or storage without having to deal with the infrastructure where it is being used.

As PaaS is built on top of virtualization technology, the vendor of such services provides the physical/virtual environment with frameworks and runtimes to manage your applications and data. Google App Engine, Red Hat's OpenShift, and Heroku are some well-known examples of Platform as a Service.

Software as a Service

SaaS comes at the top layer of cloud computing and is typically built on top of the solution given by Platform as a Service. SaaS uses the web to deliver software applications for end users, which are managed by third-party vendors. Thus, it's the most famous cloud service for the consumers, as it reduces the cost of software ownership by removing the need of technical staff to manage installation, upgrading, and licensing of the software.

The service is typically charged on a per user or per month basis and provides the flexibility to add or remove users at runtime without additional costs. Office 365, Google Apps, Dropbox, and OneDrive are some well-known examples of Software as a Service.

Creating your free Azure account

To get started with application development with Microsoft Azure, you will first need to have an Azure account and have a basic idea about the Azure portal. Before starting, let's first create an Azure account.

 If you want to learn and try Azure, Microsoft provides you 30 days' free trial to explore the cloud platform with a $200 free credit to your new account.

To get started with the $200 free credit, jump into the site at `https://azure.microsoft.com/en-us/free/` and click on the **Start Free** button:

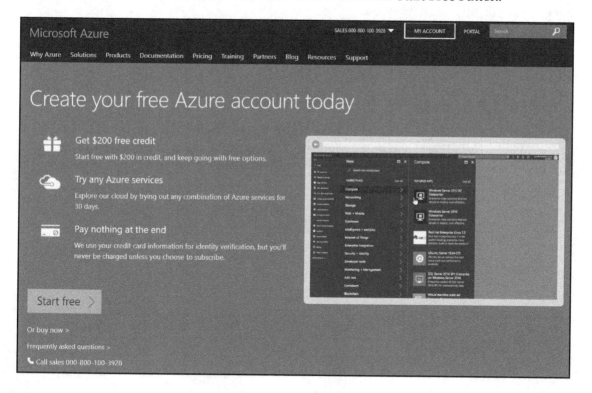

Use your Microsoft account (formerly, Windows Live ID) to log in into the portal. If you don't have a Microsoft account username, from the same screen, you will be able to create one.

Once you log in to the portal for the first time, it will ask you to verify your identity. Enter your mobile number and credit card details to verify that you are a real person. Microsoft will not charge anything on your card, but a nominal $1 charge may hold initially on your card for verification and will be removed within 3-5 days.

Once your free credit ends or you reach the expiration date, you won't be able to use the services that Azure offers unless you manually go and pay for your subscription. You can also opt for a pay-as-you-go subscription and set a monthly spending cap. In this case, when you reach that monthly spending limit, it will automatically suspend the service and won't incur you any additional costs.

Configuring Visual Studio 2017 for Azure development

Before you start building Azure applications from Visual Studio 2017, you need to configure it by installing the required workloads. If you have not already installed the Azure development workload, open your Visual Studio 2017 Installer.

As shown in the following screenshot, click on **Modify** to start customizing the instance of the IDE:

This will open the customization screen with the **Workloads** tab open. Scroll down to find the **Azure development** workload and select it. If you want to build ASP.NET applications, select the **ASP.NET and web development** workload, as shown in the following screenshot:

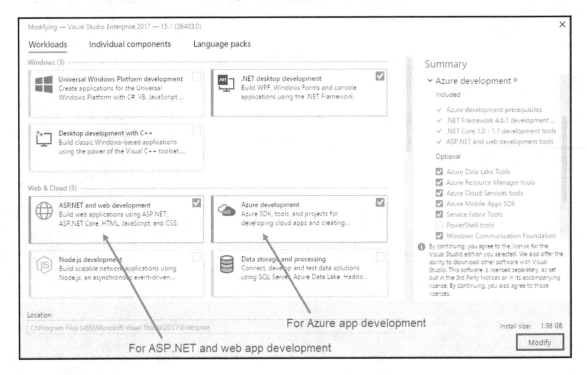

When you are ready, click the **Modify** button to start the installation process. This will take some time, based on your internet bandwidth, to download and install the required components.

Creating an Azure website from portal

Once you have your Azure account, you can visit `https://portal.azure.com` to start using the Microsoft Azure portal. When you log in to the portal, a dashboard will be shown on the screen:

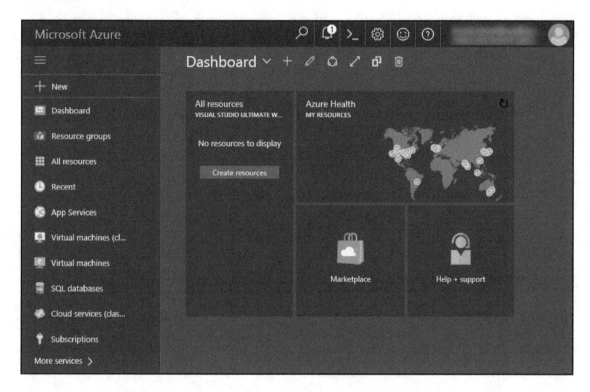

The categories present on the left side will allow you to create or manage your app services, websites, virtual machines, database, network, IoT, and many other services that Azure supports.

The Azure website comes under PaaS and provides an effortless way to build and deploy web applications. In the management portal, under the Marketplace, it's named as `Web App`. Let's start with creating our first Azure website.

Creating a web application

Once you log in to the Azure Management Portal, click on the + icon or the **+ New** label, as shown in the following screenshot. This will guide you to create any services/resources currently available in Microsoft Azure:

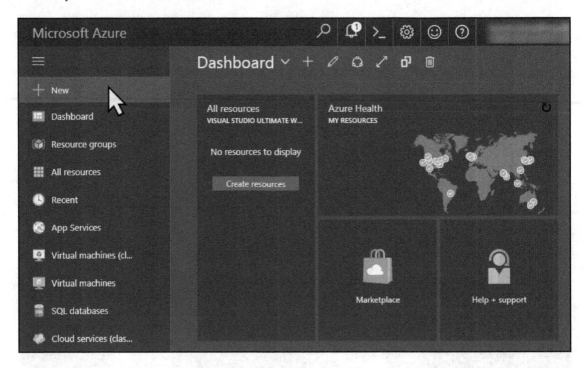

This will open a panel on the right side with a list of available resource categories from the Azure Marketplace. Select the one that you want to create. In our case, as we are going to create our website, we will select **Web + Mobile** from the list:

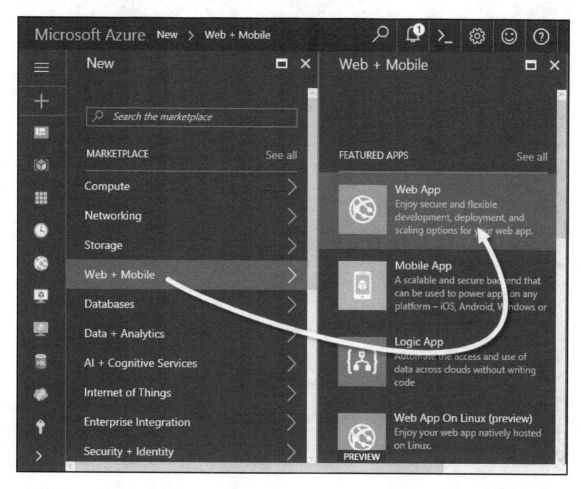

Once you select **Web + Mobile**, it will open another panel on the right side with a list of featured apps. This includes **Web App** (for websites), **Mobile App** (for secure and scalable mobile backends), **Logic App** (for automated access and use of data), **CDN** (for global distributed edge servers), **Media Services** (to encode, store and stream audio/video), and more.

As we are going to create a website, let's click the featured app titled **Web App**. This will open another new panel on the right of the screen:

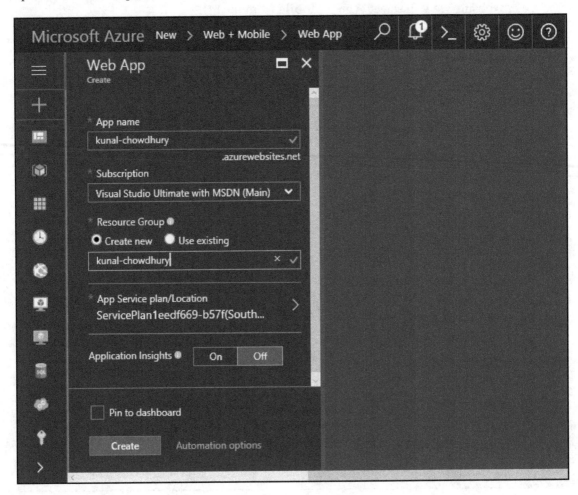

On the **Web App** screen, the wizard will ask you to input a few details. Enter a name of the application. Make sure that it is globally unique, as it's going to create a sub-domain with the same name under `azurewebsites.net`.

Select the subscription model that you are going to use. In your case, it would be different than the one shown in the preceding screenshot.

Then select the **Create new** radio button to create a new **Resource Group**. Give it a proper name. Generally, it's going to create the resource group with the same name as the application.

Creating an App Service plan

Next, you should select the **App Service plan/Location** option from the available list. **App Service plan** is the container for your app, which will determine the location, features, cost, and compute resources associated with your app. So, select it appropriately to optimize the compute cost.

In case there are no app service plans available in the list, create a new one and select it. In our case, we are going to create an App Service plan with a free pricing tier to have zero cost on hosting this demo app:

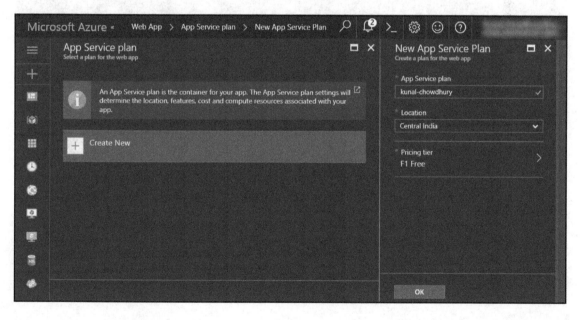

Once you select **App Service plan**, you may want to detect and diagnose the quality issues in your web applications and web services. In this case, enable **Application Insights**; otherwise, leave it as-is. When you are ready, hit the **Create** button. It will take some time for the web app to get created.

Managing Azure websites (Web Apps) from the portal

Once the web app gets created, navigate to **App Services** from the left-hand side category list as shown in the following screenshot:

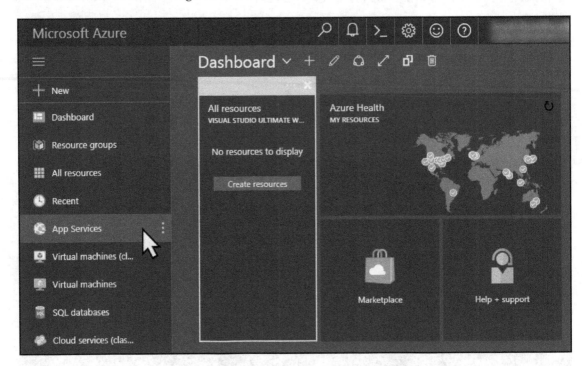

Here, it will list all the app services that you have currently hosted on your Azure account. If you have a large list, you can easily search/filter it based on the available options on this screen.

The website that we just created will get listed under this screen. Click on the name of the app that you used to create it as shown in the following screenshot:

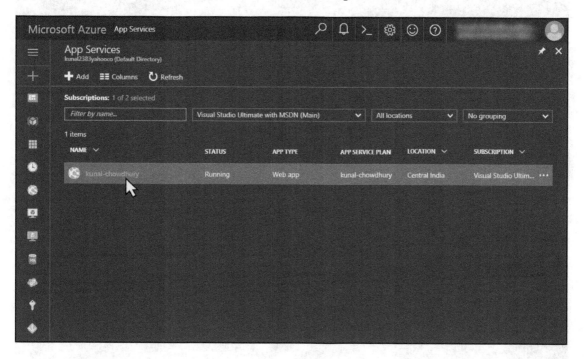

This will open another screen with detailed information about the application that you selected. Here in this screen, you can check the activity log, monitor the requests and errors, modify the access control, diagnose and solve problems, create a backup of the site, update the custom domain, and more:

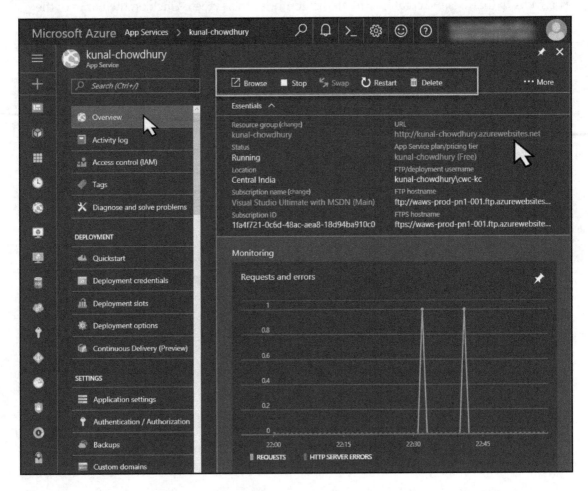

At the top of the **Overview** screen, you will find a few toolbar buttons which will allow you to browse the site, start/stop/restart the web application, and/or delete it.

The URL that was created by the name of the application (in our case, it is http://kunal-chowdhury.azurewebsites.net), when clicked, will launch the website into the browser window. A generic website from the Microsoft template will get launched, as shown in the following screenshot:

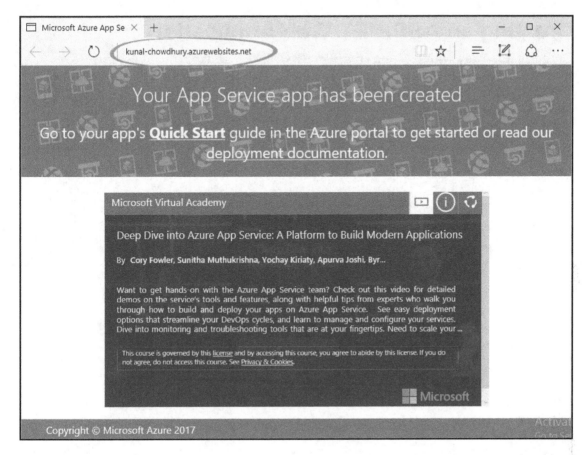

It's a default page that Microsoft provides as part of the default template. You can redesign this page and publish the entire website from Visual Studio. In the next sections, we are going to see how this can be done.

Creating an Azure website from Visual Studio

As we have already learned how to create an Azure website from the Azure Management Portal, let's learn how to create the same from Visual Studio 2017. Make sure that you have the required components/workloads already installed (see *Configuring Visual Studio 2017 for Azure development* from this chapter).

Creating an ASP.NET Web Application

Once you are ready with creating an ASP.NET website and deploying it to Azure, open your Visual Studio 2017 instance. Create a new project by navigating to **Templates** | **Visual C#** | **Cloud** and selecting **ASP.NET Web Application (.NET Framework),** as shown in the following **New Project** dialog:

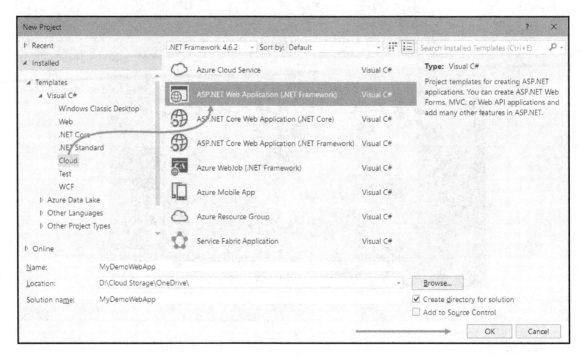

Give your project a name and click the **OK** button to start creating your web application from a template. The next screen will guide you to select the template that you want to use. There exists a number of templates (**Empty**, **Web Forms**, **MVC**, **Web API**, **Azure Mobile App**, and so on) available for you to select.

We will select **Web Forms** here with **No Authentication** support. When you are ready, click **OK** to continue:

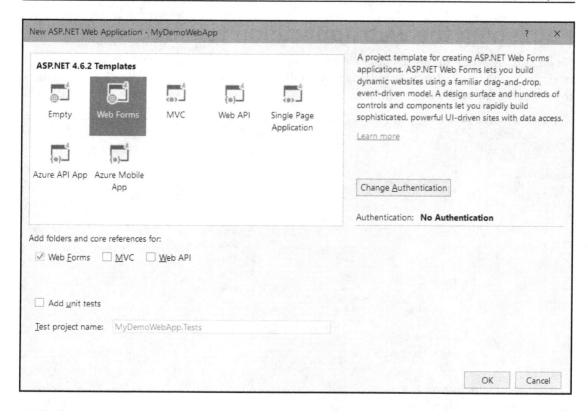

Visual Studio will then create the project based on the template and the authentication configuration that you selected on the previous screen.

Now, from the Solution Explorer, open the `Default.aspx` page. It will already have a design and content specified by Visual Studio in its template. Replace the `Content` tag with the following code:

```
<asp:Content ID="BodyContent" ContentPlaceHolderID="MainContent"
runat="server">
    <div class="jumbotron">
        <h1>Hello Azure Website</h1>
        <p class="lead">It is a demo application to build Azure
website.</p>
        <p><a href="http://www.kunal-chowdhury.com" class="btn btn-primary
btn-lg">
            Visit site &raquo;</a></p>
    </div>
</asp:Content>
```

Publishing the web application to cloud

When you are ready to publish it to cloud, as an Azure website, right-click on the project from the **Solution Explorer**. A context menu will pop up on the screen. Click **Publish...**, as shown in the following screenshot:

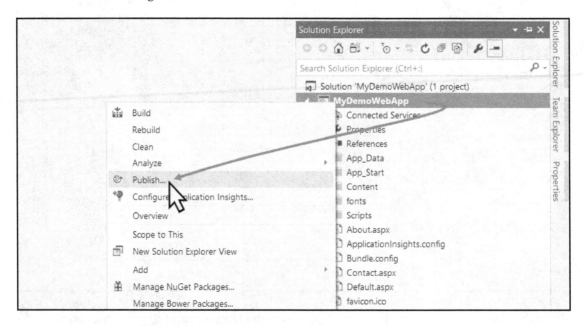

This will open the web app publishing wizard. As shown in the following screenshot, click on the **Microsoft Azure App Service** button under the **Publish** tab. There exist two radio buttons, named **Create New** and **Select Existing**. The first one will guide you to create a fresh new Azure website; whereas the other will guide you to select an existing Azure website already hosted on cloud:

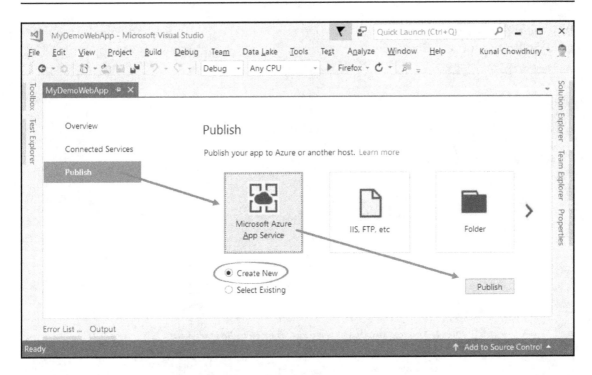

As we are going to create a new website on cloud, with a new URL, let's select the **Create New** radio option and hit on the **Publish** button.

Now, a dialog window titled **Create App Service** will pop up. On this screen, you need to first log in to your Azure account if you are not already logged in.

Provide a globally unique name for your web app, which will be used to create the website URL. Select the subscription type that you want to use to host this site:

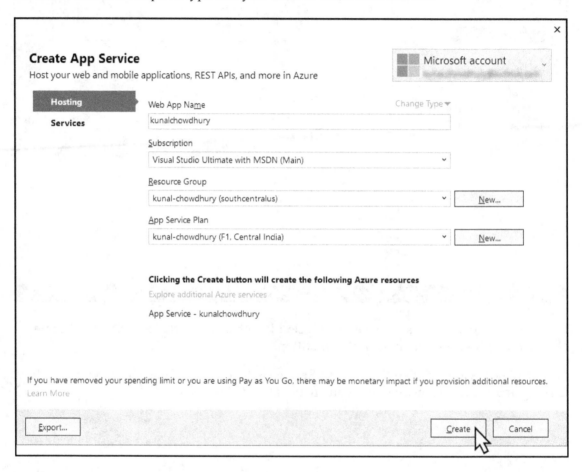

You need to select **Resource Group** from the available list. In case no resource group is available for you to use or you want to host it to a new one, hit the **New...** button and enter a name.

Now select the **App Service Plan** option from the available list. If there are no app service plans available in the list or you want to create a new plan, click on the **New...** button next to **App Service Plan**. A new window will be shown to configure a new service plan:

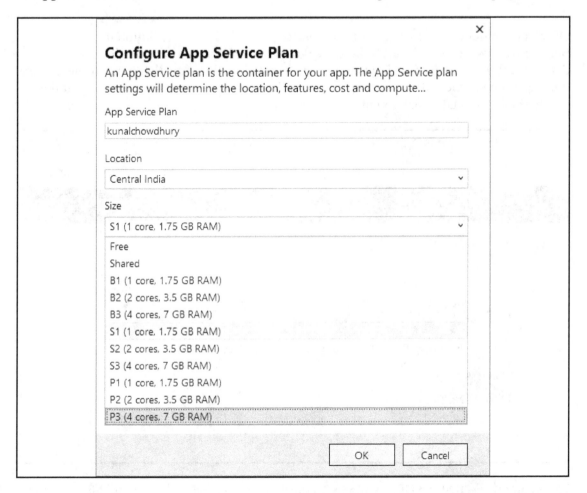

On this screen, first give your App Service plan a name so that you can easily identify it later. Select **Location**, where you want to host it. Select a proper location to optimize its usages. Lastly, select the size of the processing unit that you want to configure for this website. Select **Free** if you want it for testing/learning purpose and don't want to cut your pocket for the usages.

Do remember that, the higher the processing unit or RAM, you will find a better performance, but that will cost you more bucks due to more computing power.

Once you are done configuring your app service plan, hit the **Create** button in your **App Service** window. This will start building your project in **Release** configuration and start deploying it to Azure by creating a new website based on the name that you supplied as the Web App name. When the publishing gets complete, it will open up the browser pointing you to the website URL that you just deployed:

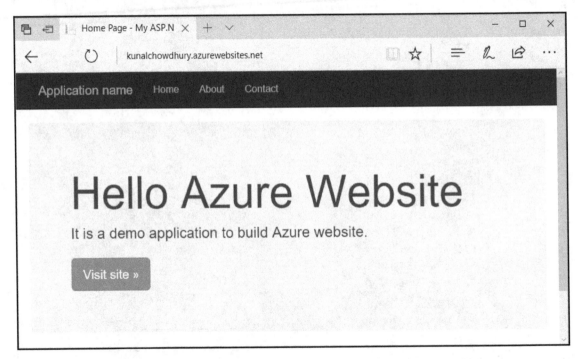

Here you can see that the URL (kunalchowdhury.azurewebsites.net) that it launched, has the same name that we provided as the app name while publishing the web app to cloud. All done! Your web app has been deployed to Azure and is running.

When you perform some updates to your web application project and want to republish the updated content to the web, right-click on the project again and click on **Publish...**. As the publishing configuration has been already created for this project, it will open the following configuration screen. You may, optionally, want to change anything here. Once you are ready, click on the **Publish** button:

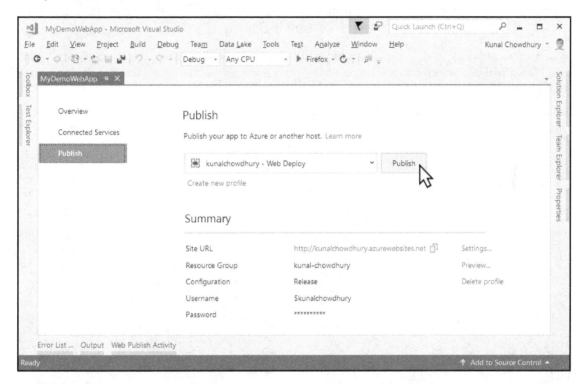

It will again build, and if there are no errors during the compilation, it will get published to the cloud account and open the browser pointing to the same URL that the app has been hosted.

Updating an existing Azure website from Visual Studio

There could be various occasions when you have a website already running on Azure and you want to update it from Visual Studio but the publishing configuration is missing in the project. In that case, perform the following simple steps:

When you are ready with your changes inside your Visual Studio project, right-click on it and click **Publish...** from the context menu. The following publishing wizard will open on the screen:

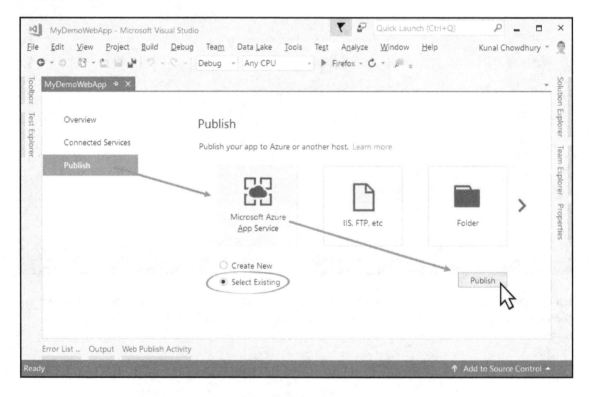

Inside the wizard, first navigate to the **Publish** tab and select the **Microsoft Azure App Service** category button, as shown in the preceding screenshot. Now, instead of selecting the **Create New** radio button, select the other one, labelled **Select Existing**, and click **Publish**.

The following **App Service** window will get launched, where you can select the already-running website to publish your current project. If you are already logged in to your Azure account, the subscription type will get populated automatically. Select the one that you want to use for this web app. Select the **Resource Group** option from the available list.

As shown in the following screenshot, another tree view list will get populated automatically based on the already-hosted apps on your Azure account. If there are no sites running, you need to go back and start from the beginning to create a new app service. In the other case, select the one where you want it to host and click **OK**:

Next, Visual Studio will show you the following screen to review the configuration details. When you are ready, just click the **Publish** button to let it compile and publish it to the website that you have already selected. Once the publishing wizard deploys to the cloud, it will open the browser window and navigate to the URL where the application got deployed:

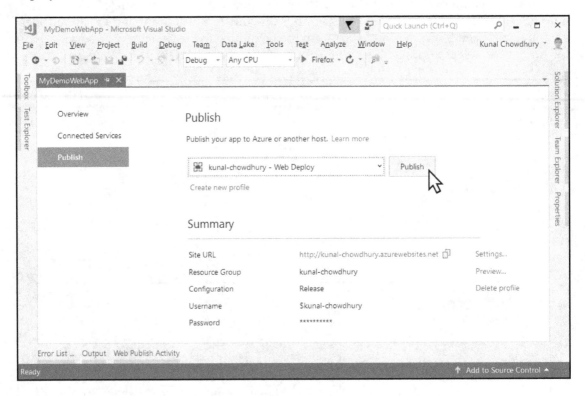

Building a Mobile App Service

Azure Mobile Apps is another type of Azure App Service run as PaaS, which runs on any platform or device, offering high scalability and global availability for enterprise-ready mobile application development platforms. Using this, you can bring a rich set of capabilities in your mobile applications.

Using the Azure Mobile Apps service, you can build native and cross-platform apps targeting Windows, iOS, and Android. You can also connect to your enterprise system or social networking sites in minutes, build offline-ready applications with data synchronization, and leverage the push notification services to engage your customers:

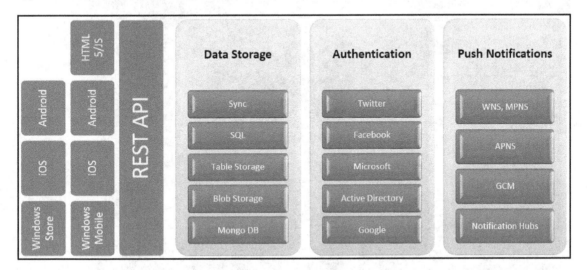

Creating Azure Mobile App

To get started, you need to create the Azure Mobile App. Log in to your Microsoft Azure portal and click on the **+** or the **+ New** button. From the wizard, select **Web + Mobile** and then **Mobile App**. This will open a new screen to enter the details about your mobile app.

Give the app a name, which should be globally unique, as it's going to create sub-domain under azurewebsites.net by the name of the app. Select the appropriate **Subscription**, create/select **Resource Group,** and select the proper **App Service plan/Location**.

When you are ready, click on the **Create** button to start creating the Azure Mobile App. This will now provision an Azure Mobile App backend which you can use in your mobile client applications. It will take some time to complete the operation:

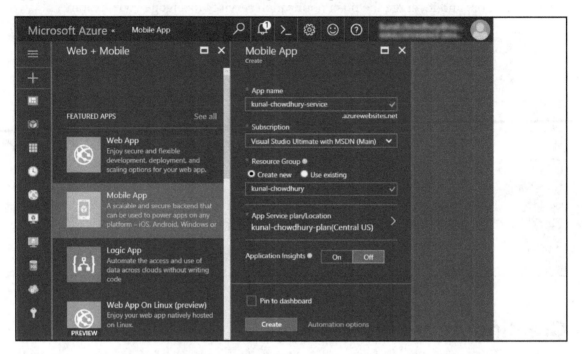

Once it gets provisioned, navigate to the **App Services** screen and click on the app name that you have just created as shown in the following screenshot:

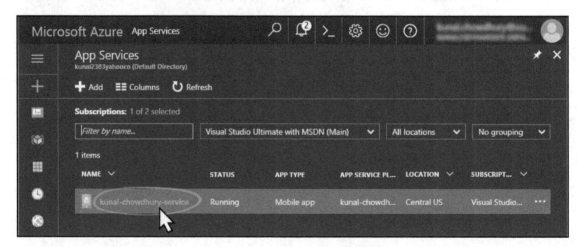

This will open the overview page of the app service, where you can get details about it. On this screen, you can also stop, restart, or delete it when you need.

Preparing Azure Mobile App for data connectivity

You may want your Azure Mobile App to connect to a SQL database hosted on Azure. To do this, you need to create the connectivity of the database and may need to create a database server too, if it is not already created.

On the service overview page, click on **Quickstart** and then select the project template that you want to integrate with. You can select Windows, iOS, Android, Xamarin, or Cordova from this screen:

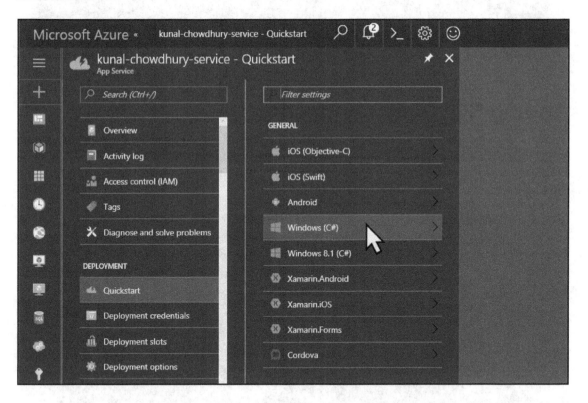

Assuming that you don't have any SQL database available on Azure, you will see the following screen. Click on the message to start creating your SQL database and then connect it with your Mobile App Service:

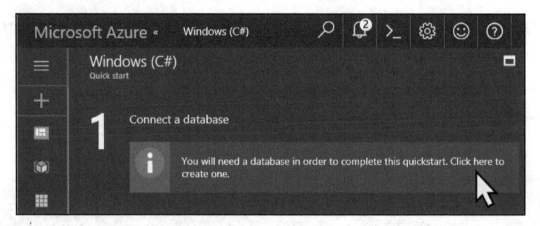

Adding SQL data connection

The following screen will pop up, asking you to create a data connection. Click on the **Add** button to add a new connection. As shown in the following screenshot, select **SQL Database** as the connection type and then click on the next item to start configuring the database settings:

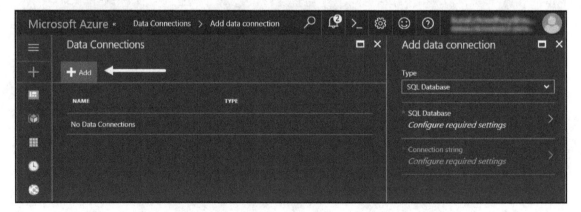

If you don't have any SQL database hosted on Azure, you need to create a new one. In case you don't have the database server, you need to create one of those too. Finally, you need to generate the connection string.

Creating a SQL Database

The Azure portal provides you with a straightforward way to create a SQL database. As shown in the following screenshot, click on the **Create a new database** button which will open another screen to ask you to enter the database name, target server, pricing tier, and so on:

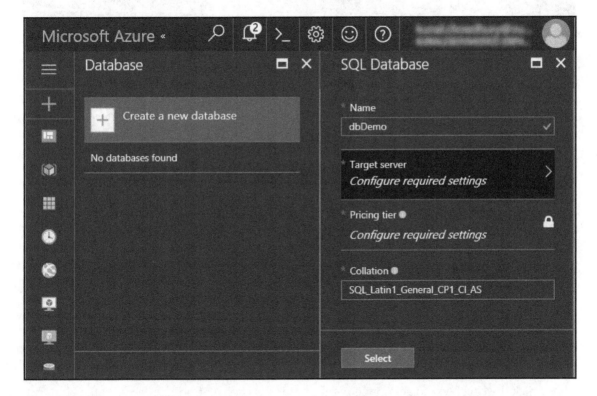

Clicking on the **Target server** option will navigate you to a different screen which will ask you to create a new DB server, if it is not already created. As shown in the following screenshot, click on the **Create a new server** button to open the **New Server** form where you need to enter details about the DB server.

Enter **Server name**, which must be globally unique, as it will create the DB server under the database.windows.net domain. Enter the other fields such as **Server admin login**, **Password**, **Location** and click on the **Select** button to continue. This will create the server and provision it, so that you can access the hosted DB server:

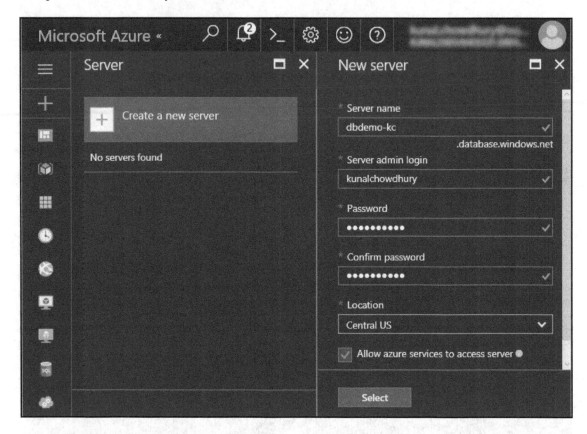

The next screen will ask you to create the Table API. You will need it to store your data to the backend. Pick the backend language from the list. You can either select **Node.js** or **C#**. Let's select **Node.js** as the language.

Now, click the checkbox to acknowledge the settings confirmation to overwrite the site content. Click on **Create TodoItem table** to continue. The `TodoItem` table is a sample DB table that the wizard will generate but if you want to create any additional tables later, you can navigate to the **Easy Tables** settings:

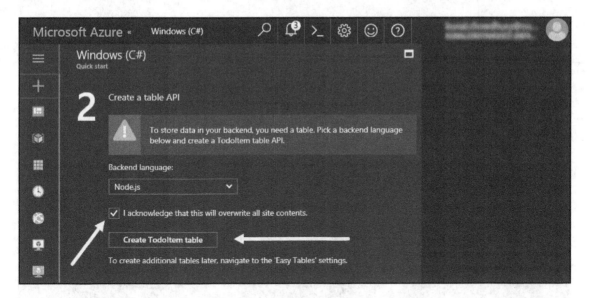

When it successfully generates a table inside your database, it will show you a green check mark beside the two settings, as shown in the following screenshot:

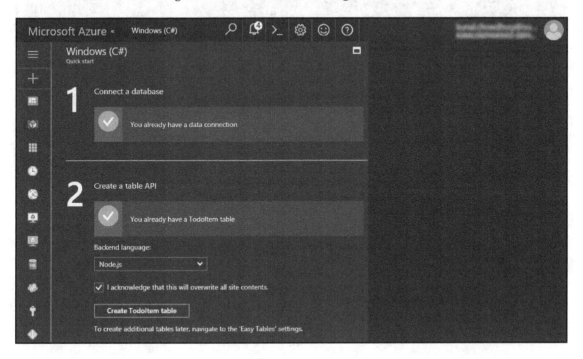

This confirms that the database has been successfully configured to use. Scroll down to view the third section, where it will generate you the configuration settings and a sample model for you to start the integration part in your application.

If you are creating the application from scratch, the **Create a new app** tab will provide you a sample Visual Studio project to kick-start. If you have an existing application and/or you want to manually insert the API configurations, navigate to the **Connect an existing app** tab page, as shown in the following screenshot:

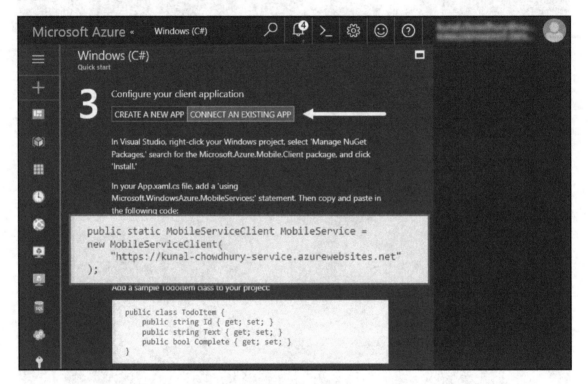

Take a note about the highlighted section, which we will need later to create the `MobileServiceClient` to integrate the mobile service in our project. The `TodoItem` model has also been generated for you to easily start with it for the first time.

Integrating Mobile App Service in a Windows application

Let's get started with integrating the Mobile App Service that we just created into an application. You can use any application, but here we will use a WPF application. Open your Visual Studio IDE and navigate to **File** | **New** | **Project...** to create a WPF project.

Creating the Model and Service Client

Once the project gets created, you need to create the Model `TodoItem` in the project. To do so, right-click on the project and navigate to **Add** | **Class...** and name it as `TodoItem`. Now copy the definition of the class from the Azure portal and replace it in the code file. Here is the code for your easy reference:

```
public class TodoItem
{
  public string Id { get; set; }
  public string Text { get; set; }
  public bool Complete { get; set; }
}
```

Now, we need to create the instance of the mobile service client, so that you can interact with Azure. Open the `App.xaml.cs` file and enter the following lines of code:

```
public static MobileServiceClient MobileService = new
MobileServiceClient("https://kunal-chowdhury-service.azurewebsites.net");
```

As our service client is hosted at `https://kunal-chowdhury-service.azurewebsites.net`, we provided it as the endpoint address to the service client object. If you have hosted it in a different endpoint, you need to set the correct one. Please update the entry accordingly, as highlighted.

The `MobileServiceClient` class is part of the `Microsoft.Azure.Mobile.Client` DLL, which you need to reference in your project. You can get it from NuGet by clicking on the lightbulb tooltip and following the context menu, as shown in the following screenshot:

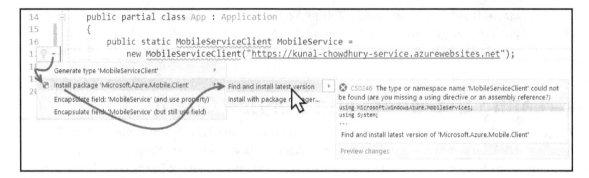

This will install the latest version of the DLLs and automatically add them as a reference in your current project. Build the solution to confirm that there are no compiler errors.

Once your service client instance has been created, you can call the API methods of it to do CRUD operations to your Azure database that you have created.

Integrating the API call

Let's first design our app UI to have a `TextBox` control to enter the description of the `ToDo` item, a checkbox to mark it as complete, and a few buttons to perform add, delete, and refresh data functionalities.

Open the `MainPage.xaml` file, where we need to change the UI. Replace the default `Grid` panel, with the following XAML code snippet:

```xml
<Grid>
  <StackPanel Width="270" Margin="10">
    <TextBlock Text="Task description:"/>
    <TextBox x:Name="txbTaskDescription" Height="26" />
    <CheckBox x:Name="chkComplete" Content="Complete?"
              Margin="0 10"/>
    <StackPanel Orientation="Horizontal"
                HorizontalAlignment="Center">
      <Button Content="Save" Width="100"
              Margin="10" Click="OnSaveButtonClicked"/>
      <Button Content="Refresh" Width="100"
              Margin="10" Click="OnRefreshButtonClicked"/>
    </StackPanel>
```

```
<ListBox x:Name="lstDetails" Height="100">
  <ListBox.ItemTemplate>
    <DataTemplate>
      <StackPanel Orientation="Horizontal">
        <CheckBox IsChecked="{Binding Complete}"/>
        <TextBlock Text="{Binding Text}" Margin="10 0"/>
      </StackPanel>
    </DataTemplate>
  </ListBox.ItemTemplate>
</ListBox>
<StackPanel Orientation="Horizontal"
            HorizontalAlignment="Center">
  <Button Content="Delete" Width="80"
          Margin="5" Click="OnDeleteButtonClicked"/>
</StackPanel>
      </StackPanel>
    </Grid>
```

In the code behind the file of the MainPage (that is, in the `MainPage.xaml.cs` file), define the button click events that we associated in the XAML page. Mark all of them with the `async` keyword. This will now look like the following code snippet:

```
private async void OnSaveButtonClicked(object sender,
  RoutedEventArgs e)
{

}

private async void OnRefreshButtonClicked(object sender,
  RoutedEventArgs e)
{

}

private async void OnDeleteButtonClicked(object sender,
  RoutedEventArgs e)
{

}
```

Now, build the solution to check for any errors and correct them if you encounter anything. Once done, run the application which will look like the following screen:

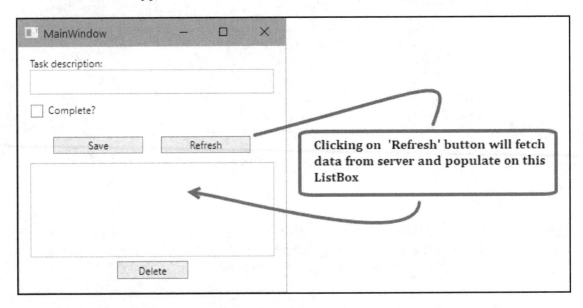

Now, it's time to integrate the Mobile Service API to perform CRUD operations to the Azure database from your application. The GetTable method of the service client object returns the handle of the table as IMobileServiceTable, where you want to perform any DB operation. Generally, it takes the table name as an argument. Alternatively, you can call the strongly typed data operations by the type of the instance of the table.

```
App.MobileService.GetTable("TodoItem"); // untyped data operation
App.MobileService.GetTable<TodoItem>(); // typed data operation
```

To fetch the contents of the remote table, we need to call the ReadAsync() method on top of the mobile service table instance and set the response as ItemsSource of the listbox that we have added in the UI. Here is the code for your reference:

```
lstDetails.ItemsSource = await
App.MobileService.GetTable<TodoItem>().ReadAsync();
```

Similarly, when you want to insert an item to the remote database table, you should call the InsertAsync method passing the instance of the model, like the following :

```
await App.MobileService.GetTable<TodoItem>().InsertAsync(todoItem);
```

Similarly, for delete operation, call the `DeleteAsync` method by passing the instance of the model. Here's how to call it:

```
await App.MobileService.GetTable<TodoItem>().DeleteAsync(item);
```

Additionally, you may want to add validations while performing the add or delete operations. When you compile and run the application, enter the task description and, optionally, select the **Complete** checkbox before hitting the **Save** button.

Once the save operation completes. or when you click on the **Refresh** button, the API call will be performed to retrieve the latest data available on the Azure DB. If you want to delete any record, select the desired data in the listbox and click the **Delete** button:

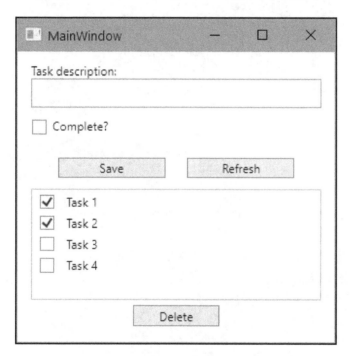

Here is the complete code snippet of the code behind the file for your reference:

```
public partial class MainWindow : Window
{
    public MainWindow()
    {
        InitializeComponent();
        OnRefreshButtonClicked(this, new RoutedEventArgs());
    }
```

```csharp
private async void OnSaveButtonClicked(object sender,
  RoutedEventArgs e)
{
  var taskDescription = txbTaskDescription.Text;

  if (!string.IsNullOrWhiteSpace(taskDescription))
  {
    var isComplete = chkComplete.IsChecked == true;
    var todoItem = new TodoItem { Text = taskDescription,
      Complete = isComplete };

    txbTaskDescription.Text = string.Empty;
    chkComplete.IsChecked = false;

    await App.MobileService.GetTable<TodoItem>().
      InsertAsync(todoItem);
    OnRefreshButtonClicked(sender, e);
  }
}

private async void OnRefreshButtonClicked(object sender,
 RoutedEventArgs e)
{
  lstDetails.ItemsSource = await App.MobileService.
   GetTable<TodoItem>().ReadAsync();
}

private async void OnDeleteButtonClicked(object sender,
 RoutedEventArgs e)
{
  if(lstDetails.SelectedItem is TodoItem item)
  {
     await App.MobileService.GetTable<TodoItem>().DeleteAsync(item);
     OnRefreshButtonClicked(sender, e);
  }
}
```

You can now navigate to the Azure portal to view the entered data into the table. Log in to the Azure dashboard, navigate to App Service, and select the Mobile App Service that you created.

Now, as shown in the following screenshot, scroll down the panel to find the option **Easy tables**. Click the **TodoItem** table to observe the data that it has. From this screen, you can also create a new table:

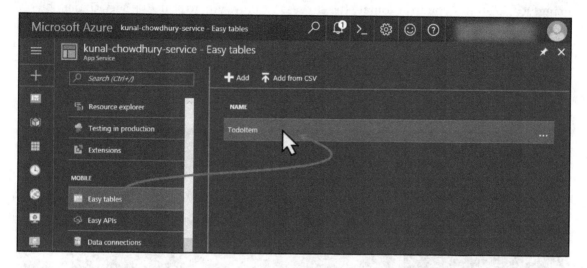

When you click the table, it will open another screen where you can see the records that the table has. On this screen, you can also change permissions to access the table, edit the script, and manage the schema of the table:

Scaling App Service plan

The portal allows you to easily scale up or scale down the App Service plan that you are using. It also allows you to automate the process to allow you to scale the service plan on demand.

First log in to the Azure portal and navigate to the app service that you want to scale. From the left side panel, scroll down to find the **Scale up (App Service plan)** link. When you click on it, a new screen will show up and will allow you to select the pricing tier for your application:

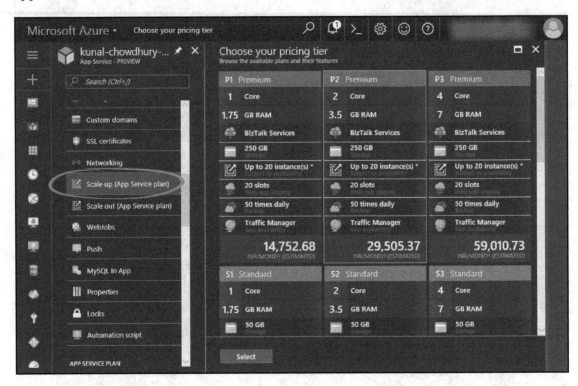

There are plenty of service plans available for you to select by choosing the correct pricing tier. The basic tiers will have less performance than the standard or the premium tier, but will allow you to save more money. The premium tier will charge you more money but will give you the best performance.

The other link, **Scale out (App Service plan),** will allow you to override the instance count. It also allows you to enable/disable the auto-scaling option. If you want to auto-scale the service based on some conditions/rules, click on **Enable autoscale**:

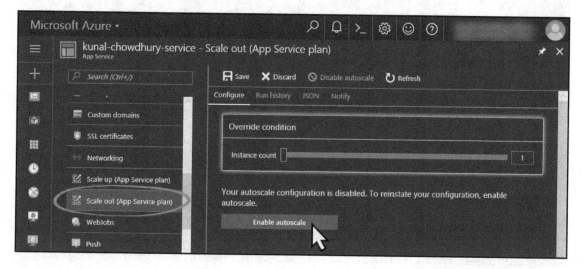

This will open another screen where you can create a condition and ask the service plan to scale based on it. You can select it either based on a metric or specific instance count. You can add more rules and conditions as per your needs. At the end, click on the **Save** button to save all your changes made on this screen.

When you don't want to run the auto-scaling option, come to this screen again and click on the button labelled **Disable autoscale**:

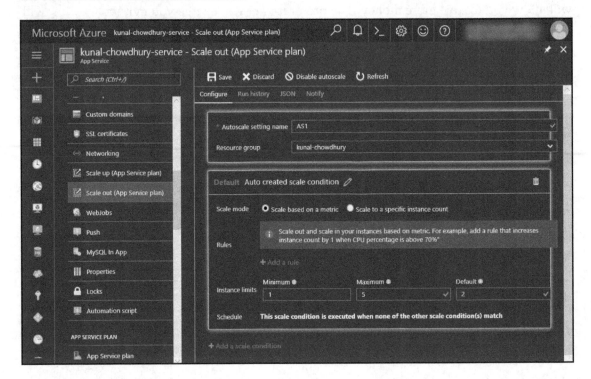

Summary

In this chapter, we learned about cloud computing basics that include IaaS, PaaS, and SaaS. We learned how to create a free Azure account and the way to configure Visual Studio 2017 for Azure development. Then we discussed creating and managing Azure websites from the portal as well as from Visual Studio. We also discussed how to update an existing website from Visual Studio.

Later, we discussed the Mobile App Service and looked in detail at how to create a mobile service, configure an Azure database, and integrate the service in a Windows application. At the end, we learned about the service API calls and scaling the app service plan based on various pricing tiers.

In the next chapter, we will learn about source controls. We will discuss how to work with Git as a source control repository with Team Services and/or GitHub from Visual Studio 2017.

10
Working with Source Controls

A **source control system** is a component of a source repository and version management system. If you are building enterprise-level applications in a distributed environment, you will want to keep your source code in a safe vault with easy-to-manage, easy-to-integrate, and easy-to-create versions of each check-in. The source control repository will help you to manage your code.

There are plenty of source control repositories available in the market. Some of the most common repositories are Git, TFS, and SVN.

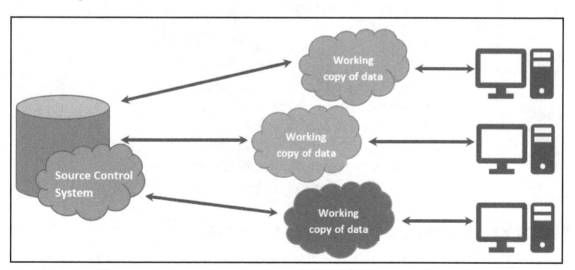

In general, repositories are being hosted on on-premise environments or in a cloud-hosted environment such as Microsoft Team Services, Team Foundation Server, GitHub, Bitbucket, and so on, and developers connect to the remote repository to clone the entire changeset on their system to perform changes on their code. When the changes are over and well tested, they push those changes to the remote.

In this chapter, we are going to discuss the following core points to use a source control repository such as **Git** and **TFS Projects** in a Visual Studio 2017 environment:

- Working with Git repositories
    - Installing Git for Visual Studio 2017
    - Connecting to the source control servers
    - Getting started with Git repositories
    - Working with Git branches
    - Working with changes, staging, and commits
    - Syncing changes between local and remote
    - Working with pull requests for code review
    - Working with Git commit history
    - Undoing your changes
    - Tagging your commits
- Working with TFS Projects
    - Connecting to a Team Project
    - Cloning an existing project folder
    - Performing a check-out operation to a file
    - Committing your changes to the repository
    - Undoing your local changes
    - Creating a code review request
    - Rolling back your existing change set

Working with Git repositories

Git for Visual Studio 2017 comes as an optional component and you need to manually install it to work with Git servers such as Team Foundation Services, GitHub, and BitBucket. In this section of the chapter, we will learn how to work with Git repositories. This will cover creating/cloning a repository, creation of a branch, working with changes, syncing, pull requests, and commit history.

Installing Git for Visual Studio 2017

To install the Git plugin for Visual Studio, run the Visual Studio 2017 installer and click on **Modify**. Once the screen loads, navigate to the **Individual Components** tab, as shown in the following screenshot. Scroll down to the **Code tools** section and select **Git for Windows & GitHub extension for Visual Studio**. Click on the **Modify** button to continue with the installation:

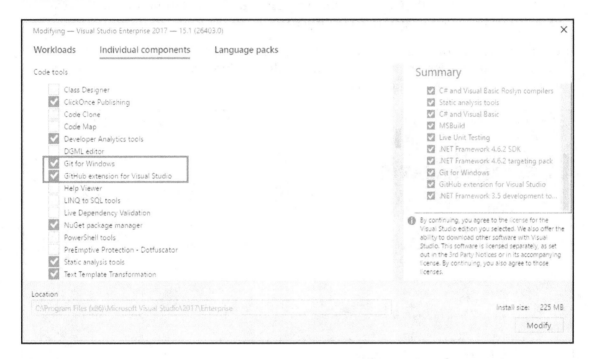

 Git for Windows will allow you to use local Git repositories as well as to perform Git commands to work with any remote repositories. If you are going to deal with GitHub, you must check **GitHub extension for Visual Studio** for having an easy access to your repository.

If you are installing it from an offline installer, it will momentarily install the required components. In the other case, it will first download it from the Microsoft server and then proceed towards the installation.

Once the installation succeeds, you are good to go with connecting to your Git repository. The next section will help you to connect with **Visual Studio Team Services** (**VSTS**)and/or the **GitHub** server.

Connecting to the source control servers

If you have an account on Visual Studio Team Services or GitHub, you can easily connect to it, directly from the Visual Studio 2017 IDE. All these connection settings are available under the Team Explorer.

To connect to a **Team Foundation Server** (**TFS**) or Visual Studio Team Services, open the Team Explorer and click the **Connect...** link present under **Visual Studio Team Services**. You will need to log in to the portal to gain access.

If you have a GitHub account and you would like to connect to it, click the **Connect...** link present under the **GitHub** panel of the **Team Explorer** window. You will need to log in with your GitHub account credentials:

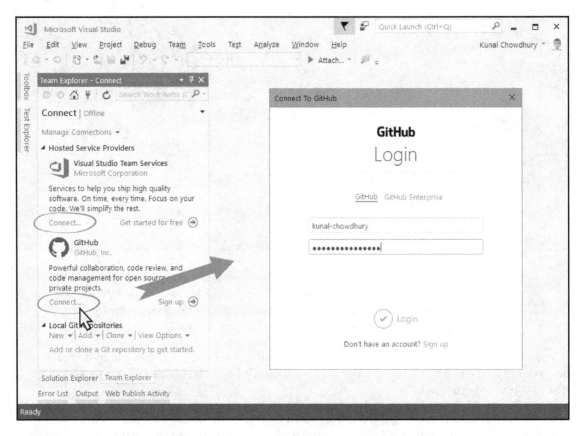

Getting started with Git repositories

Once you have signed in to the desired server of your choice, you may want to create a new code repository or would like to clone an existing one to your local from the remote server. As the process is similar for both VSTS and GitHub, we are going to demonstrate using the GitHub account.

> For details about the Git command uses from command line or bash, visit `git.kunal-chowdhury.com`.

Creating a new repository

To create a new repository on the remote GitHub server, you can directly use the Visual Studio 2017 **Team Explorer**. Once you have logged in, click on the **Create** link, as shown in the following screenshot. This will open the **Create a GitHub Repository** window on the screen. Enter the required details and select the local path of the repository. Once you have filled up everything, click on the **Create** button:

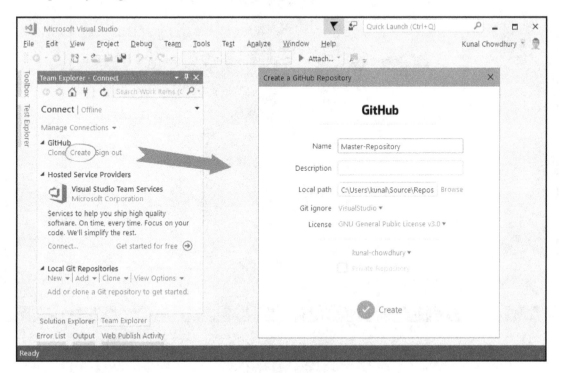

Once the process completes creation of the repository, you will find it listed on the remote server as well as in your local.

Cloning an existing repository

Visual Studio 2017 made it easy to clone an existing GitHub repository. Under the **GitHub** panel of your **Team Explorer**, click on the **Clone** link to continue. If you have already logged in, it will show you a screen with a list of repositories that you have on your Git server.

Select the repository that you want to clone, select the folder path of the local repository where you want to download the remote information, and finally click on the **Clone** button to start the process:

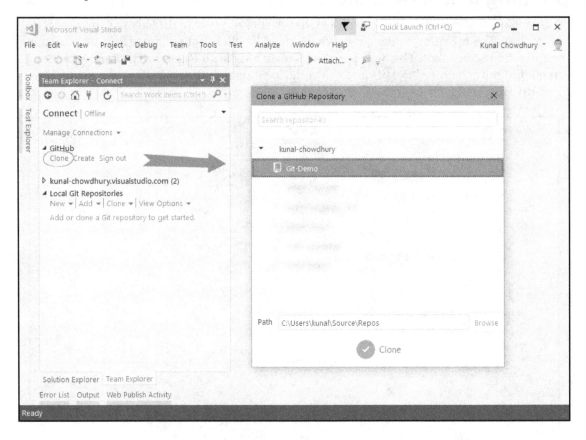

Based on the size of the remote repository and your internet bandwidth, it will take some time to download all the contents. Once the process completes, you will see it listed both under your **Local Git Repositories** and on GitHub.

In case you have a different repository, other than VSTS or GitHub, you can still clone that to your local. In such a case, as the extension or support is not available for such services in Visual Studio, you need to click on **Clone** which will expand a panel. Enter the URL of the said repository, select the local folder path of your choice and then click on the **Clone** button.

This will process the content available on remote and download a copy of it in your local repository for further processing:

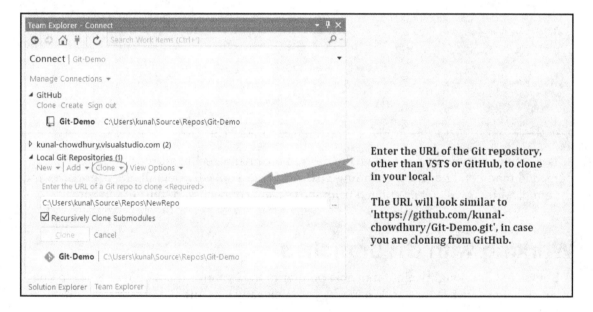

Reviewing the Git configuration settings

Once you have set up your Git repository, you may want to review the Git configuration settings. Open it up by following the path **Team Explorer** | **Settings** | **Global Settings**:

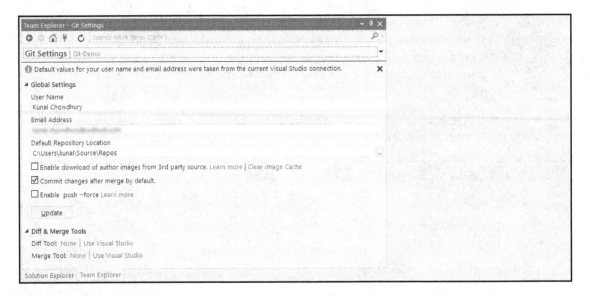

This screen will allow you to update the desired user name, email address, local repository path, and many other options including **Diff & Merge Tools**. By default, the user name and the email address will get populated from the current connection to the Git repository.

Working with Git branches

A **branch** in Git is a lightweight movable pointer to the commits that you make. The name of the default branch is master. Whenever you make any commit, it automatically moves forward.

In Git, you can create sub-branches to create another line of development from the master repository to work on a new feature or to fix a bug. Once the feature or the bug fixing is complete, it is merged back to the main/master branch and deletes the sub-branch that we worked with as shown in the following diagram:

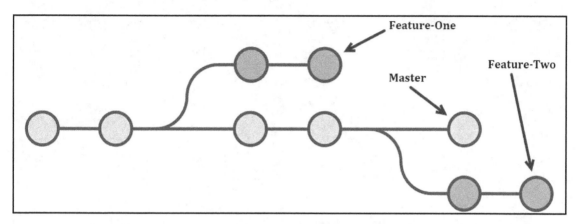

Every branch is referenced by HEAD, which points to the latest commit in that branch. Whenever you make a commit, the HEAD is updated with the latest commit.

Creating a new local branch

A Git branch is just a small reference to keep an exact commit history. It does not create multiple copies of your source. As it uses the history information stored in commits to recreate the files on a branch, it's very easy to create it. When you commit changes to a branch, it will not affect the other branches because it creates them in isolation. Later, you can share branches with other members or merge the changes into the main branch.

To create a new local branch from another one (for example, the master), right-click on that branch from Visual Studio **Team Explorer** and then, from the context menu, select the menu item **New Local Branch From...**.

Enter the name of the new branch in the input box and select the parent branch from the dropdown (which is automatically populated based on the selection). If you want to checkout to that new branch, make sure to check the box labelled **Checkout branch**. Once you are ready to create it, click on the button **Create Branch**:

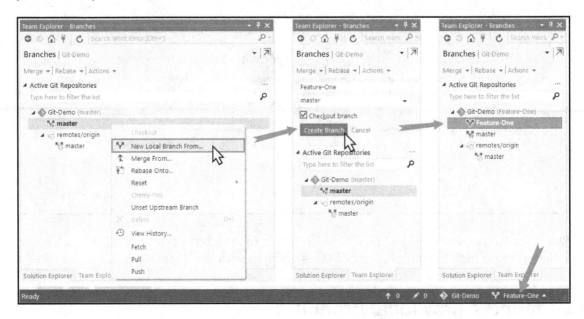

This will create the branch and checkout to it. In the **Team Explorer** window, you will see it listed as bold. Also, you will see the new branch name at the bottom-right corner of the Visual Studio status bar, as shown in the preceding screenshot.

Switching to a different branch

In Git terminology, switching to a branch is called **checkout**. Since the branches are lightweight, switching between them is very quick and easy.

You can switch/checkout to a different branch either by double-clicking on it under the **Team Explorer** window or selecting the one from the dropdown menu, when you click on the current branch name, present at the bottom-right corner of the Visual Studio status bar:

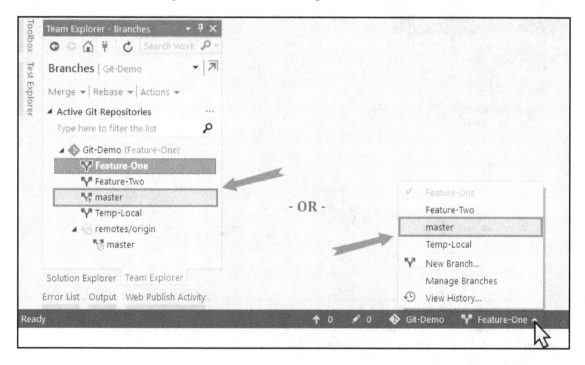

Upon checkout, the selected branch will get highlighted as bold in **Team Explorer**. Also, the name of the branch, at the bottom-right corner, will change accordingly.

Pushing a local branch to remote

When you have a local branch created on your system, you may want to push the branch (with or without any changes) to the remote so that other users can see and get the updates.

To push a local branch to the remote, right click on that branch in **Team Explorer**. From the context menu, that pops up on the screen, select **Push Branch**. This will update the remote with the details that we have just created:

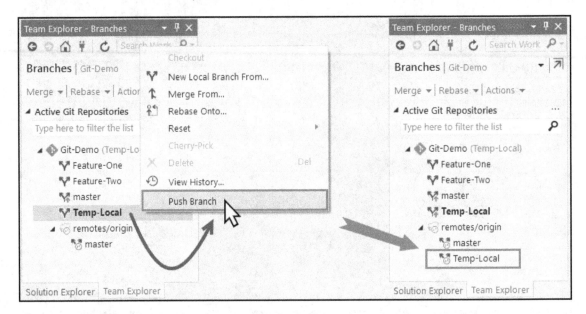

Once the remote update is successful, you will see the branch details listed under **remotes/origin** of your repository in **Team Explorer**.

Deleting an existing branch

There may be some cases when you want to remove a branch. It could be either your local branch or a remote branch available on your Git server repository. Visual Studio 2017 provides you easy access to both.

To delete a local branch, right click on it and select **Delete** from the context menu. To delete a remote branch listed under the **remotes/origin**, right click on the desired branch and select **Delete Branch From Remote** from the context menu that pops up on the screen.

Alternatively, you can select the branch that you want to delete and press the *Delete* key on your keyboard:

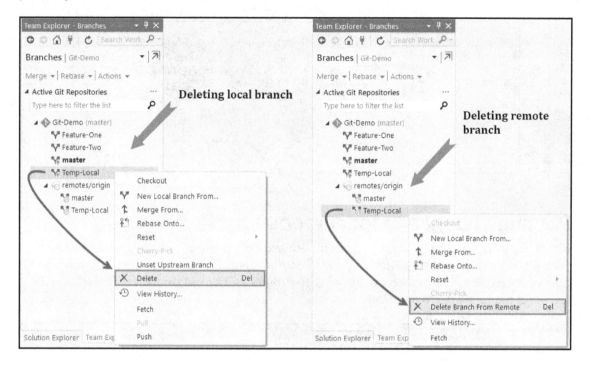

Working with changes, staging, and commits

Git is all about taking a snapshot of your code to your repository, as and when you commit your changes. There are three stages/areas where Git tracks the changes as you continue working on your repository:

- **Unmodified**: This is the area where the available files have not yet changed since your last commit to your repo. When you change some files and save them, Git will mark them as modified.
- **Modified**: These are the files which have been changed after your last commit but not yet staged for your next commit. When you stage these files, Git will move them to the staging area.

- **Staging**: This is the area where the changed files have been added for your next commit. When you commit the staged files, they will be marked as unmodified.

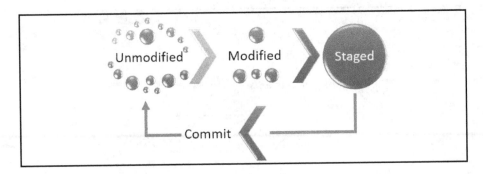

Staging changes to local repository

When you add new files to your project, modify existing ones, or delete existing files from your project or Git code base, they will be marked as modified since the last commit. You can see a list of your changes by navigating to **Project** | **Changes** under **Team Explorer**, as shown in the following screenshot:

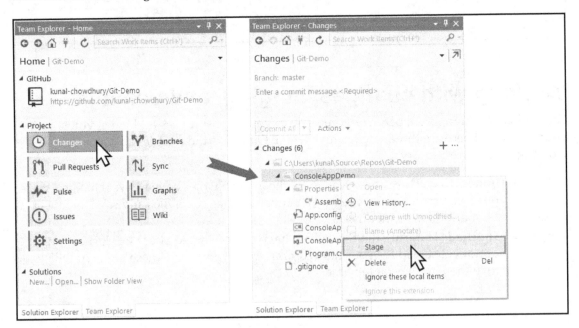

Right click on the files/folders that you want to move to the staging area and, from the context menu, click **Stage**. Later, if you want to unmark any file/folder from the staging area, right click on those files/folders and click **Unstage** from the context menu, as shown in the following screenshot:

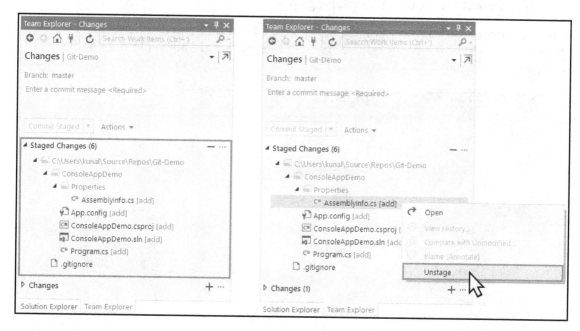

If you stage any files/folders after you staged them already, the delta will be added to the changes available in staging. When you are ready to save the changes to your repository, you need to commit those changes.

Committing changes to the local repository

To commit the staged changes to your local repository, navigate to **Team Explorer** | **Project** | **Changes**. You will see a list of staged files in the list. You will also see a list of changed files which are not yet pushed to the staging area.

Enter a comment as your commit message and click **Commit Staged** to perform a commit operation to your local repository. The changed files, which are not yet in the staging area, will not be committed:

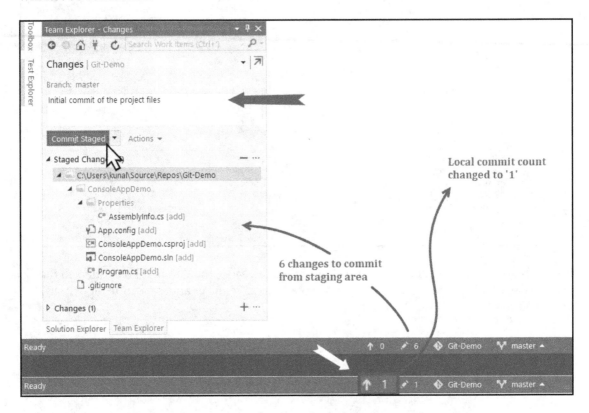

As shown in the preceding screenshot, the Visual Studio 2017 status bar will show the count of the commits performed but not yet pushed to the remote repository. As and when you commit to your local repository, the count will increase by one, but when you push all your local commits, it will reset to zero again.

Discarding uncommitted changes

There could be a set of changed files, which you don't want to commit and want to undo the changes that you have already performed. Select those files/folders and right click on them to open the Git context menu, where you can click **Undo Changes...** to discard them. The files will be reset to the unmodified stage:

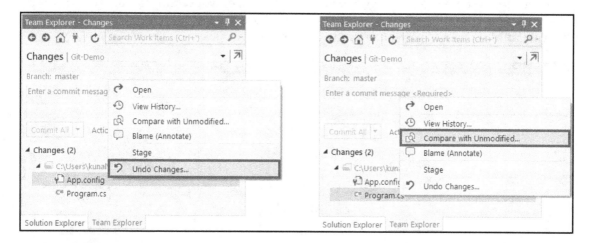

Sometimes, before performing any commit or undoing the changes, you may want to check what has been changed since your last commit. You can do so by individually selecting a file, right-clicking on that, and clicking the **Compare with Unmodified...** option from the context menu to compare the changes side-by-side, as shown in the following screenshot:

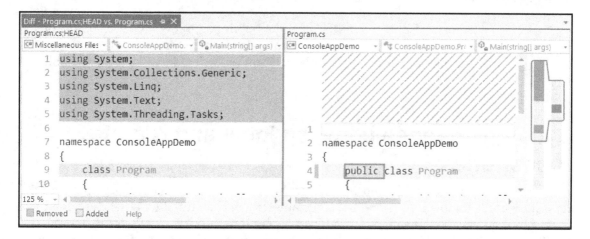

You will find the removed lines or contents marked with a reddish background, whereas the changed or added contents will be marked with a greenish background.

Amending message to an existing commit

Occasionally, in some rare cases, you may want to change the existing commit message. To do so, open the commit that you want to modify. Change the desired message and click on the **Amend Message** link, as shown in the following screenshot:

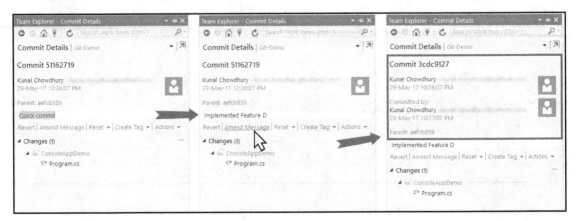

This will modify the commit message and replace the existing one with a new commit. At the end, make sure to push the changes to the remote repository for the changes to be available to other users.

It is not advisable to modify/amend a public commit, which is available on a remote repository, as it is going to replace the existing one with a new hash code. When required, only perform this operation on a local commit.

Syncing changes between local and remote repositories

The Git extension for Visual Studio 2017 allows you to easily sync changes between a local repository and a remote repository. If it finds any remote changes, it will first download those and merge with the changes available in the local repository. If it finds any merge conflict, it will immediately stop processing and ask you to resolve them first. Later, it will push all your changes to the remote repository.

To invoke a single sync operation, open the **Team Explorer** window and navigate to the **Sync** view, which may have outgoing commits ready to push:

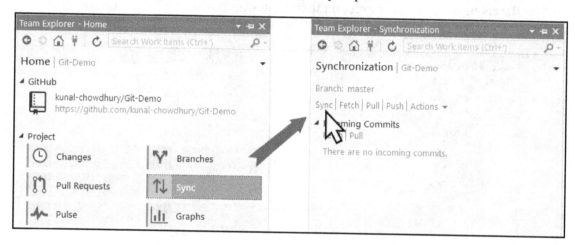

You can also perform the steps individually, rather than performing both the inbound and outbound operations in a single shot. **Push** will commit your local changes to remote, **Fetch** will download the remote changes but won't merge, whereas the **Pull** command will download the remote changes and proceed to merge the changes. Let's discuss them one by one.

Pushing changes to the remote repository

Pushing your changes can be of two types: **Push** and **Publish**. When there is a relationship between the local branch and the remote repository, push will commit the local changes to the remote repository. When there's no relation between the local branch and the remote repository, it publishes the changes to the remote repository by first creating the branch with the same name of the local branch and then pushing the local commits to it.

After you publish the branch, only push will happen as there exists a branch in the remote repository with a relationship to your local repo.

To push your changes to the remote repository, open **Team Explorer** and navigate to the **Sync** view. You will see a list of outgoing changes, as shown in the following screenshot. Review the changes for each commit and finally click on **Push** to commit those on your remote branch to make them available publicly within the same project team:

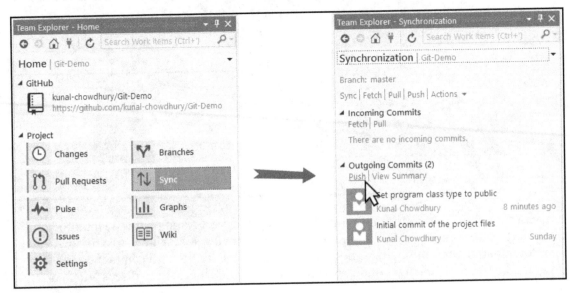

If during the push operation, it finds any conflicts between remote commits and local commits, it will break the operation immediately. You will have to first resolve these conflicts before you can push your changes.

Fetching changes available in the remote repository

When you have some latest changes in the remote repository, which you don't have in your local, you can ask Visual Studio to fetch those changes (new commits and new branches) using the Git command fetch. Fetch will just download the changes to your local, but won't merge them automatically. It will ask you to review them first.

To fetch the remote commits, open **Team Explorer**, navigate to the **Sync** view, and click on **Fetch**. A list of incoming commits will be shown, if any. You can then review them and merge those changes with your local changes:

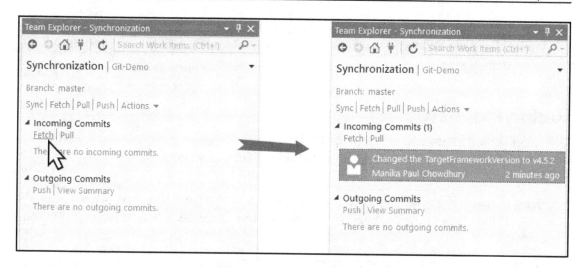

Merging changes available in the remote repository to the local repository

Pull is just like fetch, but it merges the changes automatically after downloading them. If there exist any merge conflicts, though Git takes care most of them, it will ask you to resolve them first before continuing.

To apply the remote changes to your local, open **Team Explorer** and navigate to **Sync** view. Then you can click either **Sync** or **Pull** to download the changes and merge them:

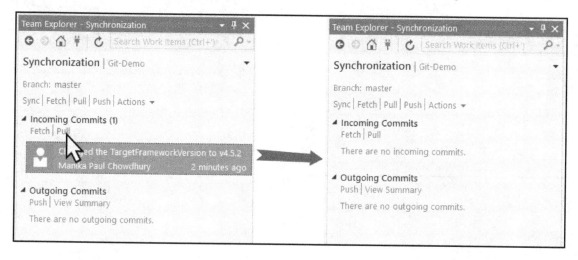

The merge operation will keep the commit history of your local changes intact, so that when you share your branch with the push command, Git will understand how others should merge your changes.

Resolving merge conflicts

Git is good at automatically merging the file changes, but it can sometimes throw merge conflicts. In such a case, you will have to manually resolve the conflicts before syncing your local and remote branch.

When there are merge conflicts, Visual Studio 2017 will list down the conflicts under the **Merge In Progress** panel of the **Sync** view. Click on the **Conflicts** link to start resolving the file conflicts:

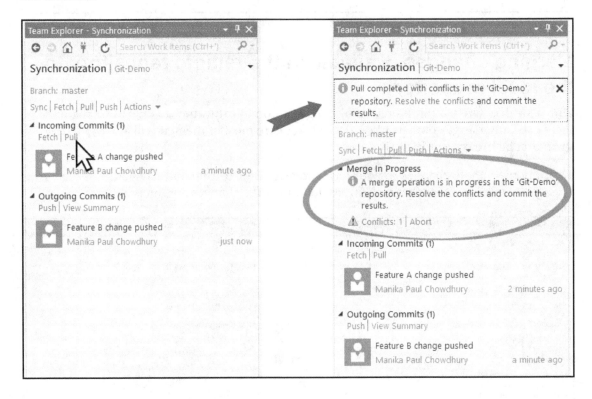

This will bring up a list of files with conflicts. Selecting a file lets you accept the changes in the source branch where you are merging. You can also compare the files by using the **Diff** link and compare with **Remote** or **Local**.

From the same screen, you can also take the remote changes or keep the local changes. If you want to review the changes and manually want to do a merge operation, click on the **Merge** button, as shown in the following screenshot:

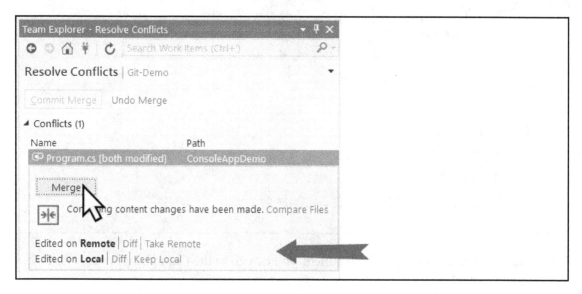

This will show you a side-by-side view of your source and target, along with the resultant changes to the file. Use the checkboxes present next to the modified lines under merge conflicts to select between the remote and the local changes. You can also modify the lines directly in the **Result** panel.

When you are done with the changes, click on the **Accept Merge** button to accept the changes performed for the conflicts. You need to perform the same for all the conflicts that you have, before continuing with the synchronization between local and remote branches, as shown in the following screenshot:

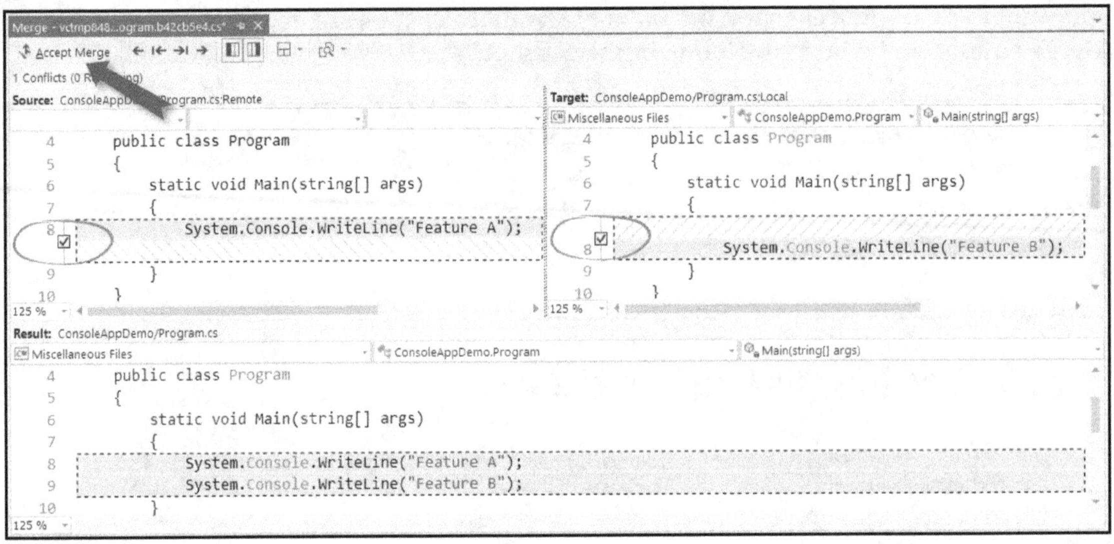

Once you are done resolving all the conflicts, you can go to the **Changes** view and commit the merged changes.

Working with Pull Requests for code review

Pull Requests is the collaborative process to discuss the changes done in a branch, get the early feedback of the changes, and merge them to the master branch once everyone approves them. You can create **Pull Request** of a work-in module even if you are not ready to merge the changes.

Creating Pull Requests for code review

If your Git repository supports it, you can create **Pull Request** directly from the Visual Studio 2017 IDE. First, you will need to push/publish the local branch changes to the remote repository. Then open **Team Explorer** and navigate to the **Pull Requests** view, as shown in the following screenshot:

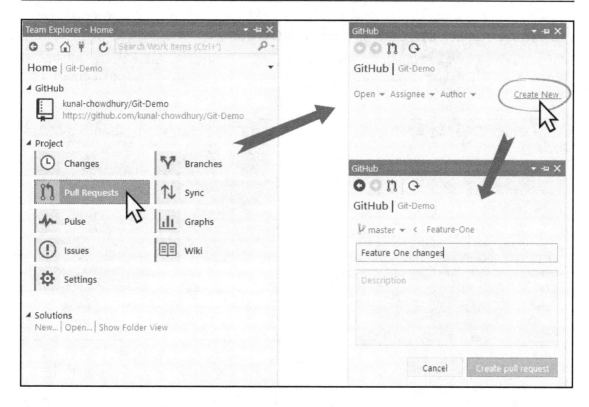

If you are using the GitHub extension, a panel will appear with a **Create New** link to create the pull request for the code review. It will automatically list the branch that you are working on and will go to merge once the reviewers approve it. Give a title to the pull request and a description of the work that you performed in this change set. Once you are ready, click on the **Create pull request** button. All the members of the project will get notification to review your changes.

If you are using Team Foundation Server or Team Services, you may get an option while creating the request to enter the reviewer's name to get it reviewed by selected people of the team project.

Reviewing an existing Pull Request

When you create a Pull Request, the selected reviewers will get the notification to review your changes. They can provide feedback and/or approve your pull request to merge into the master branch:

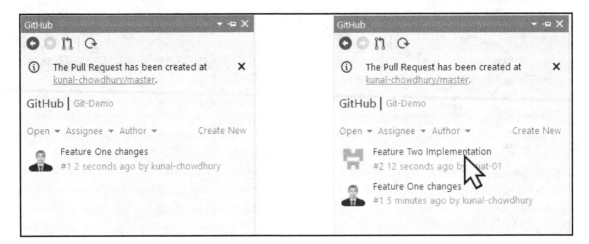

When you get a notification about someone else's Pull Request, you can click on it to open the review panel.

With the code lines, where you have some feedback or want to ask the author of this pull request to do further changes, click on the + symbol, which will appear once you hover on that line.

Clicking on the + symbol icon will provide you with an area to enter your comment description. You can use various formatting options to construct it and finally you can click on the **Start a review** button (in case you are using GitHub) to submit your feedback.

Here is a screenshot from GitHub, demonstrating the process of adding a review comment to a Pull Request:

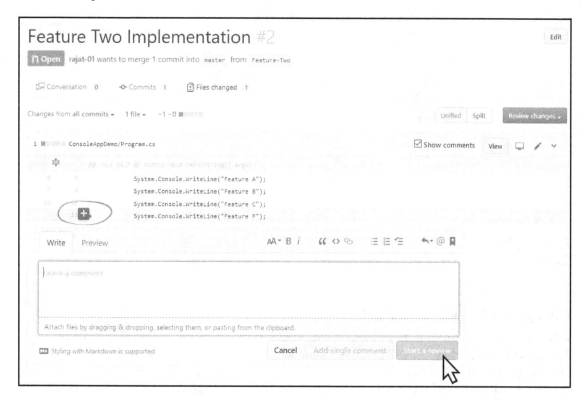

In GitHub, your comments can be of three types:

- **Comment**: To be used to submit general feedback, without providing approval to the pull request
- **Approve**: Use this option to provide approval to the code review request and to give your approval to merge the changes to the master branch
- **Request changes**: When you have some change request in mind, you can select this and ask the author of the code to address those changes before proceeding towards final approval

To select the type of comment, you can click on the **Review changes** button before submitting your feedback to the pull request. See the following screenshot:

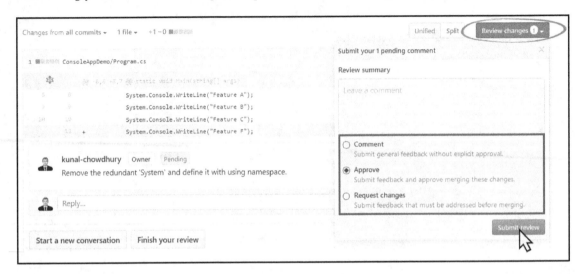

Merging a Pull Request

When everyone approves your changes, you will need to merge the code to the master branch so that the changes will be available to the other members of the team. When you are ready, open the Pull Request page which will show you a button to merge the pull request. Click on the **Merge pull request** button, as shown in the following screenshot:

During the merge, you can provide a comment to it to easily identify the changes. Generally, it auto-populates the same from the title of the pull request:

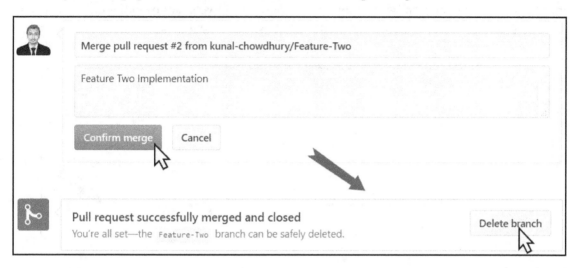

When you merge your changes to the master branch, you can delete your existing feature branch from the repository. As shown in the preceding screenshot, click on the **Delete branch** button to safely delete the said feature branch.

Working with Git commit history

Git is used for managing the history of changes, as and when you save your code as commits to your local repository and merges to the master branch after approval of pull requests.

The commit history becomes complicated when you pull remote changes, made by other team members, from the master branch to your feature branch. It then loses the linearity of the commit history, making it hard to follow.

It also makes it hard to keep track of the final feature changes when there exist multiple commits in a single feature branch. In such a case, if you want to revert a feature at a later point in time, it makes it difficult to track and revert each one of them.

To resolve this, Git provides a command called `rebase` which addresses all such issues. It takes the commits made on your current branch and replays them on a different branch. The commit history on your current branch will get rewritten to keep the granularity of the history.

For example, consider the following diagram as the commit history where you started the feature branch from the old base and saved your changes with two commits. In the meantime, some other members of your team committed two changes in the master branch. Thus, the old base will now have two branches; one points to the master and the other points to the feature:

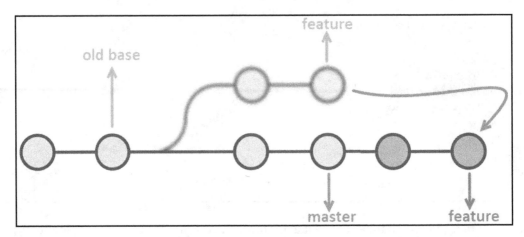

Now, when you rebase your feature branch onto the master, it will rewrite your local commit history, replaying your feature changes to the master branch. You will then see a linear commit history on your local along with the changes made by others.

Rebasing changes to rewrite the commit history

To rebase your current feature branch onto the recent changes available on the master branch, first make the feature branch current, and then navigate to the **Branches** view from **Team Explorer**.

There you will find a link called **Rebase**, which when clicked, will provide you a view to rebase the changes from your current branch to the branch where you would like to replay the commits:

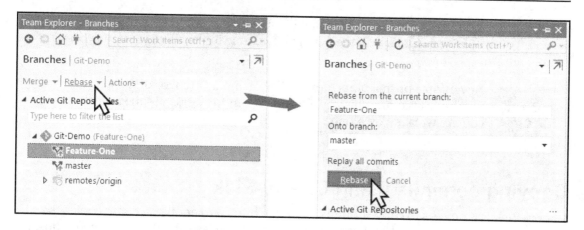

When you are ready to rebase your code, click on the **Rebase** button and wait until it completes the process. If there is a conflict, you will have to resolve those merge conflicts before completing the rebase. Click on **Continue** once you resolve all the conflicts or click **Abort** to terminate the rebasing process:

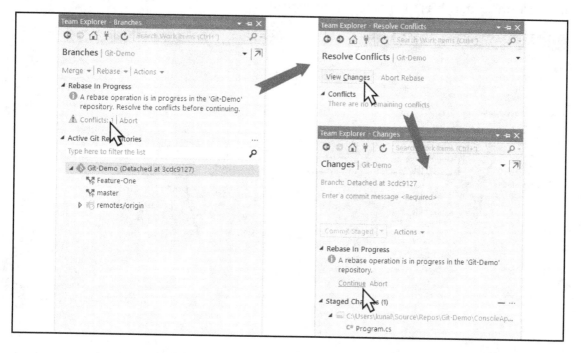

After a successful rebase, your local branch will have a different history than your remote branch. You will have to force push the changes available in your local to update in your remote branch.

> Never force push a branch that other members are working on, as it rewrites the commit history. Only perform force push to the branches that you are working on alone.

Copying commits using Cherry-Pick

Cherry-Pick is a process to copy commits from one branch to another. It only copies the changes from the commits instead of copying all the changes available in a branch. Thus, it is completely different from what a merge or rebase performs.

You will need to perform Cherry-Pick on commits when you accidentally committed to a wrong branch and/or want to pull out a set of commits from your Bug-Fix branch to the master/feature branch as soon as those are available:

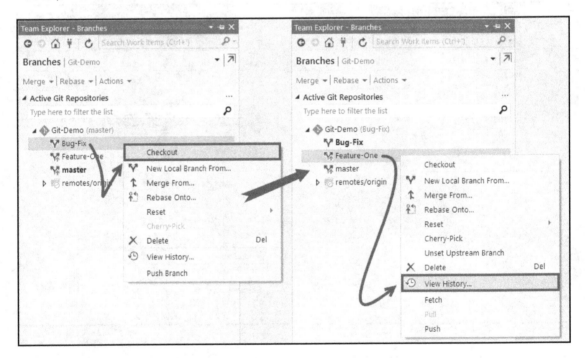

To Cherry-Pick, first checkout the branch where you want to copy a set of commits from a different branch. Then open the history of the other branch, from where you want to pull, by clicking on the **View History...** from the context menu, as shown in the preceding screenshot.

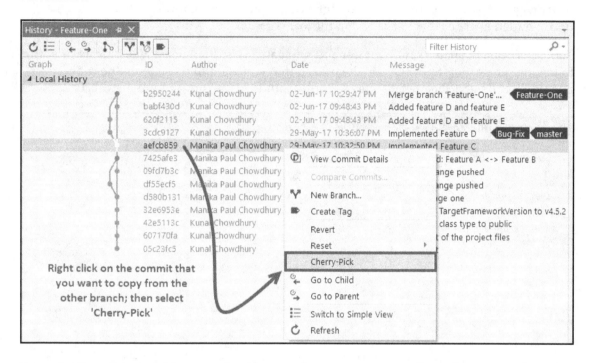

From the list of commit history, select the one that you want to pull to your current branch. Right click and select **Cherry-Pick** from the context menu, as shown in the preceding screenshot. This will pull the changes to the current branch. In case there are any merge conflicts, you will have to resolve those first before continuing.

Once the Cherry-pick process is successful, commit the changes and push them to your remote branch. You can repeat the process for each commit that you want to bring in your current checked-out branch.

Undoing your changes

You may not need all the changes to commit and push to the remote repository. There are many cases when you need to reset just the working directory/workspace to have a cleaner space, having the last committed changes, or revert a change from the remote in case you have pushed a wrong commit. In this section, we are going to discuss these two points.

Resetting a local branch to a previous state

Resetting a local branch can be done in two different ways. The first one could be resetting the branch to the last committed state available in the local repository. During this, you can select whether to keep your changes or not, but the most common way is to undo all the uncommitted changes that happened in the local branch.

To reset a branch, open **Team Explorer** and navigate to the **Branches** view. As shown in the following screenshot, right click on the branch that you want to reset. From the context menu, select **Reset | Delete Changes (--hard)** to undo all the uncommitted local changes:

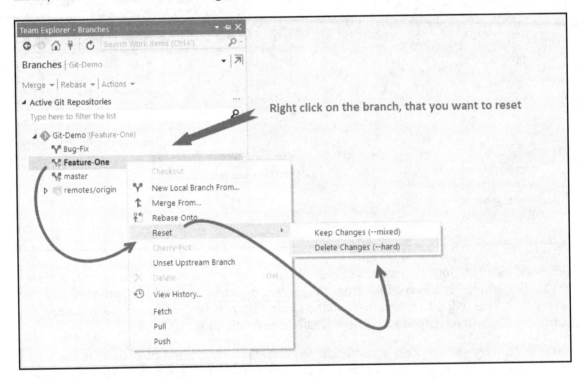

The other option could be resetting the local branch to a specific commit. All the changes available until that selected commit will be undone and will provide you with a fresh working copy of your files.

To reset a branch to a specific commit, open the **History** page of the branch and right click on the commit that you would like to reset to. From the context menu, select **Reset | Delete Changed (--hard)**, as shown in the following screenshot:

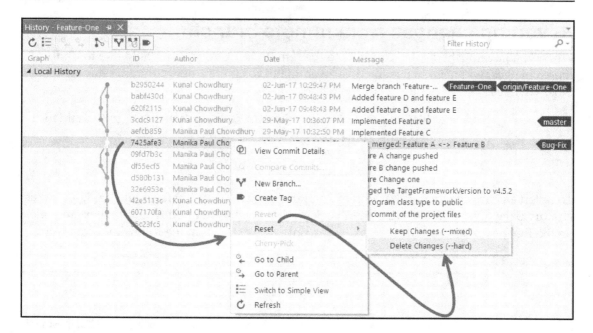

 Note that the reset operation affects the entire branch that has been selected, not just those available in your current directory.

Upon doing so, the local branch will have the changes up to the selected commit from the commit history. The **History** page will add another section that will list the incoming commits, which if needed, can be pulled to the local branch:

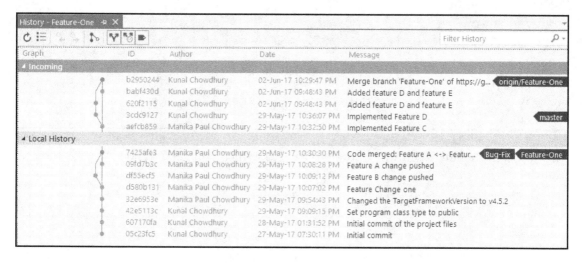

Reverting changes from remote branch

When you have pushed some commits to the remote repository and would like to undo those changes, you need to use the revert command to create a new commit, undoing all those changes.

 Note that history will not be rewritten in case of a revert. Thus, it is safe to use when working with others.

To revert a change from the shared remote branch, open **Team Explorer** and navigate to the **History** page of the branch. Now right click on the commit that you want to revert and click on the **Revert** option from the context menu entries, as shown in the following screenshot:

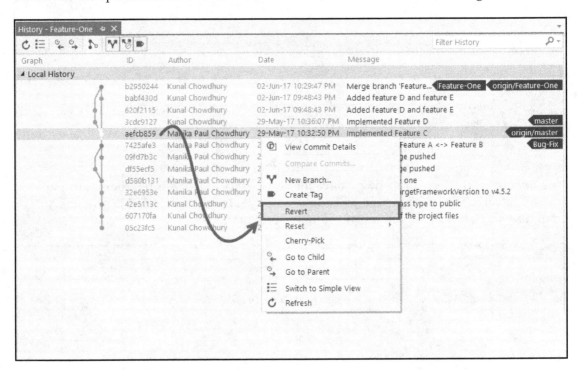

This will create a new commit to undo the changes, which you need to push to your remote branch.

Tagging your commits

Git provides you the ability to tag some specific points in your commit history as being important. Typically, people use this functionality to mark release points of the code. When you tag a commit, it becomes easy to identify the last commit that went to a specific release build.

To add a tag to a specific commit, open the **History** page from **Team Explorer**. Right click on the commit that you want to assign a tag, and click on **Create Tag** from the context menu, as shown here:

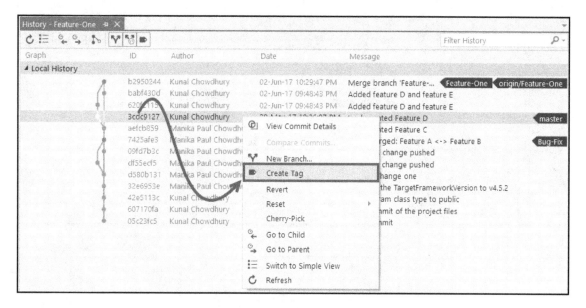

This will open the **Commit Details** dialog inside the **Team Explorer** window, with the complete details of the specific commit. Enter a tag name to it in the appropriate box, you may want to add a tag message, and then click on the **Create Tag** button.

 Remember that a tag cannot have a blank space and/or any special characters and it must be unique within the same repository.

Once the tag has been locally created, you will have to push the additional details to the remote repository so that the tag information is visible to the other team members. If the same tag name has been already created by some other team member, you won't be allowed to push the tag details that you have created:

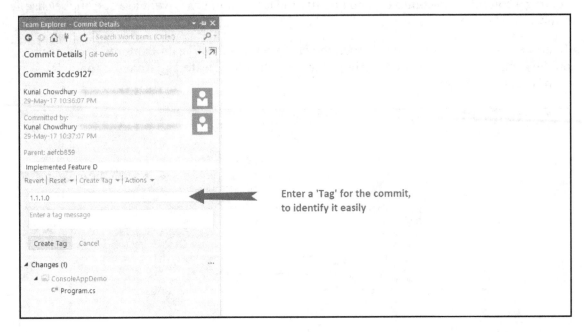

Upon creation of the tag, you will see it marked alongside the commit that you have selected to perform the tagging operation. In future, when you need to pull the remote changes up to that commit history, you can utilize it to download the specific file changes to your local:

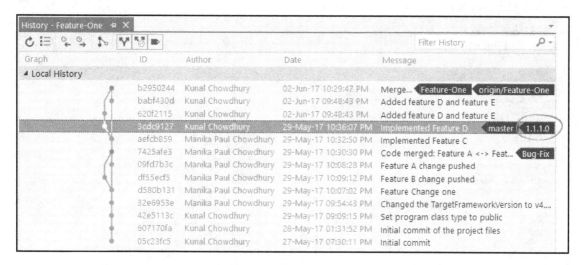

Working with Team Projects

Team Foundation Server also supports Team Projects, which is nothing but a collection of work items, code, tests, and so on, and used by a set of members of a team to work and track a set of related items.

In this section, we will learn how to use Visual Studio 2017 to connect to a Team Project, clone an existing project, sync your changes, create code review requests, and rollback any changes already committed to the repository.

Connecting to a Team Project

To connect to a Team Project in Visual Studio, open **Team Explorer** and click on the **Connect...** link, as shown in the following screenshot. This will open a page where you can add the TFS server that you want to connect:

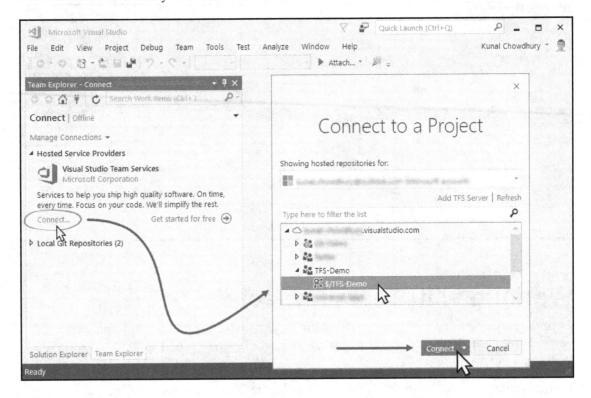

Once you add the server, you will get a list of Team Projects and Git repositories already hosted on that server. Select the one that you want to connect with. Click on the **Connect** button to continue.

Visual Studio Team Services (`https://www.visualstudio.com/vso/`) provides you with an online source control repository, where you can create unlimited Git repositories and Team Projects.

If you have a small team with a maximum of five users, you can use this for free and won't require any credit card while registering online. When your team grows, you can move on to a paid service (`https://www.visualstudio.com/team-services/pricing`) model and pay only for the users who need access.

Cloning an existing project folder

Once you have connected to the server, click on **Source Control Explorer** under your **Team Explorer**. From here, you will be able to clone/download your desired folders from the repository:

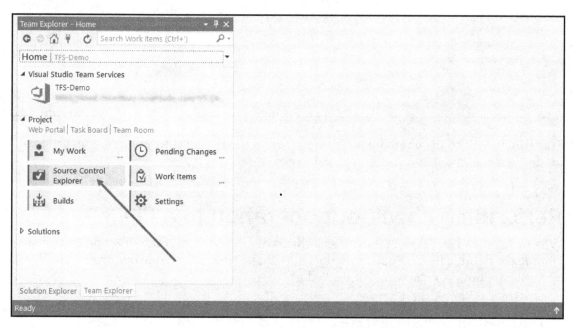

This will open **Source Control Explorer**. Select the team project from the left-side panel to view its contents at the right-side panel. Now, right click on the folder that you want to download and select **Get Latest Version** from the context menu to download it:

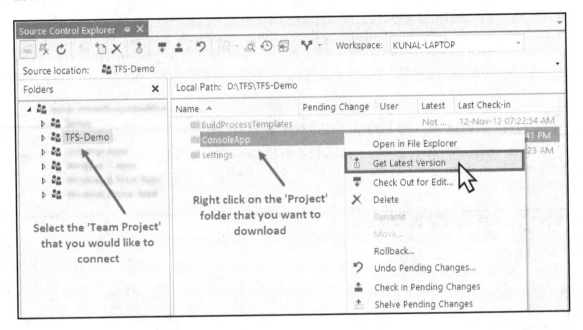

This will download the entire folder from the server to your local workspace. You can then modify any file/folder and check-in to the remote repository.

Performing check-out operation to a file

When you edit a file, it automatically gets checked out to you. In some situations, you may want to check out a file and optionally lock it to make sure that no one performs a check-in operation before your changes are checked in.

To manually perform a check-out operation, right click on the file/folder in **Solution Explorer** and click on the context menu item **Check Out for Edit...**, as shown in the following screenshot:

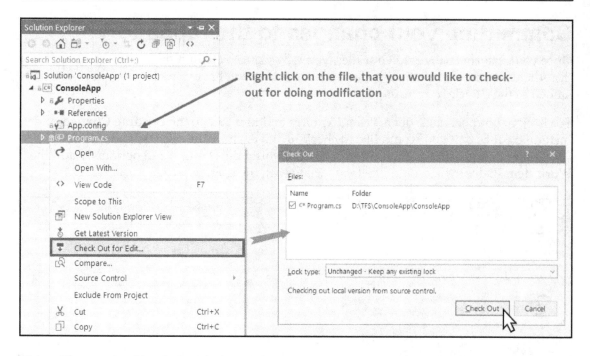

This will open the **Check Out** dialog, which will allow you to optionally lock it. From the **Lock type** dropdown, you will be allowed to select either of the following options:

- **Unchanged**: Keep any existing lock
- **Check in**: Allow other users to check out but prevent them from checking in

And when you are ready, click on the **Check Out** button. This will change the status of your selected files/folders for modification.

Committing your changes to the repository

Once you perform changes to your files, you may want to commit them to a repository for the other team members to get the latest changes that you have made. In Team Projects, it is named as the **Check-In** process.

To check-in your changes, open **Team Explorer** and navigate to the **Pending Changes** view. Include the files that you would like to check-in and exclude the ones that you don't want to check-in to the repository. Enter a comment to identify the changes and optionally add the **Work Item ID** that you would like to associate with the change set:

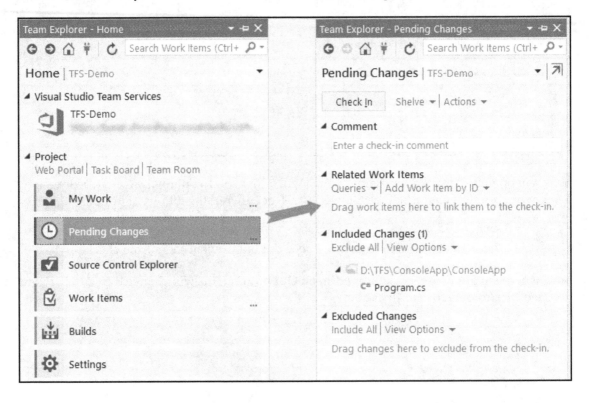

From this screen, you can also compare the files with the latest server version or the workspace version to locally review the changes that you have made. This step is recommended to make sure that you are committing the changes that you intended to push.

Right click on the individual files to open the context menu. Click on any of the following context menu items to compare them:

- **Compare with Workspace Version**: This will compare the changes with the original one that you last downloaded from the server.
- **Compare with Latest Version**: This will compare the file changes with the latest version that is available on the server.

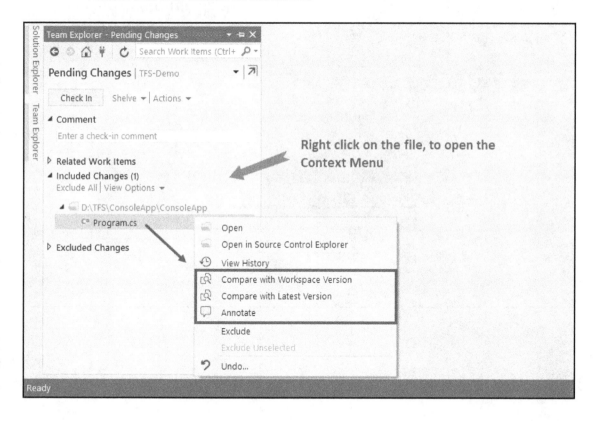

When you are ready, click on the **Check In** button to submit your changes. If there are any merge conflicts, it will ask you to resolve those first.

Alternatively, you can select the desired files/folders from **Solution Explorer** or **Source Control Explorer**, and click on **Check In...** from the right-click context menu, as shown in the following screenshot:

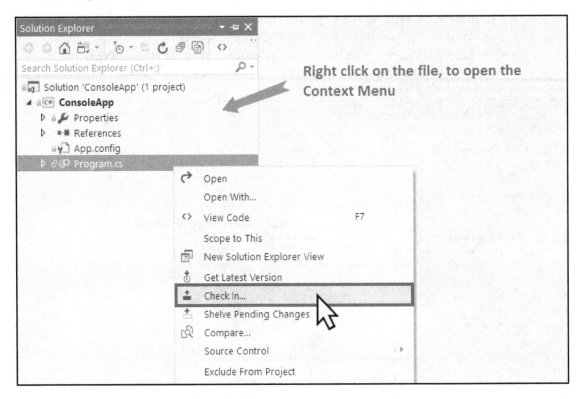

Undoing your local changes

When you want to discard any modified files/folders, right click on them under **Solution Explorer**. From the context menu, select **Source Control** | **Undo Pending Changes...**, as shown in the following screenshot:

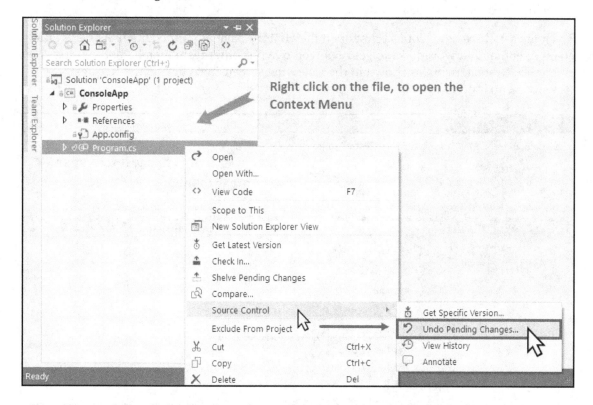

Make sure to double confirm whether you really want to undo the file/folder. Once performed, you won't be able to bring back the changes.

Creating code review request

Every product gets its success from the quality of the code and that becomes solid with a code review. Visual Studio allows you to create a code review request, directly from **Team Explorer**, and allows you to catch the defect early as it's in development stage, thus reducing the overall cost of a product.

To create a code review request, first open the **History** page of your change sets. Select the change set that you would like to get reviewed by your other team members. From the right-click context menu, as shown in the following screenshot, click on the **Request Review** menu entry:

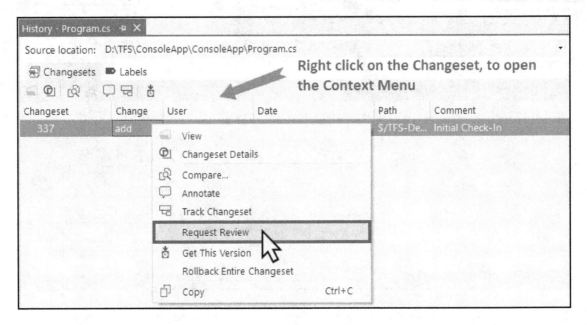

This will open the following code review request dialog where you can add one or more reviewer's name, title of the review request, and the comment/description. Fill in all the details and when you are ready, click on the **Submit Request** button:

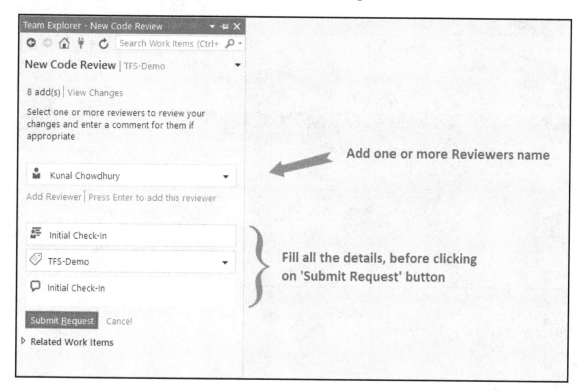

Rolling back your existing change set

In case you have checked in a wrong file or submitted a change set which was not intended to go, you may want to revert it. The condition may also arise when a specific change set is performing incorrectly in the production code and you would want to revert that.

Visual Studio allows you to easily perform a rollback of the specific change set. To do so, open the **History** page first. Right click on the change set that you want to revert, and from the context menu, select the entry **Rollback Entire Changeset**:

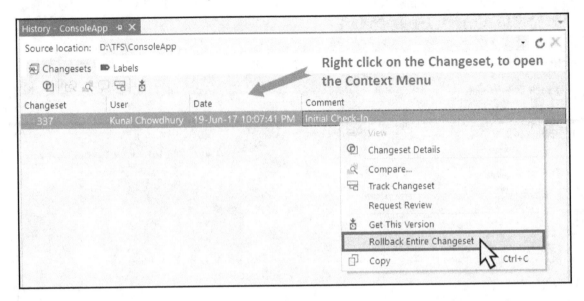

You will have to check-in the modified files/folders, which are waiting for the final commit to complete the revert/rollback process.

Summary

In this chapter, first we learned about source control repositories and the way to install Git for Visual Studio 2017. Then we discussed in depth how to use Visual Studio 2017 to interact with repositories such as GitHub or TFS.

During the discussion, we covered how to connect to a remote server and create/clone a remote repository. Then we discussed Git branches, committing changes to a branch, syncing changes between local and remote repositories, creating Pull Requests to perform code reviews, and the way to approve and merge the changes to the master branch.

We have also learned how to perform rebase, Cherry-Pick, tag a commit, and reset and revert changes. I hope the information was helpful in a broader way.

At the end of this chapter, we have also covered some basic operations on TFS projects, which includes connecting to TFS server, check-out, check-in, code review requests, and rollback of any changes.

Index

web application, publishing to cloud 362

B

BAML (Binary Application Markup Language) 91
Base Class Library (BCL) 252
breakpoints
  about 274
  actions, adding 283
  C# source code, debugging 274
  code, debugging 277
  conditions, adding 280
  exporting 287
  importing 287
  labels, adding 285
  managing, with Breakpoints window 286
  organizing, in code 274

C

C# 7.0
  literals 64
C# source code
  debugging, with breakpoints 274
Canvas
  using 117
changes tracking, in Git
  Modified 403
  Staging 404
  Unmodified 403
changes, Git repositories
  fetching, in remote repository 410
  local branch, resetting 424
  merge conflicts, resolving 412
  merging, from remote to local repository 411
  pushing, to remote repository 409
  reverting, from remote branch 426
  syncing, between local and remote repositories 408
  undoing 423
checkout 401
Cherry-Pick
  commits, copying 422
Classic Windows Apps 150
CLI (Command Line Interface) 201
cloud computing
  about 344

Infrastructure as a Service (IaaS) 346
Platform as a Service (PaaS) 346
Software as a Service (SaaS) 346
code navigation tool 32
Common Language Runtime 90
Conditional operator 78
conditions, breakpoints
  adding 280
  conditional expressions, using 281
  filters, using 282
  hit counters, using 282
Connected Services 48
Converters
  using, while data binding 129
coverage visualization 325
CTS (Common Type System) 90
custom XAML control
  building 177
  creating 179
  properties, exposing 183

D

data binding
  about 123
  Converters, using 129
  one time 125
  OneWay 124
  OneWay to Source 125
  TwoWay 124
data manipulation, UWP application
  about 168
  FlipView control 171
  GridView control 168
  ListView control 169
Data Tips
  debugging information, displaying with debugger 298
  displaying, with visualizers 295
  exporting 297
  importing 297
  inspecting, in various watch windows 290
  pinning 288
  unpinning 288
  using, while debugging 287
data trigger 134

CPSIA information can be obtained
at www.ICGtesting.com
Printed in the USA
BVHW050816080719

552847BV00024B/2136/P